THE ATTACKS ON THE

Tirpitz

SEA BATTLES IN CLOSE-UP · 8

THE ATTACKS ON THE *Tirpitz*

GERVIS FRERE-COOK

LONDON

IAN ALLAN LTD

First published 1973

ISBN 0 7110 0490 0

Published by Ian Allan Ltd, Shepperton, Surrey
and printed in the United Kingdom by
Morrison and Gibb Ltd, London and Edinburgh

Contents

Preface

The story of the *Tirpitz* is one of the strangest in naval history. Although she was the most powerful warship of her era the German High Command were determined not to risk her in action and for the four years of her life she never fired her guns except in self-defence. Yet she exercised a dominating influence over British naval strategic thinking. The Admiralty dreaded that she would break out into the Atlantic as a commerce raider and made her the target for no less than twenty-two planned attacks.

Yet if the Germans were unwilling to accept action at sea the British were just as reluctant to do so except in overwhelming force. Possibly the sinking of HMS *Hood*, the pride of the Royal Navy, in action against the *Bismarck* affected the Sea Lords' outlook, but, despite a Churchillian rebuke, the British authorities persisted in erroneously referring to the ship as '*Admiral von Tirpitz*' an indication of how great a bogey-man the Naval Staff had dreamt up. Perhaps a more realistic attitude would have been that of Captain Simpson, commanding the Tenth Submarine Flotilla in Malta, who in 1942 forwarded a patrol report of a missed attack on two Italian battleships with the comment 'but, on consideration, these battleships have never done anyone any harm'.

In writing this book I have been fortunate in being able to consult the many operational records which have now been publicly released and I acknowledge my indebtedness to the nameless writers of these excellent reports. I must also thank the staffs of the Naval Historical Branch, the Air Historical Branch and the Public Records Office for assistance in providing further information and of Illustration Research Service, the Imperial War Museum and the Photographic Section, HMS *Dolphin* for their help with illustrations and plans. I am grateful to the Controller of Her Majesty's Stationery Office, to Cassell & Co. Ltd. and to the Houghton Mifflin Co. for permission to quote copyright material. Finally I must thank my wife for her understanding and forebearance during the many evenings when I have shut myself away with pen and typewriter.

CHAPTER ONE

The Early Attacks

On the first day of April 1939 the hull of the German battleship *Tirpitz* slid down the launching slipway at Wilhelmshaven into the water, the largest warship ever to see war service in the western world,* and just two years later she was formally commissioned into the German Navy. In the four years which were to be her life-span she was to dominate the naval strategy of the Second World War more decisively than any other vessel, yet she was only once to fire her main armament offensively, and that to bombard the undefended port of Spitzbergen, and eventually she was to capsize and sink under the bombs of the Royal Air Force.

Under the Treaty of Versailles Germany had been restricted to building not more than four battleships each of 10,000tons displacement but on Hitler's election to power as Chancellor in 1933 the keels were laid for the first two battlecruisers, *Scharnhorst* and *Gneisnau*, and two years later, in 1935, the British and German governments signed the Anglo-German Naval Agreement by which Germany was allowed to build as desired up to a limit of one third of the British naval strength of surface vessels and sixty per cent (one hundred per cent if circumstances were exceptional) of British submarine numbers. Whilst signatories to the Washington Naval Agreement and the London Conference were limited to a maximum displacement for battleships of 35,000tons Germany, who had never been invited to participate in either conference, faced no such restrictions and in October 1936 the keel was laid for the *Tirpitz*, sister ship of the *Bismarck* and the second of the great German battleships. Hitler's political timetable did not envisage war with England before 1944–45 and on this basis Admiral Raeder, Commander-in-Chief of the German Navy, devised Plan Z, to include the *Scharnhorst* and *Gneisnau*, each of 26,000tons with nine 11in guns,

* *Tirpitz* displaced 43,000tons, slightly less than the later US *Missouri* class, but all were completely overshadowed by the two gigantic Japanese battleships, *Yamamoto* and *Musashi*, of 72,000tons.

the *Bismarck* and *Tirpitz* each of 45,000tons with eight 15in guns and two further battleships of some 65,000tons, as well as two aircraft carriers, cruisers, pocket battleships and destroyers.

The *Tirpitz* was actually commissioned on 25th January 1941 and even then was to spend twelve months on trials and working up in the sheltered waters of the Baltic, but long before she was considered as operational she had made her presence felt. On 2nd August 1940 Winston Churchill as Prime Minister sent to the First Lord of Admiralty and the First Sea Lord one of his famous 'Action This Day' memoranda.

> '. . . Please let me have a report of the possibility of air attack on *Bismarck* and *Tirpitz*. This seems to me to be one of the most vital steps to take.'

and two days later he followed this with a memorandum to the Secretary of State for Air and the Chief of the Air Staff.

> 'The danger of Japanese hostility makes it all the more important that the German capital ships should be put out of action. I understand that the Air Force intends to make heavy attacks on these ships as soon as there is sufficient moon. *Scharnhorst* and *Gneisnau*, both in the floating dock at Kiel, the *Bismarck* at Hamburg, and the *Tirpitz* at Wilhelmshaven are all targets of supreme importance. Even a few months delay in *Bismarck* will affect the whole balance of sea power to a serious degree. I shall be glad to hear from you.'

The Royal Air Force had not been unmindful of their responsibility for trying to eliminate the German capital ships. As early as July 1939, before the outbreak of war, they had drawn up Plan K for a very early attack on the German ports, with the intention of either damaging the ships or forcing them to leave harbour and face the might of the Royal Navy in the Heligoland Bight. Fortunately for the bomber crews Plan K had been discarded, since it had envisaged the Handley-Page Hampdens of Bomber Command making unreconnoitred attacks in daylight on Kiel and Wilhelmshaven or, if no shipping were found there, sweeping down the coastline of north Germany in hope of flushing them. The possibility of intervention by enemy fighters or anti-aircraft fire was disregarded.

However two early attempts were made to neutralise the threat of the *Tirpitz*. The Hampdens did make an unsuccessful attempt to bomb the battleship with 2,000lb AP bombs while she was still in

Wilhelmshaven and then followed this with an attempt to run 'M' mines underneath the hull during fitting out. This too was unsuccessful: both the techniques and the technology of aerial bombardment were to need a great deal of development before they could seriously damage so well protected a vessel.

So the *Tirpitz* continued her trials and work-up without further molestation throughout 1941 and the situation at sea became steadily more desperate for the British as U-boat successes against convoys mounted and the Japanese became more menacing in the Far East. The sinking of *Tirpitz*'s sister ship *Bismarck* on 27th May 1941 apparently eased matters for the Allies at the time for Winston Churchill wrote to President Roosevelt as follows:

> '. . . her removal eases our battleship situation, as we should have had to keep *King George V*, *Prince of Wales* and two *Nelsons* practically tied to Scapa Flow. . . . Now it is a different story. The effect on the Japanese will be highly beneficial. I expect they are doing all their sums again.'

But the resistance put up by the *Bismarck* and particularly the sinking of the *Hood* had affected British naval planning and at the end of August 1941 the First Sea Lord wrote a memorandum to the Prime Minister giving his reasons for the proposed 'Final Dispositions'.

> 'HOME FLEET AND FORCE H
>
> (1) The Atlantic is the vital area, as it is in that ocean alone that we can win the war at sea.
>
> (2) As long as *Tirpitz* is in being it is essential to have two ships of the *King George V* class available to work in company. . . .
>
> . . . (4) In order to have two *King George V*'s available at all times it is necessary to have three of that class in home waters, to allow for one being damaged by torpedo, bomb or mine or refitting. . . .
>
> . . . (6) If the *Tirpitz* did manage to break out she could paralyse our North Atlantic trade to such an extent that it would be essential to bring her to action at the earliest possible moment, and we could not afford to have one of the *King George V*'s absent from the scene of operations.'

Churchill replied next day.

> '. . . (3) The potency of the dispositions I ventured to suggest in my minute is illustrated by the Admiralty's own extraordinary concern about the *Tirpitz*. *Tirpitz* is doing to us exactly what a

K.G.V. in the Indian Ocean would do to the Japanese Navy. It exercises a vague general fear and menaces all points at once. It appears, and disappears, causing immediate reactions and perturbations on the other side.

(4) The fact that the Admiralty consider that three *K.G.V.*'s must be used to contain *Tirpitz* is a serious reflection upon the design of our latest ships, which through being under-gunned and weakened by hangars in the middle of their citadels, are evidently judged unfit to fight their opposite number in a single-ship action. But, after making allowances for this, I cannot feel convinced that the proposal to retain three *K.G.V.*'s in the Atlantic is sound, having regard (a) to the American dispositions which may now be counted upon, and (b) to the proved power of aircraft carriers to slow down a ship like *Tirpitz* if she were loose. It also seems unlikely that *Tirpitz* will be withdrawn from the Baltic while the Russian Fleet remains in being: and further the fate of the *Bismarck* and all her supply ships must surely be present in the German mind. How foolish they would be to send her out, when by staying where she is she contains the three strongest and newest battleships we have, and rules the Baltic as well! . . .'

Admiral Raeder was fully aware of the strategic implications of the 'fleet-in-being' and had recommended the concentration of German naval forces in northern Norway. Hitler agreed not for strategic reasons but on 'insight'. In December 1941 he convinced himself on the strength of intelligence reports that the British were planning an invasion of northern Norway and stated:

'The fate of the war will be decided in Norway.'

However mistaken Hitler's reasoning, and there can have been few more unlikely British moves than an attack through Norway, the German naval surface forces were being concentrated to their best advantage in an area from which they could not only break out as desired but where they also constituted a continual threat to the Arctic convoys which in August 1941 had begun taking supplies to Russia.

Bomber Command 28th–29th January 1942

Tirpitz was sailed from the Baltic through the Kiel Canal in January 1942 and by 22nd her presence in Trondheim was known to the

British. Churchill wasted no time in writing to General Ismay for the Chiefs of Staffs Committee.

'1. The presence of *Tirpitz* at Trondheim has now been known for three days. The destruction or even the crippling of this ship is the greatest event at sea at the present time. No other target is comparable to it. She cannot have ack-ack protection comparable to Brest or the German home ports. If she were even only crippled it would be difficult to take her back to Germany. No doubt it is better to wait for moonlight for a night attack but moonlight attacks are not comparable with day attacks. The entire naval situation throughout the world would be altered, and the naval command of the Pacific would be regained.
2. There must be no lack of co-operation between Bomber Command and the Fleet Air Arm and aircraft supplies. A plan should be made to attack both with carrier-borne torpedo aircraft and with heavy bombers by daylight or at dawn. The whole strategy of the war turns at this period on this ship, which is holding four times the number of British capital ships paralysed, to say nothing of two new American battleships retained in the Atlantic. I regard the matter as of the highest urgency and importance. I shall mention it in the Cabinet to-morrow, and it must be considered in detail at the Defence Committee on Tuesday night.'

On the night of 28/29th January the Royal Air Force made their first attack on the *Tirpitz* since her commissioning. Nine Halifaxes and seven Stirlings of Bomber Command took off from Lossiemouth for the *Tirpitz* at Trondheim. Ten-tenths cloud and severe icing conditions made it impossible for them to find the target and they returned to base without having dropped their bombs. Obviously the problem was more difficult than the Prime Minister had appreciated.

Convoy PQ 12. 1st–13th March 1942

Germany had invaded Russia on 22nd June 1941 and two months later on 21st August the first of the Arctic convoys, codenamed 'Dervish', sailed from Hvalfjord to Archangel. A month later the second convoy, PQ 1, sailed between the same ports and by 12th March 1942 a further ten convoys had reached Murmansk or Archangel. The Germans had made very little effort against these convoys during the autumn and during the winter the weather conditions prevented any serious interference.

The convoys were assembled in Iceland whence they faced a voyage of some 2,000mls through the Greenland and Barents Seas, bounded on their starboard side by the coast of Norway and to port by the edge of the Arctic pack ice. In an area of constant gales the winter wind, whipping off the ice, froze the spray on to the rigging and upper decks of the ships as they plunged and rolled in the storm-lashed seas. Occasionally there were periods of quiet which as often as not brought arctic fog. From November to February the sun remained below the horizon. Bad as conditions were for the merchantmen and their escorts, they were even worse for the U-boats. Pitching in a swell which rose far higher than their periscope standards, unable to dive (a submarine has to turn beam-on to the sea to dive and is horribly unstable while actually submerging) and anyhow virtually unable to keep periscope depth, the officer of the watch and look-outs were continually drenched as the freezing sea broke over the bridge. Their chances of finding the convoy, let alone attacking it, were very small. The same weather made reconnaissance and bombing from the air equally impossible. Of the 105 ships which set out for Russia and the 101 which sailed back only two merchantmen and one destroyer, HMS *Matabele*, were lost by the middle of March 1942. But with the coming of spring the situation was to change.

On 1st March convoy PQ 12 sailed from Reykjavik and collected its close escort, while Vice-Admiral Curteis, flying his flag in the battlecruiser *Renown*, with the battleship *Duke of York*, cruiser *Kenya* and six destroyers provided the immediate main covering force. The Commander-in-Chief Home Fleet, Admiral Sir John Tovey, in the battleship *King George V*, with the aircraft carrier *Victorious*, cruiser *Berwick* and a further six destroyers, sailed from Scapa Flow to join forces with Vice-Admiral Curteis on 6th March about 200mls east of Jan Mayen Island. At the same time as PQ 12 left Iceland a homeward-bound convoy, QP 8, left Murmansk. It was planned that they should pass each other south-west of Bear Island and indeed did so in visibility of one mile at mid-day on 7th March.

On 5th March a German reconnaissance aircraft sighted PQ 12 in the vicinity of Jan Mayen Island and that evening *Tirpitz* was ordered to put to sea to intercept. *Tirpitz*, under the command of Kapitän Topp her first commanding officer, had been lying idle in Trondheim Fjord since her arrival in January, awaiting the build-up of German naval forces. Three weeks previously the battlecruisers *Scharnhorst* and *Gneisnau*, with the cruiser *Prinz Eugen*, had made their historic

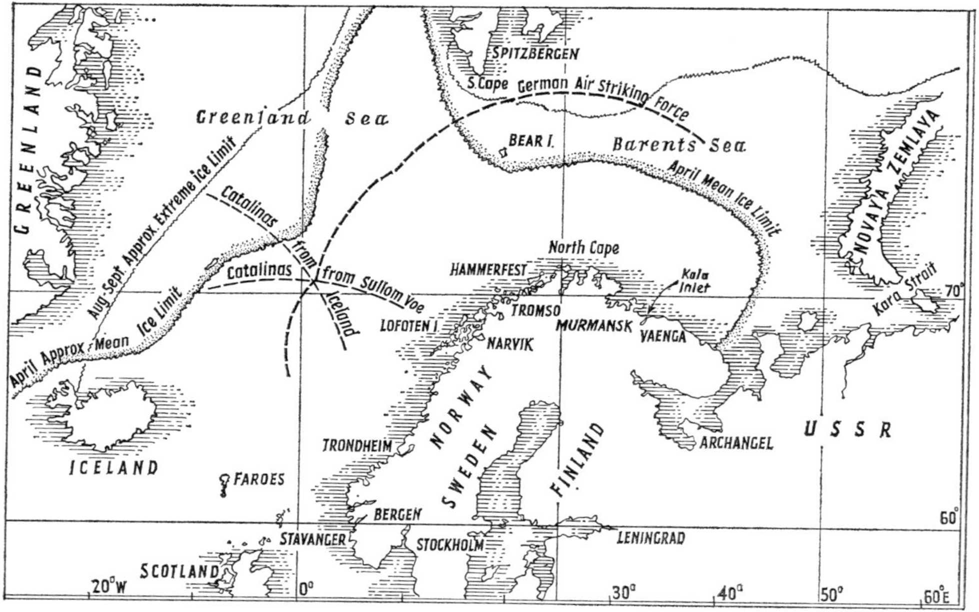

Theatre of operations for convoys proceeding to Northern Russia.

dash up the English Channel from Brest where they had been sheltering since their earlier excursions into the Atlantic. Although unaffected by British attacks either by aircraft or torpedo boats both battlecruisers had been damaged by mines and had to remain in Germany for repairs, (indeed the *Gneisnau* was never to put to sea again) but the *Prinz Eugen* and the pocket-battleship *Admiral Scheer* had steamed north in the last week of February to join *Tirpitz*. On the morning of 23rd February the *Prinz Eugen* was torpedoed off the approaches to Trondheim by the British submarine *Trident* and so damaged that although she made port she had later to return to Germany for docking.

Admiral Ciliax, who had commanded the German squadron in its dash up the Channel, joined *Tirpitz* just before she sailed on 6th March, with the destroyers *Hermann Schoemann*, *Friedrich Ihn* and *Z.25* in company. The British submarine *Seawolf*, too far away to attack, sighted the battleship shortly after she left the fjord, and at 1940 on 6th passed a sighting report giving *Tirpitz*'s course as 045° up the coast. About the same time PQ 12, with Captain Denny in *Kenya* as senior officer of the close escort, met loose pack ice at 72° N and was forced to turn south-east on a direct course for North Cape until the morning of 7th. The weather was bad and unsettled. A gale on 4th March had scattered the home-bound convoy QP 8—the Russian merchantman *Ijora* never rejoined the rest of the convoy—and with intermittent snow storms visibility varied from less than a mile to more than thirty miles.

By noon on 7th the two convoys PQ 12 and QP 8 were passing each other on courses north-east and south-west. At 0800, *Tirpitz*, steering north in a position some hundred miles south of the convoys, detached her three destroyers to sweep on a parallel course to the east of her while the British Commander-in-Chief, who was only 150mls to the west, ordered an air reconnaissance from *Victorious* which would almost certainly have located *Tirpitz* had not icing conditions prohibited any flying.

For both admirals the situation was extremely complex since neither had any information about the other. Admiral Ciliax did not even know that the Home Fleet was at sea in the immediate vicinity although he was well aware that a British covering force could be expected and that he must be most wary of being forced to action by a superior force. Admiral Tovey had a contrary problem; that of being left unguarded in enemy submarine waters while his destroyers were sent away to refuel. At 1300 the Home Fleet turned

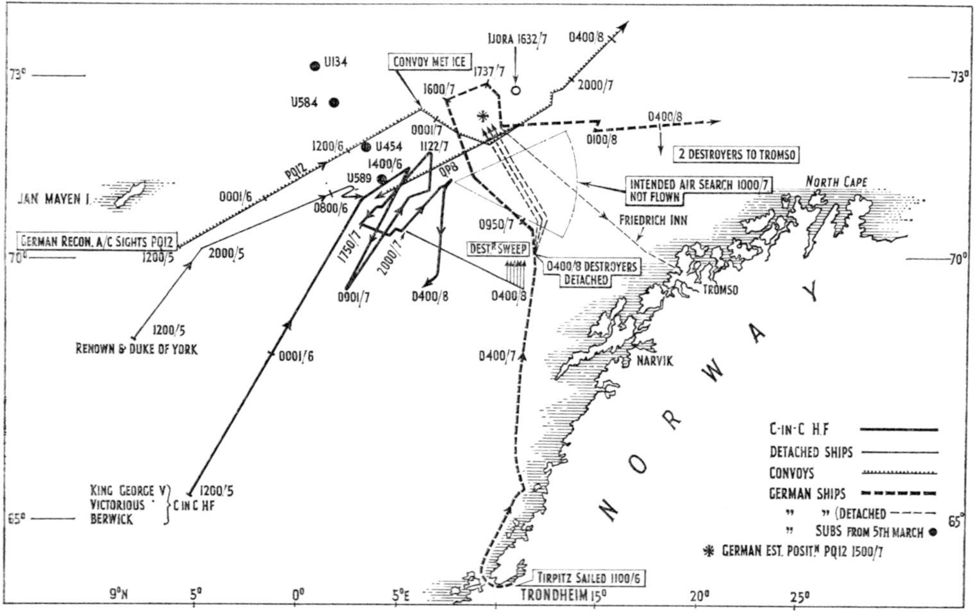

Convoys PQ12: QP8. Operations Phase 1; 1200, 5th March 1942 to 0400, 8th March 1942.

away to the south-west whilst the *Tirpitz* with her sweeping destroyers, steering north by west, crossed ahead of QP 8 without detecting it. At 1545 the *Friedrich Ihn* sighted the Russian straggler *Ijora* to the north and sank it an hour and a half later in 72° 40′ N. 10° 30′ E. Admiral Tovey received a distress signal from the *Ijora* with a garbled position and shortly afterwards a D/F bearing of a possible enemy surface vessel which suggested to him that *Tirpitz* was astern of convoy PQ 12, her expected objective. Admiral Tovey wrote: 'I thought it probable that if this was the bearing of the *Tirpitz*, whom I am convinced was highly nervous of being in such waters, she would consider her position compromised and return immediately to her base.' He turned east-south-east for an hour and a half but then receiving information that *Tirpitz* might be expected to remain at sea and operate east of Bear Island he altered course at 1923 to 040° to follow PQ 12. An hour later he detached six destroyers to steam south-east and then to search northwards, which they did without success until 0600 on 8th March.

Meanwhile Admiral Ciliax had collected his three destroyers at 1728 after the sinking of the *Ijora* and finding himself on the edge of the pack ice turned south and then east in search of the convoy. Before midnight the *Friedrich Ihn* was detached to Tromsö to refuel, and at 0400 on the 8th the other two destroyers followed her, the weather being so bad as to make refuelling from *Tirpitz* impossible.

Thus dawn on 8th March found *Tirpitz* alone some 150mls south of Bear Island and steering north in search of PQ 12, which was itself some 80mls to the south-west of Bear Island and also steaming north, which it continued to do until mid-day when the pack ice forced it once again to turn south-east. The Home Fleet was 180mls west of the Lofoten Islands, steaming south-west parallel to and 100mls south of QP 8. Admiral Tovey's intention was to return to Iceland since he was without any destroyer escort and he believed the *Tirpitz* to have abandoned her operation.

At 1045 *Tirpitz* turned on to a mean course of 255° and zig-zagged down the anticipated grain of PQ 12. The convoy was lucky: had it not been directed to go north of Bear Island, from which it was prevented by pack ice, an encounter at some time on 8th would have been almost inevitable. As it was the merchantmen passed clear to the north undetected even by a searching Focke-Wulf 200 and by nightfall was south of Bear Island and some 180mls past *Tirpitz*. Admiral Tovey with the capital ships of the Home Fleet was some 400mls to the west of Norway and reasonably clear of the risk of air attack.

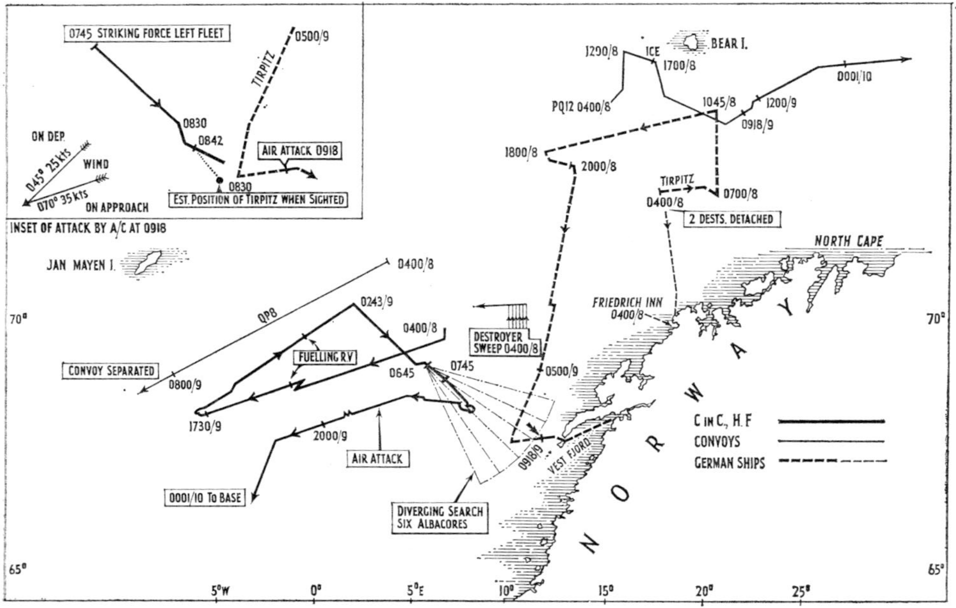

Convoys PQ12: QP8. Operations Phase 2; 0400, 8th March 1942 to 0001, 10th March 1942.

At 1816 on the evening of 8th March, German Group Command North advised Admiral Ciliax that it was quite possible that the convoy had turned back three days earlier after the sighting off Jan Mayen Island. There seem to have been no grounds for this report for neither PQ 12 nor QP 8 appear to have been subsequently reported, but it placed the responsibility for continuing the search on Admiral Ciliax and at 2025 that evening he altered course to 191° to rendezvous with his destroyers off Vest Fjord before returning to base. Four minutes after Admiral Ciliax had received his unhelpful signal Admiral Tovey, acting on a suggestion from Admiralty that *Tirpitz* was still at sea far to the north, turned his fleet back towards Bear Island. The German battleship steamed steadily south throughout the night.

At 0240 on 9th further information from Admiralty indicated to Admiral Tovey that *Tirpitz* was steaming south and not searching the waters off Bear Island and he altered course from north-east to 120° towards the Lofoten Islands and increased speed to 26knots. (Had the Home Fleet steamed directly east all night, daybreak might well have found them within gunshot of *Tirpitz*.)

At 0640 on 9th March the Commander-in-Chief ordered *Victorious* to fly off a reconnaissance force of six Albacores on a diverging search between 105° and 155° to a depth of 150mls and fifty minutes later a strike force of twelve torpedo-carrying Albacores under the command of Lieut-Commander W. J. Lucas, RN was flown off behind them. The wind which was blowing at 25knots from 045° veered and increased in velocity to 35knots from 070° and although visibility was good between snow storms there was seven-tenths cloud at 2,000ft with icing down to sea-level. The orders to the strike force were to make good a course of 135° and to act on any intercepted enemy reports. The Commander-in-Chief had sped them on their way with the signal:

> 'A wonderful chance which may achieve most valuable results. God be with you.'

At 0802 Albacore Duty F sighted *Tirpitz* with the *Friedrich Ihn* in company and made a report which was received by the strike commander leading his squadron at 500ft and he altered course to 163°. At about 0810 *Tirpitz* sighted the reconnaissance aircraft and at 0830 catapulted off two Arado aircraft 'as a defence measure against submarine and aerial attack'. *Tirpitz* then turned on to a course of

082° and increased speed to 29knots for Vest Fjord, an alteration which was duly reported by the shadowing Albacore. Two shadowing aircraft were engaged in an indeterminate scrap with the Arados but a third Albacore was attacked and the navigator wounded by cannon fire although the Albacore made a successful return to *Victorious*. (The German aircraft was identified as a JU 87 by the Albacore but German records complain of the lack of fighter support from the Luftwaffe at Bodo and Bardufoss and it was more probably one of *Tirpitz*'s Arados.)

At 0842 Lieut-Cdr Lucas sighted *Tirpitz* bearing 140° at a range of 20 miles. He altered course directly towards *Tirpitz* and the formation began to climb to 3,500ft with the intention of getting ahead of the enemy, having established contact on airborne radar at a range of 16mls. However the maximum speed of the Albacore was 155knots and *Tirpitz* was steaming at 29knots into a near head wind of 35knots, so that the very best that Lucas could hope for was an overtaking speed of 95knots. This would mean half-an-hour's flying before they could be in the most favourable position for attack, a half-hour to be spent in cloud in icing conditions during which time fighters from the Norwegian airfields might well arrive. In fact the closing rate was only 40knots as the Albacores were both heavily laden and trying to climb and Lucas gave the order to his sub-flights to act independently.

At 0917 as the Albacores were directly above *Tirpitz* they suddenly became visible and at the same time sighted their target through a break in the clouds. *Tirpitz* did not immediately open fire and Lucas, mistakenly thinking that the Germans were still unaware of his presence, ordered 'Dive to attack'. The first sub-flight dived parallel to the port beam of *Tirpitz*, about 1,800yds distant, swung right-handed to discharge their torpedoes from 1,500yds on a 90° track and ran into the start of a heavy ack-ack barrage. A minute later *Tirpitz* turned hard to port as the second sub-flight launched its torpedoes from 2,000yds against an already swinging target. Both salvoes missed, though not necessarily by much. All the torpedoes were set for a speed of 40knots and a depth of 25ft with contact only pistols. The second two sub-flights attacked four minutes later, coming in on a big sweep from the starboard side and dropping their torpedoes in less organised salvoes. By then the ack-ack fire from *Tirpitz*, both long and close range, was at full force and one aircraft from each of these sub-flights was shot down on the approach. The Albacores missed again. Much chastened but undamaged, *Tirpitz*

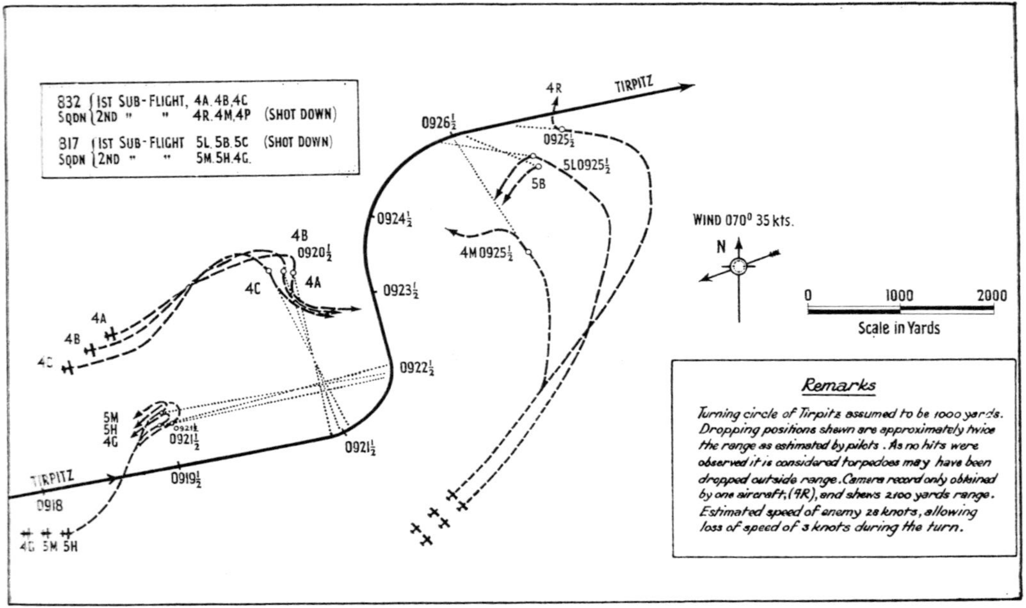

Track chart of the Fleet Air Arm torpedo bomber attack on *Tirpitz*, 9th March 1942.

continued at full speed for the shelter of Vest Fjord while the disappointed airmen returned to *Victorious*.

The only camera record taken by one of the attacking aircraft suggested that the torpedoes had been dropped at an excessive range, double that estimated by the pilots, but the German reports mentioned the courage of the British airmen in pressing home their attacks to a range of between 400 and 1,200yds. Basically it was inexperience and lack of training which saved *Tirpitz*. Lieut-Cdr Lucas had only just joined his squadron, had never flown with them before and had himself had very little torpedo practice since 1937: the pilots had had very little opportunity to practise together as a squadron the complicated manoeuvres for making a diverse but concerted attack. However the attack caused the German High Command to exercise yet greater caution in sending *Tirpitz* to sea and for a time they deflected part of their ship-building effort in Germany in an abortive attempt to complete the aircraft carrier *Graf Zeppelin*.

Admiral Tovey, bitterly disappointed, headed the Home Fleet back to Britain, shadowed by a Blohm und Voss 138 which he endeavoured to drive off with *Victorious*' Fireflies until in the late afternoon three JU 88s unsuccessfully tried to bomb the carrier. Admiral Ciliax waited in Vest Fjord until 13th March, then slipped down to Trondheim in thick weather, eluding the Allied submarines lying in wait for his passage. Convoys PQ 12 and QP 8 reached harbour safely, but the threat to the southern flank of the convoy route remained.

Bomber Command 31st March–29th April 1942

The failure of the covering force for PQ 12 to damage *Tirpitz* and the threat which she continued to pose meant that further efforts must be made to sink her. Bomber Command therefore flew three sorties against the battleship in her berth at Foetten Fjord near Trondheim. The first attack was carried out early on 31st March by thirty-four Halifax bombers. The battleship was extremely difficult to attack. She was secured close alongside the shore in a narrow fjord with high mountains on either side and covered with camouflage nets. On receipt of any air-raid warning an elaborate system of smoke pots was set alight and the area rapidly obscured by a smoke screen. These defensive measures combined with bad weather made the attack abortive. Only one aircraft succeeded in locating the target and dropped one 4,000lb and four 500lb bombs without causing any damage. Five aircraft were lost.

On 28th April Bomber Command struck again. Of the forty-three aircraft which took off, thirty-two attacked the *Tirpitz* in two waves, a first attack of high-flying Lancasters followed by an attack by low-level Halifaxes, these led by Wing-Commander Bennett who was subsequently to found the Pathfinder Force. Twenty 4,000lb bombs were dropped and thirty smaller ones, none of which hit, and forty-four 1,000lb Mark XIX mines with hydrostatic fuses set to 30ft. The intention was that these should be dropped as near-misses either in the fjord or on the mountainside to roll down to *Tirpitz*'s berth and explode underneath her. It was a clever idea which unhappily did not work and it is doubtful if the 100lb of explosive in the mines would have caused much damage, but it worried the Germans and forced them to take even more defensive measures. Five bombers were shot down including Bennett's, but he and his radio-operator evaded a German sentry and successfully made their way across country to Sweden.

On the following night there was a repeat attack by thirty bombers which was again foiled by the German smoke screen. Bombs and mines were dropped around the obscured battleship, but again without any success, for the loss of two bombers. In a month Bomber Command had managed to make three attacks, a not inconsiderable achievement in view of the weather conditions, and had lost twelve aircraft out of the one hundred and seven which had set out; they had failed to inflict any damage whatsoever. Something else was required but before it could be planned *Tirpitz* was to achieve her greatest indirect success.

Convoy PQ 17. 27th June–24th July 1942

After the successful passage of PQ 12 in March the British Government had continued to send convoys of supplies to Russia as the northern summer advanced and seventy ships out of an original sailing of one hundred and three had been safely escorted through for the cost of a cruiser and a destroyer; only sixteen merchantmen were lost, seventeen having to return to their port of departure owing to ice and weather. PQ 16, which had sailed at the end of May, had fought its way through against heavy air attack and the losses it received had encouraged the Germans to reinforce their torpedo bombers and to plan for a more intensive effort in the future.

Convoy PQ 17 sailed from Reykjavik on 27th June with a close escort of destroyers and corvettes, a close covering force of four cruisers, two British and two American, commanded by Rear-Admiral Hamilton, and a stand-off covering force of two battleships and an aircraft carrier of the Home Fleet under the Commander-in-Chief, Admiral Sir John Tovey. Admiralty policy however was quite clear; the safety of the convoy against surface forces which might attack west of Bear Island must be guaranteed by our own surface forces; east of Bear Island it must be provided by submarines.

Although the British Commander-in-Chief had a shrewd appreciation of the German attitude he was not aware of the crippling restrictions which Hitler was imposing on the surface forces. Admiral Schniewind, Commander-in-Chief Afloat, was anxious to employ his capital ships, yet after obtaining Hitler's approval for a sortie by the capital ships (*Operation Rosselspring*—'Knight's Move') Grand Admiral Raeder felt it necessary to warn Group Command North that a reverse would be most undesirable, and Group Command North thereupon signalled to Admiral Schniewind—'Better short-lived operations with partial success than a prolonged attempt at complete success. Should the situation appear doubtful, do not hesitate to disengage. On no account allow the enemy to score success against the main body of the fleet.'

On 2nd July the Germans began to concentrate their forces. *Tirpitz* and *Hipper* left Trondheim for Vest Fjord, and *Scheer* and *Lutzow* left Narvik for Alten Fjord. *Lutzow* and three of the *Tirpitz* group of destroyers managed to ground themselves on passage and were out of the operation before it had properly begun.

By the morning of the 4th July convoy PQ 17 was some 60mls north of Bear Island where the first ship was torpedoed by an aircraft. Rear-Admiral Hamilton with the cruisers was given discretion to cruise eastward as close cover, subject to orders from Admiral Tovey, who decided to adhere to the original plan and ordered the cruisers to turn back unless assured by the Admiralty that they would not encounter *Tirpitz*. At 1809 that evening Rear-Admiral Hamilton signalled his intention to turn westward at about 2200 on completion of fuelling his destroyers, but at 1930 the Admiralty signalled him to remain with the convoy pending further instructions. Rarely can a naval operation have been more confused. The responsibility for the convoy rested with the senior officer of the escort, Commander J. E. Broome, RN in HMS *Keppel*, in conjunction with the convoy commodore, Captain J. C. K. Dowding, DSO, RD, RNR. Yet the

Senior Officer Escorts was under the orders of the Rear-Admiral, First Cruiser Squadron, who was again under the operational control of the Commander-in-Chief, at sea some 300 miles away, with the Admiralty trying to tell everyone what to do.

By 2100 on 4th July the convoy had successfully fought off a determined torpedo-bomber attack—two ships had been sunk and one damaged but three aircraft had been shot down—and the cruisers had been left unmolested although only 10mls ahead. At Admiralty however they knew that the German heavy ships had sailed from Trondheim and Narvik but had lost contact with them thereafter, although in fact they were to remain in Alten Fjord until noon on 5th, awaiting Hitler's permission to put to sea. The First Sea Lord, Admiral Sir Dudley Pound, decided that a major assault on the convoy by heavy German surface forces was imminent, that the cruisers and escorts could not defend them, and that the best hope was dispersal. The following signals were sent.

'Most immediate. Cruiser force withdraw westward at high speed.'
DTG 2111 B/4

'Immediate. Owing to threat from surface ships, convoy is to disperse and proceed to Russian ports.' DTG 2123 B/4

'Most immediate. My 2123/4. Convoy is to scatter.'
DTG 2136 B/4

Commander Broome passed the signal to the convoy, then took his destroyers to join the cruisers in accordance with the Commander-in-Chief's standing instructions that in the event of surface attack by a force overwhelmingly superior to the escort, the prime object of the latter was to shadow the enemy, and, should a favourable opportunity occur, to attack them.

Tirpitz, *Scheer* and *Hipper* with six destroyers actually sailed at 1137 on 5th in search of the convoy, knowing that the British battleships and cruisers were well to the westward and heading for home. At 1700 the Russian submarine *K.21* reported the Germans as steering 045° some 45mls northwest of North Cape and claimed to have hit *Tirpitz* with two torpedoes. However no mention of a submarine attack is to be found in the battleship's war diary and she sustained no damage. A reconnaissance aircraft reported them an hour later and the British submarine *P.54* likewise at 2029, having tried desperately for an hour to close to an attacking position. German naval command intercepted these reports and, fearful of an air

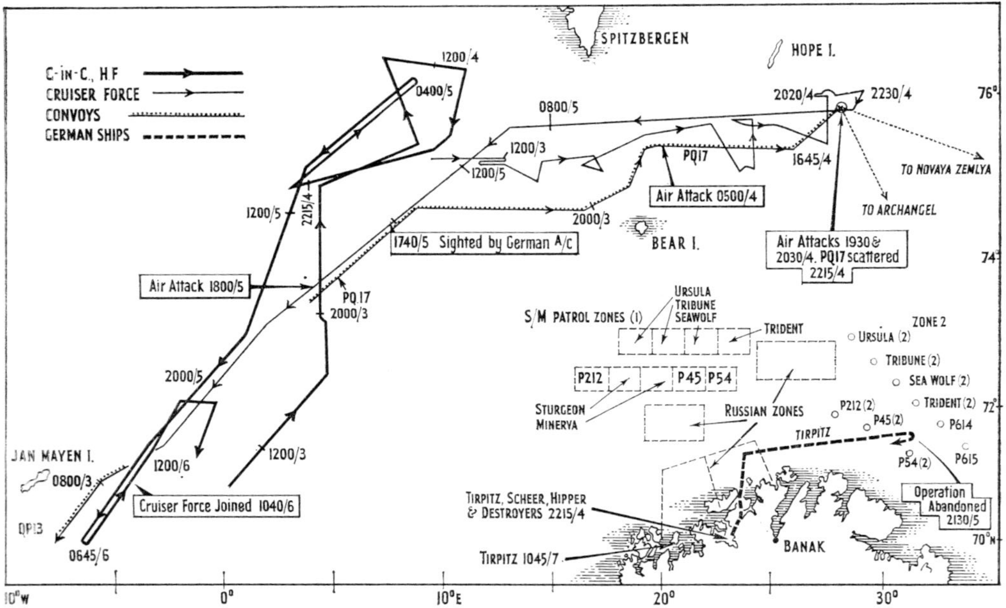

Convoys PQ17: QP13. Operations, 3rd July 1942 to 6th July 1942.

attack from *Victorious* if the operations against the convoy continued after 0100 on 6th, at 2132 ordered Admiral Schniewind to discontinue the operation and return to Alten Fjord.

Too late the Admiralty signalled to Admiral Tovey that *Tirpitz* 'might be reluctant to go as far as the convoy' if the battle fleet steamed eastward. The threat of the surface attack had worked, the convoy was scattered and unprotected. Nineteen ships were to be sunk by bombs or torpedoes in the next three days. Of the thirty-six merchant vessels which had sailed two turned back and eleven reached Russia; twenty-three were sunk. Without firing a gun, without even getting within 300mls of the convoy, *Tirpitz* had achieved one of the outstanding naval successes of the war.

CHAPTER TWO

Operation 'Title', 26th October—1st November 1942

The failures of Bomber Command in the spring and the terrible effect which even the threat of an excursion had produced on Convoy PQ 17 made it essential to try some other means of eliminating *Tirpitz*. On the night of 18th December 1941 the Italians had launched three two-man 'human torpedoes' into Alexandria Harbour and had seriously damaged the battleships *Queen Elizabeth* and *Valiant*. A month later the Prime Minister was enquiring what action was being taken to copy this achievement. Using as a model an Italian chariot salvaged after an abortive attack on Gibraltar Harbour, the British soon had a working vehicle.

At about the same time a naval officer at Lunna Voe, Lieut David Howarth, RNVR, put forward an idea for an attack on *Tirpitz* using torpedoes slung under a fishing vessel, but heard no more about it. Lunna Voe was then the base for the Shetland 'Bus, the fishing boat organisation which brought refugees from Norway and sent back resistance fighters. Amongst those who had escaped from Norway was Leif Larsen who, in October 1941, had taken part in a mine-laying operation off Kristiansund in the fishing vessel *Nordsjon*. The *Nordsjon* had been sunk in a gale but all her crew had survived and returned to Britain, Larsen and four of his shipmates by stealing the newly completed fishing boat *Arthur*. Larsen was now invited to consider taking *Arthur* back to Norway with two chariots and their crews for an attack on *Tirpitz*.

As early as April 1942 a prototype British chariot, as the 'human torpedoes' were called, had been built and the training of charioteers had begun under Commander Geoffrey Sladen, RN. In June 1942 the first chariot was ready for testing and a base had been set up at Loch Erisfort with HMS *Titania* as depot ship. The chariot was virtually a 21in diameter torpedo powered by an electric battery which had a capacity to drive it at about 3knots for six hours. A crew of two, dressed in waterproof suits and breathing from an adapted submarine escape set, sat astride the torpedo; the forward crew member drove the chariot, having a control column which operated a rudder and a pair of stern hydroplanes, whilst his companion acted as far as possible as navigator and was responsible for the negotiating of nets and securing the war-head to the target. The war-head was 600lb of high explosive on the nose of the chariot from which it could be detached and was fitted with a delayed action fuse to allow the charioteers time to get well clear after an attack.

Larsen immediately accepted the offer of a chance to attack *Tirpitz* and planning of the operation was begun. It was decided that two chariots should be used which meant a team of six British sailors, a crew of two for each chariot and a dresser for each crew to help them into their diving suits and to be reserve crewman, and that the best means of getting the chariots within striking distance of *Tirpitz* would be to carry them in a small Norwegian fishing trader. The *Arthur*, 'liberated' a year earlier by Larsen, was selected and a crew of Norwegians chosen; Björnöy as engineer, Strand as radio operator and Kalve as deck hand.

The first requirement was to adapt *Arthur* to take the chariots and to provide a safe hiding place for the charioteers and their equipment while passing the German patrols in the fjords. *Arthur* was to be carrying a cargo of peat to Trondheim, a bulky, easily obtainable and untraceable cargo, and initially the chariots were to be stowed in chocks on the deck for the passage across the North Sea. On reaching the Norwegian coast *Arthur* would be moored amongst the small islands off Smölen and the chariots hoisted overboard to be towed submerged by wire pendants fixed to eyebolts in *Arthur*'s keel. A small petrol generator was carried for recharging the chariots' batteries at this time, which was to be thrown overboard after use and its vacant space filled up with spare peat carried on deck. An extra bulkhead was built at the after end of the hold some two feet forward of the genuine one dividing the hold from the engineroom and access to this space was from a door in the engineroom concealed behind the switchboard. Here was the stowage for the charioteers' gear and for the British party themselves during routine searches. A complete set of forged papers was provided; fishing pass, registration papers, crew list and movements certificate, made out for a similar craft still in Norway, rubber stamped and suitably well-handled. Thus equipped *Arthur* sailed to a remote Shetland loch to join the depot ship *Alecto* and the battleship *Rodney* which was to act as a target for the practice attacks by the chariots.

The crews for the chariots consisted of Lieut Brewster, in command, with AB Brown as his number two, and Sergeant Craig, RE, with AB Evans as his number two, with ABs Causer and Tebb as dressers. (Causer was subsequently to be commissioned and awarded a DSO for a chariot attack on the Italian cruiser *Bolzano* in La Spezia.) After a series of successful practice attacks on *Rodney*, Larsen took *Arthur* to Lunna Voe to prepare for the operation. The boat was carefully checked over and any British fittings removed and replaced with Norwegian ones, the crew were dressed only in Norwegian clothing and even the fresh food, bread, wrapped butter etc., was found from a refugee boat which had recently arrived. Final details for the escape were arranged.

The whole operation had been meticulously planned in collaboration with the Norwegian resistance movement. The proper German inspecting officers' signatures had been taken off fishing papers, details of the inspection points recorded and the defences around *Tirpitz* surveyed. All this information had been brought to England via Sweden by a young Norwegian officer, Odd Sörli, disguised as a Lutheran pastor. He had also brought the details of the escape arrangements. After the attack the chariots crews were to land on the south shore of the fjord where a car would be waiting to take them to the Swedish border. Meanwhile the dressers and Norwegian crew were to scuttle *Arthur* and to row ashore to another rendezvous where more cars would await them. If either of these plans failed they were all to meet on the following night on a nearby hill-top.

On the morning of 26th October *Arthur* sailed for Norway. The weather was rough with a strong easterly wind; pitching heavily the fishing boat ploughed on and sighted the mountains around Smölen on the evening of Tuesday 27th. During the afternoon of Wednesday 28th as *Arthur* was approaching the entrance to the fjord the engine stopped. It was three hours before Björnöy could get it going again.

During Thursday 29th the generator was started to recharge the chariots' batteries but after a quarter of an hour it broke down, damaged by the rough crossing, and there was nothing to do but to throw it overboard and hope that the chariot batteries had retained their original charge. Throughout the day they made several attempts to uncover and hoist overboard the chariots, always to be thwarted by the aircraft which constantly patrolled the fjord. When the first 'plane flew over Tebb completely forgot himself and started towards a hidden machine-gun, but fortunately was stopped by a furious outburst from Larsen. Then the weather blew up and made it impossible to hoist out the chariots, which had to be postponed until early on 30th. No sooner was this task safely accomplished and Brewster and Evans back inboard than an inquisitive elderly fisherman arrived and had to be talked off with the information that the chariots, which he could clearly see below *Arthur*'s hull, were German minesweeping devices. Everything British was then thrown overboard, the machine-gun hidden in the hide-out between the engineroom and the hold, and at 1400 Larsen unmoored *Arthur* and started for the entrance to Trondheimsfjord, the chariots towing below. By late afternoon the engine began making unsatisfactory noises and at 2300 Larsen anchored off Hestvik for repairs and to contact Nils Strom, a resistance worker ashore. Larsen started a pre-arranged conversation about peat but Strom was not thinking and it was some time before Larsen could extract the correct reply! With the help of a local blacksmith Björnöy was able to make and fit a copper patch to the fractured head of the piston and by 0900 on Saturday 31st October *Arthur* was again under way. An hour later they reached the examination boat.

The examination passed off successfully though not without apprehension. Everything was in order except the weather: a flat calm and bright sunshine left the chariots clearly visible below *Arthur*'s keel when she lay stopped, something which had not been foreseen back at Lunna Voe. A slight fracas with a heaving line distracted the attention of the German sailors as the two boats came close together and the chariots remained unnoticed for the quarter of an hour that the examining officer took with Larsen, checking the forged papers and enquiring about a colleague doing a like task further down the fjord. Eventually *Arthur* was permitted to proceed, her wake concealing the chariots from further observation.

Arthur continued without trouble for the rest of the forenoon and all afternoon up the fjord towards Trondheim, east-north-east to the Agdenes lighthouse, then south-south-east to Gjeiten and the entrance to Korsfjord, where the main fjord again turned so that the course up to Trondheim where it widened was again north of east. The charioteers had remained concealed all day, resting as best they could, and as daylight faded they prepared for the night's attack as they altered course off Korsfjord. The weather was fine but for a stiff easterly breeze and the lights of Trondheim were readily visible. (The Germans were very casual about maintaining a black-out.)

Top: Launching of *Tirpitz*, 1st April 1939./*IWM*
Above: The battleship *Tirpitz*./*IWM*

Above: Destroyer—*Friedrich Ihn.*/*IWM*
Top right: Halifax bomber taking off./*IWM*
Right: HMS *Victorious* with Albacores ranged on the flight-deck. /*IWM*

OO R

Above: Albacore torpedo-bombers in formation./*IWM*
Top right: Albacores of the second flight attacking *Tirpitz*, 9th March 1942./*Captain Reinicke*
Right: *Tirpitz* taking avoiding action—the track of a torpedo which missed can be seen across *Tirpitz*'s wake./*Captain Reinicke*

Right: Lief Larsen.
/D. Howarth
Below: The Norwegian fishing boat *Arthur*.
/D. Howarth

Top: A chariot with charioteer—no warhead fitted./*Submarine Museum*
Above: Charioteers in action./*IWM*

Left: HMS *Belfast.*/*IWM*

Bottom left: The main armament of a *King George V* class battleship iced up by freezing spray in the arctic winter./*IWM*

Below: Escorts refuelling from a tanker in a northern anchorage./*IWM*

Left: Lt B. C. G. Place, VC, DSC, RN./*IWM*

Bottom left: Lt. D. Cameron, VC, RNR./*IWM*

Top right: T-class submarine in a Scottish loch./*IWM*

Right: HMS *Sceptre.*/*IWM*

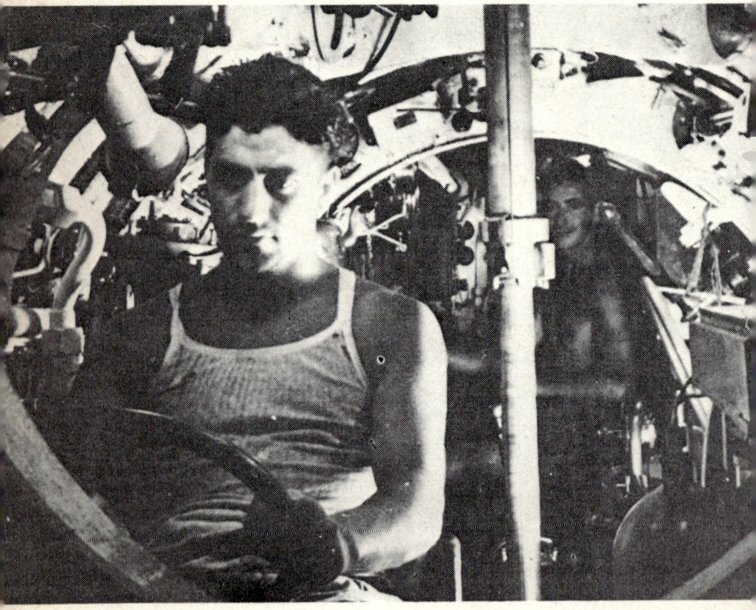

Left: HMS *Thrasher* towing X-5 out of Loch Cairnbawn. The head and shoulders of the passage CO can be seen in the open hatchway of the 'wet-and-dry'./*IWM*

Bottom left: Interior of an X-craft—the helmsman as seen from the 'wet-and-dry'./*Submarine Museum*

Below: Interior of an X-craft—the CO at the periscope./*Submarine Museum*

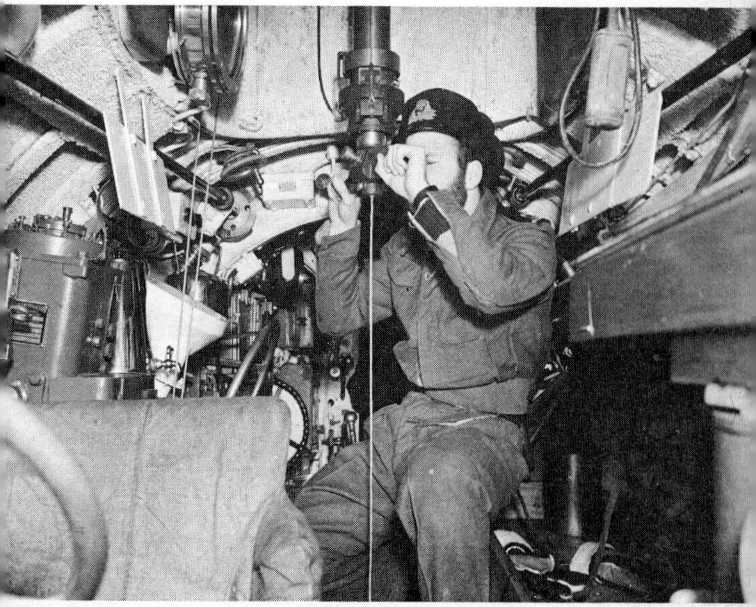

Above: The First Lieutenant at the diving controls of an X-craft. /*Submarine Museum*

Top right: An X-craft diving./*Submarine Museum*

Right: Aerial view of *Tirpitz* moored in Kaa Fjord, taken by a Russian aircraft./*IWM*

ALTEN FJORD
TIRPITZ
KAA FJORD

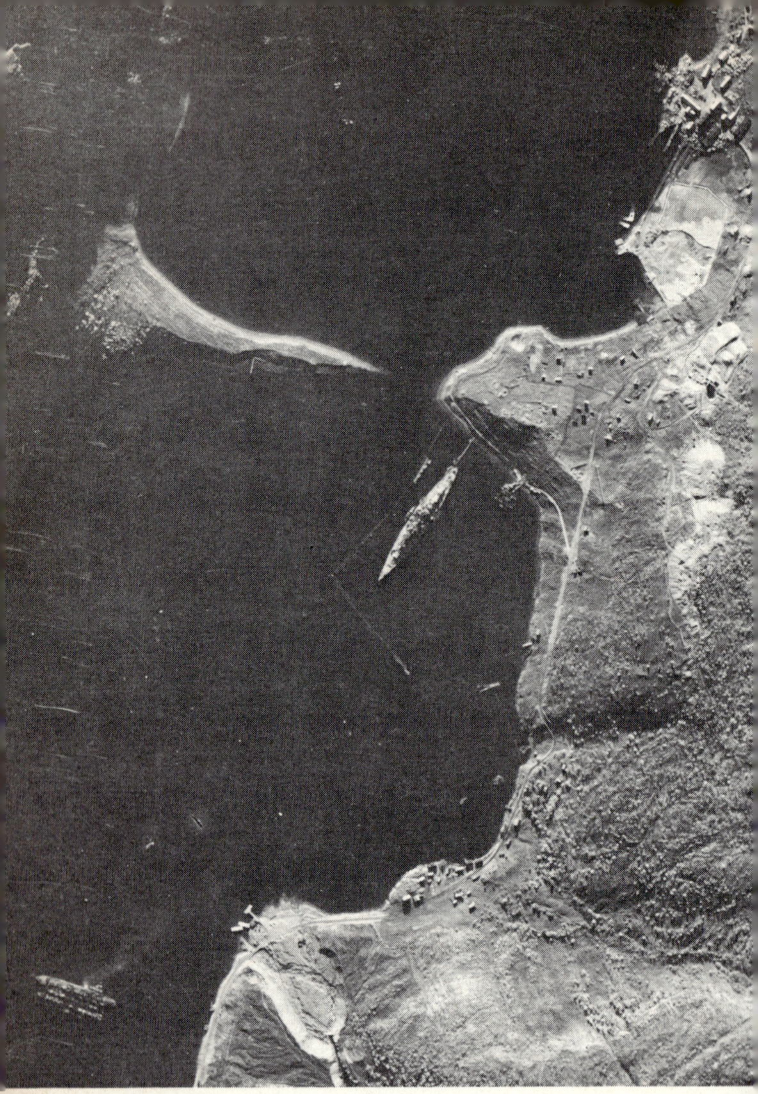

Reconnaissance photograph of *Tirpitz* moored in Kaa Fjord, September 1943. The nets, and particularly the boat gap, can be clearly seen./*MOD Crown Copyright*

There remained about fifteen miles to go to the slipping position before the final approach by the chariots. Craig and Evans completed their preliminary dressing and Brewster and Brown began as Trondheim came abeam to starboard. The east wind increased steadily and *Arthur* began to pitch into the steep sea set up in the fjord. There was nothing to do but press on at reduced speed in the hope that the sudden storm would blow itself out before they reached the entrance to Asenfjord where *Tirpitz* was berthed. Their luck was out. The chariots could be heard bumping erratically against *Arthur*'s keel and just after 2200 they heard a 'loud, grinding, tearing noise' and then a jerk and a shudder as something hit *Arthur*'s propellor. One of the chariots had broken adrift.

Larsen eased *Arthur* into sheltered water and Brewster ordered Evans, who was fully dressed, to go over the side and inspect the remaining chariot. It too was gone. Both chariots had broken adrift and were lost, the towing lugs torn from them and still shackled to the wires secured to *Arthur*'s keel. They had come undetected within ten miles of their target and their disappointment was intense. Brewster wrote:

> 'We were dismayed. The chariots were gone and the attempt was off. I don't think anyone has ever been so disappointed as we were that night. We were within ten miles of the pride of the German Navy; all our obstacles were behind us; and we might as well have been at the North Pole. Looking back, I don't remember a single curse. We were all too unhappy for that.'

Brewster and Larsen held a quick consultation. Although undetected they decided against trying to steam back to the Shetlands; they would have to sell the peat to obtain the necessary clearance papers for a start and it was very doubtful if *Arthur*'s patched engine would last out the voyage. They could only scuttle the boat and make their way to Sweden as planned. At about 0100 on 1st November, in flat calm water in the lee of the land, they went ashore in two parties by dinghy and scuttled *Arthur* by opening the sea-cocks and boring holes in her bottom. They were in the wrong place for help from the Norwegian resistance movement as arranged and so had to walk to the Swedish frontier. They split into two parties, Larsen, Kalve, Craig, Evans and Tebb in one, Björnöy, Strand, Brewster, Brown and Causer in the other. Just short of the frontier Larsen's group were accosted by two armed police. Bluff proved unavailing and in the ensuing gun fight Evans was shot in the stomach. His companions were forced to leave him for dead. Larsen and the rest of his party crossed the frontier that night, as did Björnöy and Brewster's group. It had taken both groups four days and nights of hard going since they had left *Arthur*. A fortnight later they were flown back from Sweden to England, where Larsen was awarded the Conspicuous Gallantry Medal, the first non-Briton so to be honoured, and Brewster the Distinguished Service Cross.

Evans in fact had not died from the shot which hit him in the skirmish. The Germans took him to hospital and restored him to health. Then they interrogated him and on the express orders of the High Command he was shot as a spy.

The Germans also located *Arthur* which had drifted inshore and finally sunk with her masts still above water. A careful investigation revealed the hidden compartment and the Germans were able to make an intelligent deduction of the kind of attack which had been attempted. Operation 'Title' had only just failed.

Winter–Spring 1942–43

Tirpitz remained at her anchorage in Trondheimfjord all through the winter of 1942–43, carrying out an extensive programme of self-maintenance which even included making a caisson so that the rudder could be changed while the ship was still afloat. The loss of *Gneisnau*, bombed in dry dock after the Channel dash, had dissuaded Hitler from risking the return to Germany of *Tirpitz* and there was no dry dock big enough to take her in Norway. But while *Tirpitz* was refitting there occurred an episode which was to have far reaching political effects on her future.

On 30th December 1942 Vice-Admiral Kummetz put to sea from Alten Fjord in the *Hipper*, with *Lutzow* and six destroyers in company, to attack convoy JW 51B which had been reported by a U-boat as 'weakly protected'. (The Arctic convoy numbering had recently been changed for security reasons from PQ and QP, outward and inward respectively, to JW and RA with a numerical sequence beginning at 51.) JW 51B had as close escort six destroyers under Captain Sherbrooke in HMS *Onslow*, two corvettes, two trawlers and a minesweeper. Rear-Admiral Burnett with two cruisers and two destroyers was giving support at long range while some 500 miles to the west the Commander-in-Chief cruised with units of the Home Fleet in the hope of a chance at *Tirpitz*.

At 0930 on New Year's Eve the German forces opened fire on the first British destroyer and attempted to attack the convoy. Five and a half hours later it was all over. Courageous and skilful handling of the destroyers and the arrival of Rear-Admiral Burnett with the cruisers had driven off the enemy. The British lost the destroyer *Achates* and the minesweeper *Bramble* sunk, the destroyers *Onslow*, *Obedient* and *Obdurate* damaged; the Germans lost the destroyer *Friedrich Eckholdt* sunk and the cruiser *Hipper* severely damaged. The only merchant ship to be hit was the *Calobre*. Just at the moment when the Germans had had a very fair chance of inflicting a great deal of damage on the British Vice-Admiral Kummetz had received a signal ordering him to take no risks and he had been forced to disengage without subjecting the British cruisers to the *Lutzow*'s 11in guns. As with convoy PQ 17 interference from ashore at a vital tactical moment had again been proved ill-advised.

The results of this abortive sortie were to be very important. Hitler was dismayed over the disaster of Stalingrad and was anxiously awaiting a victory over the Arctic convoy to brighten the New Year and to show as a credit in the campaign against Russia. Kummetz's failure caused the Führer to lose his temper and to attempt to immobilise his big ships. He proposed to land their big guns and to mount them ashore to repel the anticipated Allied invasion, to convert the cruisers and pocket battleships into aircraft carriers and to put all available effort into a submarine building programme. Hitler asked Grand Admiral Raeder to comment on these proposals. Raeder submitted his comments and his resignation and on 30th January 1943, after twenty-five years as Commander-in-Chief of the German Navy, he handed over this responsibility to Admiral Karl Dönitz.

Although Dönitz was already Admiral Submarines he was too far-seeing a naval strategist to desire the disbandment of the capital ships and the consequent release of British naval forces for use elsewhere, and he persuaded Hitler to reconsider the order which he had said was 'Irrevocable'. The capital ships remained but always with the uncertain feeling that they were viewed with suspicion at the Führer's headquarters, the target for snide comment by Field-Marshall Goering for their expensive uselessness, particularly since a shortage of oil and oilers to transport it was becoming steadily more embarrassing to the Naval Command.

In March 1943 *Tirpitz* left Trondheim after her winter of self-refitting and joined *Scharnhorst* and six destroyers at Alten Fjord at the northernmost tip of Norway. Here was a constant source of trouble for the Allies; a fast and heavily-gunned pair of ships poised either to strike out into the Atlantic or to swoop on the Arctic convoys at will, yet almost inaccessible in their mountain-ringed anchorages, guarded by two fighter airfields at Bardufoss and Banak, out of range of land-based bombers except by the use of the primitive Russian facilities, their potential for destruction was enormous. As it transpired their actual achievement was farcical.

Spitzbergen—9th September 1943

One hundred and fifty miles north of Bear Island and four hundred miles north of Alten Fjord and North Cape, the most northerly point of Norway and the Continent of Europe, is South Cape, the most southerly point of the island of Spitzbergen. A bleak island which before the war had some 3,000 inhabitants, Norwegian and Russian, whose livelihood had been coal mining, its inhabitants had been evacuated by the Allies in August 1941 and the mines smashed. A month later the Germans had set up a weather reporting station on the island. A rival Norwegian station had been established in the summer of 1942 and the Germans had been forced to evacuate their weathermen by submarine.

At dawn on 9th September 1943 *Tirpitz* and *Scharnhorst* opened fire with their main armament against the two 3in guns which comprised the defences of Barentsberg and the destroyers ran inshore with landing parties. Before noon it was all over: some prisoners had been taken, a supply dump destroyed, the wireless station wrecked and the landing parties had returned on board. The German ships retired unmolested to the apparently safe waters of Alten Fjord. For the only time in her existence *Tirpitz* had fired her main armament offensively at low trajectory. Although those on board were not to know it *Tirpitz* had carried out her last operation. In the fourteen months remaining to her she was to be nothing but a target for attack—almost her only voyage was that from Alten Fjord to the shallow anchorage of Tromsö.

CHAPTER THREE

The Attack by the X-Craft

Building and Trials

Although there had been proposals for small submarines to attack enemy targets in harbour, mostly put forward during and after the Great War by two distinguished submariners, Commanders Geoffrey Layton and Max Horton (both of whom were to become Admirals and Commanders-in-Chief), the ideas had never been favourably received and it was left to a retired officer, Commander Cromwell Varley, DSC, to design and have built the first prototype X-craft which was launched into the Hamble River near Southampton. This vessel was designated X-3, X-1 being the letter and number given to the 3,500ton cruiser submarine commissioned in 1929 whose armament had included four 5·2in guns, and X-2 the number given to the Italian submarine *Galileo Galilei* which had surrendered off Aden to the gun-boat *Moonstone* shortly after Italy had entered the war. However except in actual size and armament X-3 and her successors were to differ very little from any normal submarine, and indeed were but little shorter overall than the Holland class boats which were first accepted into the Royal Navy in 1902.

Overall the X-craft had a length of 51ft with a pressure hull diameter of 5½ft, and a diving depth of 300ft. They were powered by a Gardner diesel engine for propulsion on the surface and for charging the battery by means of a generator which itself acted as a motor to drive the craft when dived. Initially there was a crew of three, later increased to four, cramped into whatsoever space there was left inside the pressure hull that was not required for machinery, with a deck-head height of only four and a half feet. In two respects the X-craft differed from a conventional submarine. Between the forward compartment which was the control room and the midships section which contained the battery was a space known as the wet-and-dry (or W&D) with a hatch in the pressure-hull overhead and pressure tight hatches fore and aft into the two compartments.* This was the means of exit and entry for a diver when submerged and also for the officer of the watch when keeping watch on the surface. It also served the secondary purpose of housing the 'head' or lavatory with its complex pressure-assisted flushing arrangements. The second difference was the armament. Instead of torpedoes the X-craft was fitted with side-cargoes, detachable ground mines each containing two tons of amatol and fitted with a time switch operated fuse which could be set from inside the craft and allowed up to a 36hr delay.

That the X-craft ever got beyond the drawing board or prototype stage was due to the most fortunate succession of chances. Cromwell Varley had retired from the Navy to direct an engineering business and as a submarine commanding officer of the Great War had been a contemporary and friend of Admiral Sir Max Horton, Flag Officer, Submarines, for the first two years of the war prior to his appointment as Commander-in-Chief, Western Approaches. Horton himself had endeavoured to interest the Admiralty in at least three designs of midget submarine in the period between the wars and since the Prime Minister, Winston Churchill, was an enthusiastic supporter of any ideas for carrying the war to the enemy X-3 received a very favourable reception. (By contrast it was to take Barnes Wallis three years to get anyone to give him support for the Tallboy 12,000lb bombs which were finally to sink the *Tirpitz*.) Thus as early as midsummer 1941 the first naval personnel were appointed to this unusual organisation. These were Lieut W. D. Meeke, DSC, RN, Lieut Donald Cameron, RNR and Chief ERA Richardson. A drifter named *Present Help* was provided as a tender and by the end of the year experimental side cargoes had been satisfactorily exploded.

X-3 was launched at 2300 on 15th March 1942 and made her first dive on 24th. A month later the first newly-commissioned volunteer officers were selected for 'special duties' and in late May they began their theoretical and practical training at Fort Blockhouse, Gosport, (HMS *Dolphin*, the submariners' alma mater), and in X-3 in the Hamble River. After further submarine training at Blythe and Rothesay they reported to the newly set-up X-craft base at the Kyles of Bute Hydropathic Hotel, Port Bannatyne on the Isle of Bute, commis-

* This arrangement of compartments was peculiar to X-3 and X-4. In all subsequent craft it was reversed so that the control room was in its more normal place amidships and the battery was stored in the forward compartment.

sioned as HMS *Varbel*. This name must be unique amongst ships' names of the Royal Navy since it was concocted by combining the surnames of Commander Var(ley) and Commander T. I. S. Bel(l), DSC, RN who was the serving officer in charge of personnel and training. Had its significance been appreciated when it was proposed to Admiralty it would no doubt have been rejected. Varley remained as a civilian throughout the war, conspicuous in his tweed suit amongst the naval uniforms. Port Bannatyne was an excellent base, near the main submarine base of HMS *Cyclops* in Rothesay Bay yet hidden from curious eyes by a little spit of land, with direct access to Loch Striven and northwards through the Kyles of Bute, a waterway too narrow and purposeless to interest anything larger than a fishing boat. It is remarkable that although eighteen months were to elapse from the launching of X-3 until the first operation, during which time craft had to be built and tested and crews trained, the Germans appear to have been quite ignorant of their existence.

On 26th August, after a series of successful trials in Portland Harbour, X-3 was loaded on to a railway truck and taken by land from Southampton to Faslane, where she was hoisted into the waters of the Clyde and escorted by HMS *Alecto* to Loch Striven. Ardtaraig House, at the head of the loch, was taken over as *Varbel II* and while Meeke went to Vickers-Armstrong to supervise the building of six operational craft the training of crews was continued in X-3 under Cameron and his new first lieutenant, John Lorimer.

In November the first major accident occurred. Since the X-craft had so little freeboard they were fitted with an air induction pipe to allow them to use the main engine on the surface without being swamped in a sea-way—it could in fact be used as a snort mast although not designed as such and the practice was not advisable. Where the induction pipe entered the craft a valve could be screwed shut to seal the pressure hull before diving. During an afternoon's training a piece of flotsam jammed unnoticed in the valve and as the craft dived, water poured into the pressure hull. Lorimer, who was in command, immediately ordered the blowing of all main ballast but in the confusion the only wheel spanner was dropped and lost under the deck boards. As the water continued to pour in the craft dropped stern first to the bottom of Loch Striven in a hundred and ten feet of water.

Lorimer quickly appreciated that they would have to escape from the steadily flooding craft and he and the two trainees, Sub-Lts Gay and Laites, put on their DSEA breathing sets. It took some forty minutes for the X-craft to flood up completely, even with the opening of additional valves, during which time the three of them had to stand crouched in the dark, their eyes troubled by the chlorine gas given off from the flooded battery, while the cold water rose slowly up their legs and bodies. With the pressure inside and outside the craft equalled Gay was able to open the hatch and to pull himself out. Laites however was in trouble having exhausted all the oxygen in his DSEA set and was losing consciousness. With great courage Lorimer removed the set from Laites, put a fresh one on him and then physically manhandled him up through the hatch. The fresh set was torn off as Laites went through the hatch but he surfaced and was picked up by the dinghy from *Present Help*. Lorimer, exhausted by cold and the effort of getting Laites out, and almost unconscious himself from lack of oxygen in his own now-exhausted bottle, managed to clamber out of the hatch and rise successfully to the surface.

Present Help had seen the accident occur and had immediately signalled 'Tripper', the code-word to denote a submarine disaster. By 2300 that evening HMS *Tedworth*, the salvage vessel, had not only arrived but had raised X-3 from the bottom, a remarkable achievement even allowing for the fact that everything had been favourable. X-3 was taken to Portsmouth for refit.

Training continued on the Clyde with X-4, which had newly arrived with Lieut Godfrey Place, DSC, RN as commanding officer, and in December the first fatal casualty occurred. While the craft was on the surface for an endurance exercise Sub-Lt Morgan Thomas, RNVR climbed out of the wet-and-dry to take over the watch on the casing from Place, who went below and shut himself initially into the control-room forward. It was a dirty night and Thomas was caught by an unexpected wave which not only washed him overboard but flooded the wet-and-dry which still had its upper hatch open. X-4 took on a near vertical angle with the bows out of water and drifted helplessly, Place in the forward compartment and ERA Whitely aft, separated from each other by the flooded wet-and-dry and unable to communicate. Place managed to send a distress signal to *Present Help* anchored near-by in Loch Ranza. After a couple of hours the drifter was able to pass a hawser round X-4's stern and haul the craft horizontal so that the wet-and-dry could be baled out.

On New Year's Eve 1942 X-5 was launched at Faslane; X-6 arrived on 11th January 1943 and the remaining four craft shortly after. The lessons learnt in training had been incorporated as modifications. Apart from the major change of lay-out in bringing the control-room amidships and putting the battery forward the new craft were much as before, but the wet-and-dry hatch could now be shut from the control-room and the induction pipe had a bar and strap on it for the officer of the watch, both arising from X-4's mishap. As well as the operational craft their new depot ship, HMS *Bonaventure* under the command of Captain W. E. Banks, DSC, RN, came to Loch Striven.

It had been the intention of the Naval Staff for the attack on *Tirpitz* to be carried out in the spring of 1943. The timing was critical: the weather had to be reasonably good to permit the use of X-craft (which precluded the winter) as well as their need for sufficient daylight for navigation, yet there had to be sufficient darkness to cover the approach (which precluded the summer). Against a target berthed five degrees north of the Arctic circle this limited the periods to the March and September equinoxes, the exact dates being further dependent on the phases of the moon. There remained too a still unsolved problem; how to get the X-craft within striking distance of *Tirpitz*. Although the craft had an operational range of 1,500mls at 4knots, just sufficient to make the passage to and return from Alten Fjord, the living conditions were so uncomfortable that the crew would be exhausted long before they reached the target. Reluctantly Flag Officer, Submarines, Rear-Admiral Barry who had relieved Admiral Sir Max Horton in November 1942, had to advise the Naval Staff that a spring attack was not possible and that it would have to be postponed until the autumn. This delay was probably the best thing possible, since it allowed for further specialised training and for the intelligence and planning of the operation to be detailed rather than rushed. However it was hardly likely to have pleased the Prime Minister who, while suffering from pneumonia in North Africa, had cheered himself by dictating a series of memoranda including one on 13th February 1943 to the Chief of Combined Operations, Paymaster-General, First Sea Lord, Chief of the Air Staff and C-in-C Bomber Command.

> 'Have you given up all plans for doing anything to *Tirpitz* while she is in Trondheim? We heard a lot of talk about it five months ago, which all petered out. At least four or five plans were under consideration. It seems very discreditable that the Italians should show themselves so much better at attacking ships in harbour than we do.
>
> What has happened to the chariots and diving mines?* I should

* This was probably a reference to the 'Johnnie Walker' mine which was conceived as a weapon for use against *Tirpitz* and used by the Royal Air Force in September 1944.

be much obliged if you would take stock of the position, if possible together, and thereafter give me a report. It is a terrible thing that this prize should be waiting and no one be able to think of a way of winning it.'

Apart from the proposal that the X-craft should make their own way to and from Norway, two other ideas were considered. The first was that they should be towed by Norwegian fishing boats, like *Arthur*, to within striking distance but this was rejected for two reasons; a practical trial had shown the fishing boat to be insufficiently powered for the tow, and the boats available were not from the Narvik area and would be suspect since Norwegian fishing boats have noticeable local characteristics. The second suggestion was that they should be carried aboard the depot ship and launched near the Norwegian coast. Such an expedition, however, would be bound to attract attention, however carefully the actual launching was screened from reconnaissance aircraft, and thus alert all enemy naval forces just at the moment when this was least desirable. It was finally decided that the best method would be to tow each X-craft with a large submarine, which would also help to recover it and tow it back to base after the attack. With this decided the detailed planning for the operation in the autumn could be begun.

Throughout the summer of 1943 the X-craft, now formed with the charioteers into the 12th Submarine Flotilla, carried out arduous and specialised training under Commander D. C. Ingram, DSC, RN. HMS *Bonaventure*, commanded by Captain P. Q. Roberts, RN, moved to Loch Cairnbawn, remotely hidden just north of Loch Ewe, where exercises were carried out against capital ships of the Home Fleet, carefully protected by nets. Net cutting was practised back in Loch Striven and in May Sub-Lt Locke was lost after cutting X-7 through a net. As a result the operational crew of each X-craft was increased from three to four, the extra man being a specially trained diver recruited from the charioteers. The passage crew remained at three, an officer, a stoker and an electrical rating, their prime task being to ensure that the craft was handed over in a fully functioning condition at the end of the tow. Everything that could be done in preparation and training was done during the summer of 1943.

Operational Preparations and the Passage

The code-name for the midget submarine attack on *Tirpitz* was Operation 'Source', but even within this overall plan there were three separate sets of plans to be prepared. Operation 'Funnel' was the attack on the target in Alten Fjord; Operation 'Empire' was for the Narvik area between 67° and 69° north; and Operation 'Forced' for the Trondheim area between 63° and 65° north. What was essential was a knowledge of the enemy's whereabouts, his intentions and his defences. There were two ways of obtaining the necessary information, by aerial reconnaissance and by signalled information, from members of the Norwegian Resistance, and both were used to the full.

Torstein Raaby, who was later to gain fame as a member of Kon-Tiki's crew, had spent most of 1941 sending meteorological reports from a deserted Arctic island and later from a secret transmitter in Tromsö, before being forced to flee to Sweden and thence to England. He was returned to Norway near Trondheim in the Submarine *Ula* and from there made his way first to Hammerfest and then to Alten. Here he was helped to obtain a job, and working in close association with two other Norwegians, Karl Rasmussen and Harry Pettersen, Raaby began sending daily radio reports to London about the German ships. He lived next door to a German officer and delighted in the impertinence of using his neighbour's receiving aerial to do duty for his transmitter!

Air reconnaissance was equally complicated to arrange. Alten Fjord was out of range of aircraft from any Scottish base and it was necessary therefore to have a reconnaissance unit based in Russia. The Admiralty were unwilling to rely on Russian reconnaissance. Nearly every signal or memorandum during the war shows a frightening lack of co-operation from the Russian authorities for any facilities for their allies, whether it were for the setting up of a medical unit or for recreational facilities in Murmansk for convoy crews, and there was no reason to suppose that their reconnaissance would be either effective or accurate. In May the Admiralty asked that a British photo-reconnaissance be laid on and in July the Royal Air Force agreed. Thanks to the efforts of Admiral Fisher in Moscow Russian approval was obtained and on 21st August a Mosquito unit was due to fly to Vaenga but they were delayed for six days by bad weather and the non-arrival of the photographers' visas! They left on 27th, their equipment going in the destroyers *Musketeer* and *Mahratta* to Kola Inlet. In the event no Mosquito reconnaissance was possible and the task had to be carried out by PR Spitfires which arrived at Vaenga on 3rd September, just eight days before the X-craft were scheduled to leave Loch Cairnbawn on their passage.

In order to give the X-craft sufficient darkness and at the same time sufficient moonlight to make their approach up the fjords the attack had to be made during the period 20–25th September, and the former was therefore chosen as the latest date for slipping from the towing submarines. This entailed a departure from the Loch Cairnbawn base on the 11th September. On 30th August HMS *Titania*, under the command of Commander W. R. Fell, OBE, DSC, RN, arrived at Loch Cairnbawn as depot ship for towing submarines and within the next two days the six towing submarines arrived: *Thrasher* (Lieut A. R. Hezlet, DSC, RN), *Truculent* (Lieut R. L. Alexander, DSO, RN), *Syrtis* (Lieut M. H. Jupp, DSC, RN), *Seanymph* (Lieut J. P. H. Oakley, DSC, RN), *Stubborn* (Lieut A. A. Duff, RN) and *Sceptre* (Lieut I. S. McIntosh, MBE, DSC, RN). *Satyr* and *Sea-Dog* were held in reserve at Scapa Flow at twenty-four hours' notice. On 1st September all leave was stopped at Loch Cairnbawn.

All the towing submarines were fitted with a special towing tube and slip, as were the two reserve submarines, and five days were spent in trials, towing, slipping and recovery. There were two types of rope, a special hemp hawser with a telephone cable laid into its centre as a core, and a new type made of nylon. Cameron had been to some pains to ensure that he acquired a nylon hawser for X-6. On 6th September after a final swinging of compasses the X-craft were hoisted inboard of *Bonaventure* for final preparations and the fitting of side cargoes. There remained only the briefing of the crews.

Normal photographic reconnaissance and messages signalled by the Norwegian Resistance had kept the Admiralty well advised of *Tirpitz*'s presence in Kaa Fjord, in company with *Scharnhorst* and *Lutzow*, the latter in the adjacent Lange Fjord. On 7th September the first Spitfire reconnaissance for several days was flown and reported *Tirpitz* and *Scharnhorst* absent from their berths, confirming a message received from Raaby. The situation for Flag Officer, Submarines and the Naval Staff was very tense. (Unbeknown to them *Tirpitz* and *Scharnhorst* had sailed for the bombardment of Spitzbergen.) However by 10th September reconnaissance showed that the big ships were back at their normal berths and Admiral Barry flew to Loch Cairnbawn to speed the X-craft on their journey.

It had been hoped that before the X-craft left a Catalina could fly back from Russia with photographs taken of *Tirpitz*, but this could not be done so all details had to be analysed in Russia and signalled. However Flag Officer, Submarines remarked:

> 'The subsequent reconnaissances flown by this unit were invaluable. Full details of the disposition of the enemy units and net defences

were signalled from Russia and given to all the personnel taking part before they left harbour. The first photographs taken by this unit did not arrive until a few hours after the X-craft had sailed; but this did not in fact matter, as the relevant information was complete in the signalled report.'

The date for the slipping of the X-craft was known as D-day (subsequently to be used for a far more notable occasion). The towing submarines after leaving Loch Cairnbawn were to make their way independently to a position 75 miles west of the Shetlands and then to proceed on parallel courses twenty miles apart until about 150 miles west of Alten Fjord, when they were to steer for their landfalls. Each submarine had an area off Söröy Island where it was to slip its X-craft just outside the declared mined area after dusk on D-day and was then to patrol there until 27th September before attempting to recover the returning X-craft. The X-craft themselves were to cross the mined area on the surface and to make their way via Stjernsund to Alten Fjord, bottoming during the daylight of 21st. They were to enter Kaa Fjord at dawn on 22nd.

At 1600 on 11th September *Truculent* with X-6 and *Syrtis* with X-9 on tow left Loch Cairnbawn, followed at intervals of two hours by *Thrasher* with X-5, *Seanymph* with X-8 and *Stubborn* with X-7. *Sceptre* with X-10 having the shortest route sailed at 1300 on 12th. The passage for the first four days was uneventfully made in fine weather, the T-class making good an average speed of 10knots, the S-class $8\frac{1}{2}$knots. The X-craft were towed dived, surfacing every six hours or so for fifteen minutes to ventilate the craft.

On 14th September the Spitfire photographs were received in England and Flag Officer, Submarines was able to signal details of the defences and to allocate targets to the X-craft. Target plan No. 4 was adopted: X-5, X-6 and X-7 were to attack *Tirpitz*, X-9 and X-10 *Scharnhorst*, and X-8 *Lutzow* in Lange Fjord, a long arm on the west side of Alten Fjord some 10 miles from Kaa Fjord at its head. Snow which had been on the high ground in August was falling low down the mountainside; by the day after the attack there was to be light snow on the low ground. The defences were signalled as follows:

'Photographs confirm two single nets average width 410ft, probably A/S across entrance to Kaa Fjord which may possibly be secured to bottom. NW end joins shore—gap 900ft between S.E. end and shore.

> Double A/T net from shore parallel to *Tirpitz* and 170ft from starboard side then across bow to gate. Centre of gate 600ft north of ship's bow. Thence single net to shore with 4 small rafts incorporated. There is NO gap.
>
> *Scharnhorst* enclosed on either side by double line of A/T nets: movable portion of nets is ahead of ship.
>
> *Lutzow* protected by double A/T net not across anchorage.'

The Germans had listening posts and small submarine chasers in the approaches and also maintained a boat with constant hydrophone watch some 600yds E.S.E. of the gap in the nets by Jemmeluftneset at the entrance to Kaa Fjord, stopping and checking all craft entering. The gap in *Tirpitz*'s anti-torpedo nets was closed after the last boat had gone through for the night until next morning, and *Tirpitz* kept hydrophone watch during the hours of darkness. By chance on the night of 21st–22nd September communications between *Tirpitz* and Bossekop ashore broke down so that a continuous flow of boat traffic was necessary. The gap remained open and was patrolled all night by a ship's boat and hydrophone watch kept until 0600 on the morning of 22nd, but this break from routine of course was not to be known by the X-craft.

The next two days of the passage, 15th and 16th, were to be very eventful for three out of the six X-craft. At 0100 on the morning of 15th the telephone link between X-8 and *Seanymph* failed and three hours later the tow parted at 0400. X-8 surfaced five minutes later but was unable to see *Seanymph* although the visibility was about five miles, so half-an-hour later X-8 set course 029° at 3knots on main engine, her estimated position being 69° 04′ N. 08° 14′ E. *Seanymph* did not discover the broken tow for another couple of hours when X-8 was due to surface and ventilate. She immediately turned to retrace her course and to search for the lost midget, which she did in vain.

Meanwhile at 1213 *Stubborn* sighted what she took to be a U-boat and dived for an hour and ten minutes, surfacing when it seemed safe to do so and there was nothing in sight. This sighting was probably X-8 searching hopefully for *Seanymph*. At 1550 the tow between *Stubborn* and X-7 parted but X-7 surfaced immediately and an auxiliary tow was passed. While this was being secured X-8 sighted them and closed and at 1718 *Stubborn* with X-7 securely in tow and X-8 keeping thankful company began searching for *Seanymph*. They had no success and as dusk fell at 1900 course was altered to the northward and a signal sent to Flag Officer, Submarines who broad-

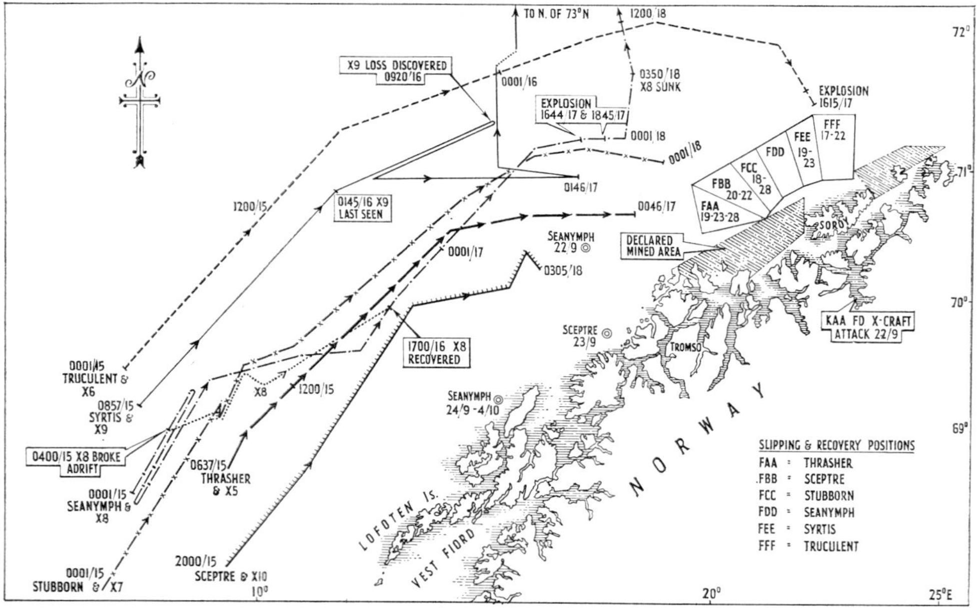

Track chart for Operation 'Source', 15th September 1943 to 4th October 1943.

cast the information back to *Seanymph*. (For this operation all signals between Flag Officer, Submarines, the operating authority, and the submarines were coded by a sytem of individual one-time pads; whilst ensuring the maximum security in the event of any mishap or capture of the towing submarines it meant that only the operating authority could encode or decode the submarines' signals and they were unable to read each others'.)

At midnight 15/16th X-8 lost contact with *Stubborn* and X-7 by steering the wrong course. By a misunderstanding in the turn-over of the watch the middle watch helmsman steered 146° instead of 046° and the mistake was not appreciated until 0400. At about 0300 on 16th dawn revealed to *Stubborn* that her foundling had gone astray in the dark but as the day lightened *Seanymph* was sighted and signals exchanged in position 69° 35′ N. 10° 16′ E. *Stubborn* and X-7 headed back northwards while *Seanymph* continued the search for her wayward sibling, whom she eventually found at 1700 that evening, barely two hours before dusk. They had been parted for over thirty-six hours and while the new tow was being secured in good weather the operational crew took over from the exhausted passage crew. By 2005 *Seanymph* resumed course for Alten Fjord with X-8 firmly back in tow astern.

However *Syrtis* and X-9 were not to be so fortunate. On 15th the telephone link between them had failed making communication impossible when the submarine was dived. At 0120 on 16th after a period on the surface for ventilation and battery charging X-9 dived. *Syrtis* increased speed gradually to 8½knots and set course east-north-east until 0855 when she dropped hand grenades as a signal to X-9 to surface. Nothing happened and when twenty minutes later the tow was hauled in it was found to have parted. *Syrtis* turned to retrace her course but in doing so a bight of the towing rope was washed overboard and took a couple of hours to clear from the entanglement near the propeller. A careful comparison of log readings and fuel consumption indicated that X-9 had broken the tow shortly after diving—probably between 0145 and 0300—and at 1145 *Syrtis* began to steam back along her tracks, only to run into fog with a visibility which varied from 2 miles to as little as 2 cables. At 1545 *Syrtis* sighted an oil slick along a course 090°—the course for the slipping position 200 miles to the east—and altered course to follow it. No further trace of X-9 was ever seen. By 0146 on the 17th *Syrtis* had approached within about a hundred miles of the Norwegian coast without finding X-9 and had reached the midget's 'furthest-on' position if all had been well. To continue surfaced so close to the enemy might prejudice the whole operation, so *Syrtis* turned to sweep back along the hoped-for track until 0620 when she turned to go north of the 73° parallel where she could break wireless silence. From 0128 until 0554 on the 18th *Syrtis* tried to pass a message to Flag Officer, Submarines, but without success, so finally she broadcast it. Even so it was not received and not until 2nd October did Flag Officer, Submarines know that X-9 had been lost and had taken no part in the attack.

The reason for the loss of X-9 is of course unknown but it was probably caused by the unexpected weight of the breaking tow rope and the loss of forward movement. Conditions during the latter part of the passage were far from calm, a generally quartering swell caused the towing submarines to lift and drop their sterns and to jerk the tow rope, and the best way for the X-craft to overcome a tendency to be jerked to the surface was to trim the craft heavy and use the hydroplanes to counteract this as necessary. The breaking of the tow would not only have removed the upward pull but would have made the craft even more bow heavy by the weight of the rope, and the loss of forward movement would diminish the effect of the hydroplanes. Once started on a bow down plunge an X-craft could be very hard to stop before reaching a depth at which the pressure hull would collapse.

X-8 and *Seanymph* were again having difficulties throughout the 17th. At 0725 X-8 began to have trouble keeping a trim and air could be heard escaping from the starboard side-cargo. Steadily the craft became heavier and listed further and further to starboard until by 1630 with the compensating tank dry and No. 2 main ballast tank fully blown the commanding officer (Lieut Macfarlane, RAN), decided that there was nothing else to do but to jettison the charge. This he did with the fuse set to 'safe' but a quarter of an hour later the side cargo exploded at a range of about half a mile, fortunately doing no damage. However the jettisoning of the starboard side-cargo caused X-8 to list to port, a sure indication that the port side-cargo was flooding and at 1655 Macfarlane decided that this too must be released. Warned by the previous premature explosion he set the fuse to a 2-hour delay, surfaced and let go the side-cargo. An hour and three quarters later, at 1840, this side-cargo exploded with tremendous force, severely damaging X-8, flooding the wet-and-dry, distorting water-tight doors and rendering her unable to dive, although the explosion was estimated to be $3\frac{1}{2}$ miles away.

In *Seanymph*, which was dived at the time, lights were broken.

Seanymph surfaced as darkness fell and after a prolonged effort of exchanging signals by lamp (the telephone was totally useless) turned to seaward until dawn when the crew of X-8 were taken off and the craft scuttled in position 71° 41′ N. 18° 11′ E. at 0350. *Seanymph* followed *Syrtis* to the area north of 73° N. to report to Flag Officer, Submarines. In his subsequent report the latter wrote:

> 'It is not clear why the second explosion caused such damage, at an apparent range of 3½ miles while the first explosion at only 1,000yds did none. Both charges had been dropped in approximately the same depth of water (180 fathoms). It may be that only partial detonation occurred in the first charge which had been set to "safe". Whatever the reason, the force of the second explosion would appear to have illustrated the efficiency of the charges. I find it hard to believe that the explosion was in fact 3½ miles away; but whatever the horizontal range was, there is no doubt about the depth of water, so that in any event the result of the explosion was indeed remarkable.'

Throughout the 18th September the remaining submarines continued to tow the X-craft satisfactorily. *Truculent* and *Thrasher* had experienced little if any difficulties and had made their landfalls on the preceding day; *Sceptre* who likewise had an uneventful passage made a landfall on 19th. It is worth noting that these three submarines and their X-craft were using the new nylon tow ropes; it was the hemp tows which gave trouble and parted. The original plan had been for the exchange of operational and passage crews to take place on 17th but bad weather prevented this and it was not until the evening of the 18th that *Stubborn* began the transfer to X-7. The transfer was difficult, the waves washing the rubber dinghy on to the craft and the submarine's ballast tanks, but with relief the passage crew handed over to their successors and anticipated the luxury of an S-class submarine. They were too optimistic. As *Stubborn* got under way the auxiliary tow rope, rigged three days earlier, parted. For an hour and a half Lieut Philip, SANF, the passage CO, bobbed perilously around in the rubber dinghy making attempts to pass a 2½in wire as a tow rope before it was successfully secured. *Stubborn* went ahead and the two parted again as the securing shackle came apart. Philip and Place, the operational CO, had been so cold in their fingers that they had been unable to screw the shackle properly tight. The tow was passed again, by heaving line, and at

0125 on 19th *Stubborn* set course for the slipping area with X-7 in tow. The whole operation had taken five hours in the dark, in a rough sea and in the cold of an Arctic autumn. During the following day the other three operational crews were successfully transferred to their craft.

Much of the credit for the success of the whole operation must be given to the passage crews. For eight or nine days these crews of three men had lived in appalling conditions, unable to stand upright, only in one place being able to stretch out more or less straight, tossed, jerked and rolled by the sea and the tow, cold, damp or just plain soaking wet, somehow they had managed to keep their craft in working order for their successors. They had ventilated and dried out their little submarines, charged the batteries, repaired faulty pieces of equipment, navigated, especially when the tow had broken and they had got lost, cooked their meals in a double saucepan like a carpenter's glue-pot with an electric element beneath it or boiled water for cocoa in an electric kettle, and when off watch slept fitfully on the bunk on top of the battery cells forward. It was selfless team-work of the highest order.

The Attack

By dawn on D-day—20th September—all four of the towing submarines with their X-craft were in their respective slipping zones, the operational crews safely transferred. *Seanymph* had been ordered to a patrol position some 60 miles west of Alten Fjord, but *Syrtis*, the loss of X-9 unknown to Flag Officer, Submarines, had received no new orders and so had taken station in her originally scheduled area to help with recovery after the attack. It was to be a frustrating operation for *Syrtis*'s commanding officer, Lieut Jupp. At 1843 on the 19th he had sighted a submarine which had dived five minutes later, and again at 0300 on 20th, in position 71° 00′ N. 22° 10′ E he again sighted a surfaced U-boat, steering 235° at 9knots at a range of 3,500yds. His orders were quite precise. In order not to compromise the operation submarine commanding officers were forbidden to attack anything below a capital ship either while they were on passage or awaiting the X-craft attack, and Jupp had no choice but to let a sitting target cross his bows unmolested at 1,500yds. Flag Officer, Submarines wrote:

> 'It reflects great credit on the look-out kept by our submarines that, with six of them in the vicinity, and four of them with

X-craft in tow, none were sighted. A single sighting might have compromised the whole operation.'

Meanwhile *Stubborn* and X-7 were making an eventful approach to their slipping position. Already delayed by the parting of the tow, at 0105 on 20th *Stubborn* sighted a mine and took avoiding action. The submarine cleared the mine but in so doing the mine's mooring line caught in the tow rope and the mine drifted slowly down towards X-7 until it came to rest firmly against the craft's bow. There was no telephone between *Stubborn* and X-7 as the tow was a makeshift affair so it was not until Place, realising through the periscope that something untoward had caused *Stubborn* to stop, came up on to the casing of X-7 so that he could see what had happened. He tried first to submerge the tow but this was no use, so gingerly pushing the mine away with his feet he cleared the mooring wire from the tow rope and finally kicked it clear, calling over to *Stubborn* as he did so, 'That's the first time I ever shoved a mine clear by its horns'. Peter Philip, the passage CO, had watched with dismay, not only at the danger to X-7 but because Place had borrowed his sea-boots on changing over crews; 'enormous, fleece-lined jobs, five guineas at Gieves and the apple of my eye'. Place was still wearing the boots when he was taken prisoner.

Between 1830 and 2000 on the evening of 20th September X-5, X-6, X-7 and X-10 all slipped from their towing submarines and began to make their way on the surface across the declared minefield towards Söröy Sund. The weather was very quiet, cold and still with some moonlight. X-6 had a certain amount of trouble due to flooding of the starboard charge but by throwing out all unnecessary gear, mostly food, and putting all stores to port the list was kept at 10° to 15°. The periscope was tending to cloud up and the automatic pilot refused to function but otherwise all was in fine order.

X-6 continued on the surface until 0125 when she dived at first light and continued up Söröy Sund submerged to the entrance of Stjern Sund and by dusk she was nearing Tommelholm, one of the Brattholm group of islands off the entrance to Kaa Fjord where the X-craft were to rendezvous if possible. X-6 surfaced to recharge batteries but had to make an emergency dive at the approach of a patrol boat. By 2100, back on the surface, X-6's crew was treated to a display of starshell and searchlights from the destroyer base at Lieffshaven. Shortly before midnight Cameron tucked X-6's bows between a couple of rocks to await first light.

X-7 had a comparatively uneventful passage up to the rendezvous. At 2315 Place exchanged shouts of good luck with Lieut Henty-Creer in X-5, the last time the latter was to be seen, and at 1630 sighted a large ship, probably *Scharnhorst*, steaming north in the lee of Aaroy Island. X-7 also spent the dark hours among the Brattholm group of islands, charging her batteries and undertaking final maintenance, but no contact was made with X-6.

X-10 had been handed over with a defective periscope hoisting motor which rapidly got worse. Then the gyro compass failed. Lieut Hudspeth decided to seek a discreet shelter on the north side of Stjernöy to try and repair them. They spent all day of the 21st making repairs though with little success, but at 1750 set off for Kaa Fjord. At 0135 an approaching vessel forced them to dive. The gyro compass was still defective and the light for the projector magnetic compass, accessible only from outside the craft, failed, leaving the X-craft with no means of steering any given course. Hudspeth decided to try and con the craft visually and raised the periscope, only for the motor to burn out, filling the craft with fumes. Hudspeth surfaced to ventilate the craft and unable in any way to navigate while dived made for Tommelholm on the surface. At 0215 he bottomed for the day in 195ft of water and the crew set to work to try and repair the defects, hoping to be able to attack their target, *Scharnhorst*, during the night of 22nd–23rd. As X-10 dived the floodlit A/S nets across the entrance to Kaa Fjord could be clearly seen four and a half miles away.

In order that the X-craft should not damage each other a careful schedule had been laid down. The first period for attacking was from 0100 to 0800 on 22nd with a firing period for any side cargo of one hour after this, i.e. from 0800 to 0900. Thereafter there was to be an alternating cycle of three hour attack periods and one hour firing periods.

X-6

Cameron planned to attack *Tirpitz* at 0630 on 22nd and to set his fuses with a six hour delay to explode at 1230 in the second firing period, thus leaving X-6 a reasonable chance of getting out of Kaa Fjord before the explosion revealed to the Germans that an attack had taken place. He set the time-fuse switch on the starboard (flooded) charge with no difficulty but the port time switch refused to function except on the two-hour setting. Cameron weighed up the situation very thoughtfully. X-6 had a flooded starboard charge which might

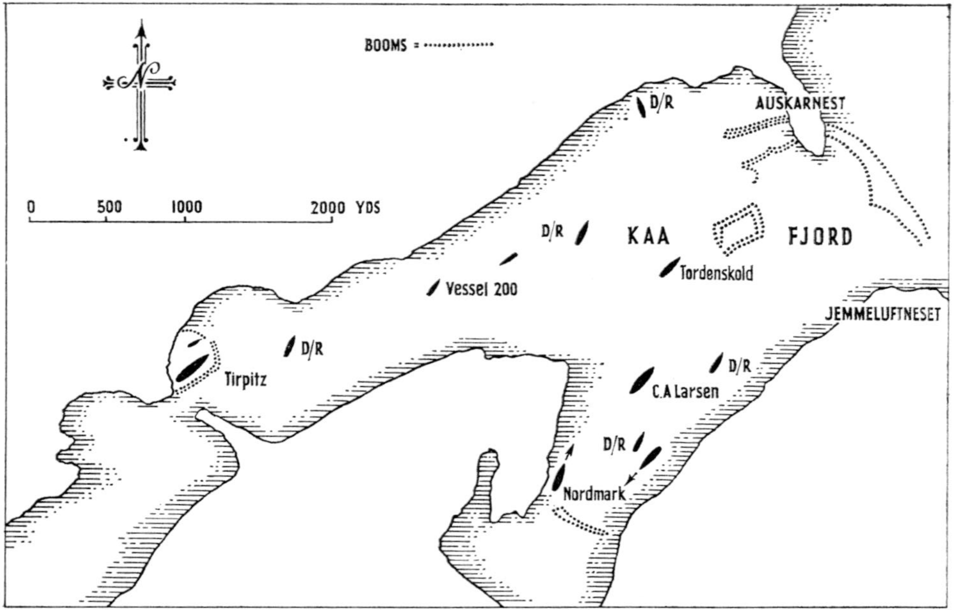

Operation 'Source'. Location of shipping and defensive booms in Kaa Fjord based on a reconnaissance sortie flown on 23rd September 1943, the day following the midget submarine attack.

not explode but was anyhow causing the greatest difficulty with the trim and might make the craft unmanageable if Kaa Fjord proved to be less saline than the outer waters, the firing clock for the port charge was unreliable, the periscope was leaking and continually misting up and there was an air leak in the forward ballast tank. If he attacked he might compromise the chances of X-5 and X-7, but he had not seen them and had no means of knowing whether or not they were still operational. Delay would not improve his chances and at 0145 X-6 set off for Kaa Fjord. The weather was dull and overcast and a stiffish breeze was raising white horses, ruffling the surface of the water and making conditions ideal for a submarine attack.

At 0400 Cameron could see nothing through the periscope. He ordered an alteration of course to the north and stripped the eyepiece, then turned back again to try and continue the attack. He raised the periscope and, as had happened in X-10, the hoist motor burnt out. ERA Goddard stripped it down, fudged a repair using an earth return, and X-6 went on. At 0445, hardly able to see, Cameron approached the nets at the entrance to Kaa Fjord. Broad on X-6's port bow the patrol boat could be discerned stopped by Jemmeluftneset, the south-eastern point at the entrance to Kaa Fjord, but X-6 was forced to pass close by to her by a ferry boat heading north. Cameron altered course for the hoped-for entrance when he heard more propellor noises and was just able to see a coaster preceding him through the boom. X-6 was too slow and too blind with a flooded periscope to follow submerged, so Cameron took an enormous chance. He surfaced and proceeded in the coaster's wake using the diesel, trusting that in the early morning no one would notice the craft, or if they did would not realise what it was, and that his noise would be lost in that of the coaster. After a few minutes X-6 was safely through the boom and dived again. The gamble had paid off.

For the third time during the attack Cameron stripped down the flooded periscope while X-6 proceeded at 60ft towards *Tirpitz*, some two miles up the fjord: when they came to periscope depth again they were forced to go deep suddenly to avoid knocking off the periscope on a destroyer's mooring cable. *Scharnhorst*'s berth by Auskarneset was empty but *Tirpitz* was secured behind her anti-torpedo nets. There was also anchored in the fjord the repair ship *Neumark*, a tanker and a Norwegian ship, three destroyers, *Z.30*, *Z.31* and *Erich Steinbrink*, and the very old Norwegian coastal defence ship *Tordenskold*, re-named by the Germans *Nymphe* and

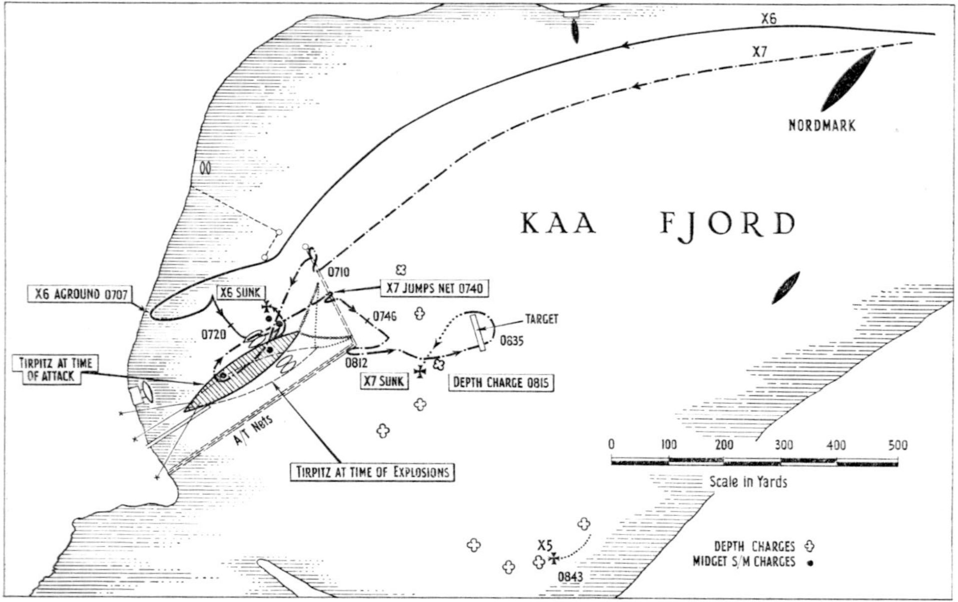

Operation 'Source' the attack on the *Tirpitz* by the midget submarines on 22nd September 1943 based on reports by the commanding officers of the midget submarines X6 and X7 and a German plan.

fitted out as an ack-ack ship. Cameron kept over to the northern shore by dead reckoning, scraped under an unexpected pontoon, and just after 0700 slipped unseen through the boat gap in the A/T net. At 0707 X-6 ran aground at the western shore and broke surface. She was seen aboard *Tirpitz* and reported but mistakenly considered to have been a porpoise and was disregarded! At about 0712 X-6 again broke surface about 30yds abeam of *Tirpitz* and was identified correctly. The periscope was again flooded and the gyro compass had stopped due to the violence of grounding and the subsequent large angles of dive and rise to which it had been subjected. Cameron groped his way blindly in what he believed was the right direction and was caught in what he thought were the starboard side A/T nets surrounding *Tirpitz*. He broke clear and surfaced close under *Tirpitz*'s port bow to be met with a fusilade of small arms fire and hand grenades—X-6 was too close for any of the battleship's guns to be brought to bear. It was obvious that escape was impossible so Cameron and his crew destroyed their more secret papers while he backed the submarine alongside *Tirpitz* and released both side-cargoes beside 'B' turret. Then they all climbed out from inside the craft on to the casing to surrender to a German picket-boat, which not only took them prisoner but put a line on to X-6 to tow her inshore. In this the Germans were unsuccessful. The Kingston valves had been opened and the motor put astern as the last of the crew had left the inside of the craft and the Germans were forced to cut their tow-rope to avoid the risk of being pulled under as X-6 remorselessly sank. Cameron and his crew were taken aboard *Tirpitz*.

X-7

At almost the same moment that X-6 was releasing her charges by 'B' turret of *Tirpitz* X-7 was doing likewise just a little further astern.

Place with X-7 had left Brattholme Island at 0045, an hour earlier than X-6, and had passed unseen and without incident through the boom at the entrance to Kaa Fjord at 0350. Then X-7 ran into trouble. Proceeding deep and blind up the fjord the craft became severely entangled in a rectangle of nets which protected a berth in the middle of the fjord.* Here X-7 remained enmeshed for an hour before her violent exertions enabled her to break free, but only at the expense of a defective gyro and a broken trim pump. By 0600 X-7 was free and Place decided to go deep beneath the anti-torpedo nets

* Possibly this was planned for *Lutzow*, but in fact the berth was never observed to have been used.

surrounding the target. This proved to be a mistake although a perfectly reasonable one. Intelligence and experience had led Place to expect the nets to reach some 60ft or so down from the surface but in fact another net covered the space below to the bottom of the sea-bed and X-7 was again entangled. She worked herself free but broke surface unnoticed and had to dive again, only to become enmeshed yet again at 95ft. These erratic manoeuvres rendered the gyro completely useless and Place let the craft come slowly to the surface so that he could see where he was. By some 'extraordinary lucky chance' (Place's own subsequent report) X-7 had broken clear of the A/T nets and was inside them with nothing between her and *Tirpitz* 30yds ahead. Place ordered the craft to 40ft and struck the battleship abreast of 'B' turret where he released his first side-cargo under the keel. He then went to 60ft and having turned went astern under *Tirpitz* for some 180ft and released his other side-cargo as nearly under 'X' turret as he could estimate. The first grenades thrown against X-6 were heard as X-7 hit *Tirpitz*, so X-7 must have laid her first side-cargo at about 0723 and the second a couple of minutes later.

After releasing both side-cargoes X-7 was taken down to 100ft and course altered to try and get her out through the gap where she had entered. However the compass was still not functioning and with no proper idea of a course to steer she was again caught in the nets. For about three quarters of an hour Place worked the craft on motors and by blowing ballast to clear her, but each time he won free it was to become enmeshed again. At 0740 X-7 broke surface and came under small arms fire, but cleared the net and dived to the bottom in 120ft. Getting under way but still blind X-7 again ran into a net somewhere off *Tirpitz*'s starboard bow until at 0812 a violent explosion shook the craft free. Place again bottomed to inspect the damage but although the pressure hull was still intact the machinery was so damaged that it was clearly impossible to try and make the return passage. Place therefore brought X-7 to the surface close to a battle-practice target and climbed out on to the casing under a hail of fire, waving his sweater in surrender. He had just time to step on the target before X-7, her ballast tanks leaking, sank beneath him at 0835.

Place was taken prisoner and nearly three hours later Sub-Lt Aitken made a successful escape from the craft but his two companions, Sub-Lt Whittam and ERA Whiteley failed to follow him and died, having exhausted their oxygen supply before they could get out of the hatch. All three had been forced to breathe their escape oxygen for much of the time while flooding up as the water reacted with the battery acid to produce chlorine, exactly as had happened in X-3 in the previous November.

Tirpitz

On board *Tirpitz* the day had begun much as usual. At 0500 the hydrophone listening watch had been secured and maintenance on the sets had been started when at 0707 an object was briefly sighted but mistaken for a porpoise and disregarded: it was X-6 running aground inside the A/T net. At 0712 X-6 was correctly identified when she again broke surface some 75yds off the port beam (a note in *Tirpitz*'s log states that times between 0710 and 0730 are inaccurate) and the power boat was manned at the gangway. At the same time the alarm was raised throughout the battleship by the alarm bell.

A certain amount of confusion seems to have arisen here by the misuse of the alarm bell. Instead of the correct number of rings for 'submarine danger' the bell was rung for 'close water-tight doors', so that the actual threat to *Tirpitz* was unknown to most of her ship's company. The anti-aircraft armament was manned but X-6 was too close to the battleship and her attendant craft to allow them to open fire. The X-craft was seen to dive and then resurface some minutes later when a power boat went alongside, embarked the crew and endeavoured to take the craft in tow. At 0736 water-tight doors were all closed and the prisoners brought on board where their demeanour caused the Germans to believe that they had successfully completed their task. The order was given for *Tirpitz* to raise steam.

At 0740 a second midget submarine was sighted outside the A/T net boom—this was X-7 forcing her way out. A.A. guns opened fire, grenades were thrown and the destroyers *Z.27* (*Erich Steinbeck*) and *Z.30* told to drop depth-charges. The boom gate to the net enclosure was shut.

On the sinking of X-6 close beside *Tirpitz* at about 0730 it had been Captain Meyer's intention to take the battleship to sea as quickly as possible away from any danger that might have been left by X-6; already divers were preparing to check the hull for limpet mines and a wire was being drawn along the battleship's bottom. However the sighting of X-7 outside the nets caused Captain Meyer to change his plan as there was obviously a possibility of danger in the fjord and he had no means of knowing whether the attackers carried a locomotive torpedo or merely some form of static mine.

Moreover it would probably take at least an hour before *Tirpitz* could be under way. Since X-6 had been sighted on *Tirpitz*'s port side it was probable that any explosive charge would have been laid on that side and *Tirpitz*'s bows were hauled over to starboard with her anchors and cable-holders. Moving the stern, which was secured to the shore by wires, was not readily feasible.

At 0812 there were two violent explosions, almost simultaneously, and *Tirpitz* leapt upwards several feet. A very considerable amount of damage occurred. All the lighting circuits and much of the power supply were put out of action and the ship settled down with a slight list to port with No. 2 generator room flooded, as well as other adjacent compartments. Some minutes later a second midget submarine (X-7) was seen to surface and was fired on as a member of the crew came out and stepped on to a practice target. After the submarine was seen to sink the destroyer *Z.27* dropped five depth-charges in the vicinity.

At 0843 yet another submarine was sighted about 650yds away broad on *Tirpitz*'s starboard bow. Both heavy and light AA guns opened fire and several hits were seen as the craft went under water, probably damaged. Two minutes later a destroyer dropped a pattern of five depth-charges over the spot. This must have been X-5 and is all that is known of the craft since Place and Henty-Creer had exchanged shouts of good-luck off Söröy at 2315 on 20th, thirty-three hours earlier. It is probable that Henty-Creer was waiting until the next 'safe-to-attack' period after 0900 before attempting to force the nets.*

The damage to *Tirpitz* was severe. There were splits in the bottom of the hull and buckling and distortion underneath and to outlet pipes. No. 2 generator room was flooded and all the other electrical generators shocked so that no power was available in the ship for two hours, which effectively prevented the starting of boilers and the ship putting to sea. Much of the machinery was shocked on its mountings and put out of action: the propeller shafts could not be turned and 'A' and 'X' turrets jumped off their roller paths and temporarily made unserviceable. P III twin AA mounting was jammed, range-finders and fire control equipment were severely damaged and W/T and radar equipment rendered useless. Two aircraft were severely damaged and the port rudder was put out of action.

Two power supply ships were sent to aid the battleship, the *Karl*

* See Appendix 10.

Junge and the *Watt*, the latter arriving in the afternoon from Lange Fjord. On 25th September the German Naval Staff decided, with the approval of the Führer and the C-in-C Navy, that repairs should be carried out in a northern port, but it was appreciated that the battleship might never again be completely and operationally efficient.

At daybreak on 24th September the tugs *Arngast* and *Bardenfleth* began searching for the X-craft 750yds off *Tirpitz*'s starboard bow (X-5) but three days later the *Arngast* located the remains of X-7 only about 400yds from *Tirpitz*, lying on the bottom with a list and the hatch open; the forward part had been sheered off by depth-charging. The help of an expert Norwegian diver having been declined, probably very wisely from the German point of view, the craft was beached on the east side of Straumneset on 11th October and the documents therefrom sent to Germany. A week later the wreckage of X-6 was discovered and the stern raised but the remainder was too disintegrated to justify any further effort. The search for X-5 was discontinued on 12th October.

X-10

X-10 spent all the daylight hours of 22nd September dived by Tommelholm, trying to make good her defects. At 0815 two very heavy explosions were heard, followed five minutes later by an irregular series of explosions which were repeated twice later on during the forenoon. By sunset X-10's defects were still uncured and very reluctantly Hudspeth decided that any attempt to attack an alerted enemy in his defective craft would be virtual suicide. At 1800 X-10 surfaced and began her homeward journey.* At 1825 both side-cargoes were set to 'safe' and jettisoned in 135 fathoms of water —unlike X-8's they did not explode improperly. By midnight X-10 was at the western end of Stjern Sund but as it was too late to cross the minefield in darkness Hudspeth went back to the comparative shelter of Smalfjord on the north side of the island, arriving at 0215. As the fjord was completely deserted and the weather had deteriorated into frequent snow showers they remained surfaced all day, secured to the shore. The light of the magnetic projector compass was replaced and the periscope locked in the raised position and at 1100 on 23rd X-10 dived and set course for the minefield, surfacing

* In fact X-10 would not have found *Scharnhorst*. The battlecruiser had gone out on a gunnery exercise on 21st—sighted by X-7 off Aaroy Island, making her way to attack—and on hearing of the damage to *Tirpitz*, *Sharnhorst* was diverted to Lange Fjord.

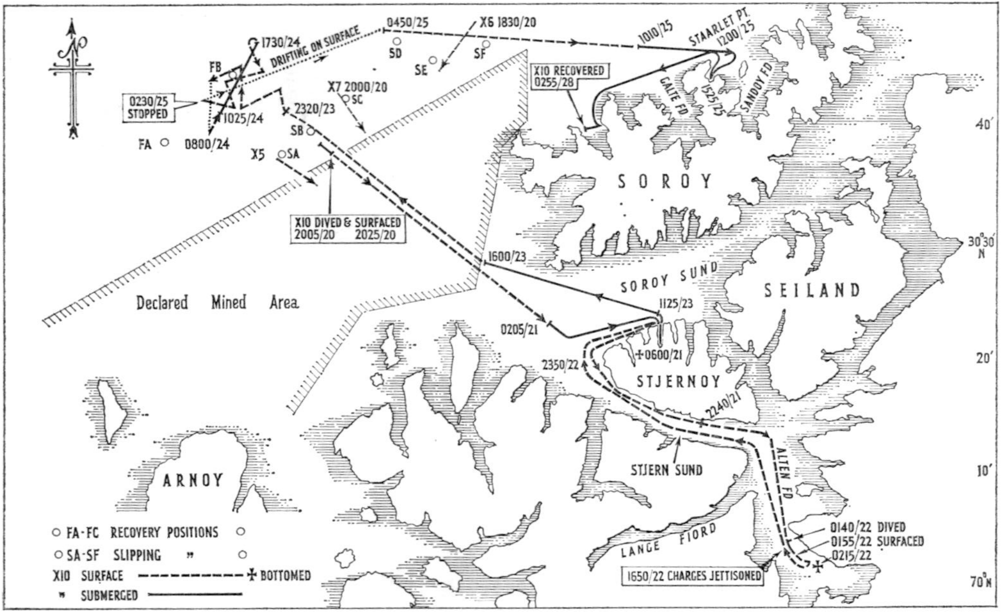

Operation 'Source'. Approaches to Kaa Fjord showing the movements of X10, 20th–28th September 1943.

at 1800 and reaching the rendezvous position (FB) at about 2300. For a day and a half Hudspeth manoeuvred in the area, dived and surfaced, trying to contact a towing submarine, but without success and at 0430 on 25th he set course for Sandöy Fjord, securing there towards dusk alongside the beach of Ytre Rappafjord. Here the crew of X-10 rested and cleaned up. They were all very cold. George Harding took off six pairs of trousers before he gave up counting, but after washing in the icy sea and cooking a special meal they felt better.

At dawn on 27th X-10 again set off, this time for O Fjord twenty miles to the west, where a submarine was due to rendezvous that night. At 0055 on 28th, five minutes before they were going to give up hope and start to make for Russia or Iceland by themselves their RG search gear picked up an infra-red transmission from a submarine and by 0150 X-10 was in tow of *Stubborn*. The coming of dawn and deteriorating weather prevented a change-over of crews and it was not until 2200 on 29th September, exactly ten days after he had taken over from Sub-Lt Page, his passage CO, that Hudspeth handed X-10 back to Peter Philip, X-7's original passage CO.

Twenty-five hours later at 2330 on 30th the tow between *Stubborn* and X-10 parted and it was four hours before *Stubborn* could again proceed, even as slowly as three knots. Next day *Truculent* and *Syrtis* were ordered to keep pace but a planned fleet operation caused their course to be modified. By 2nd October the weather had improved so that speed was increased to 6knots but at 1230 on 3rd the tow parted yet again. By 1700 the tow was once more renewed but at 1807 a signal from Flag Officer, Submarines, warned them of an imminent gale and instructed Lieut Duff in *Stubborn* to embark the passage crew and scuttle X-10 at his discretion. Very reluctantly Duff decided that this was the proper course of action and at 2045 X-10 was sunk in 66° 13′ N. 04° 02′ E. The expected gale broke two days later, by which time the submarines were all safely in Lerwick.

The Towing Submarines

Except for *Seanymph* who had been ordered to patrol to the westward, the other five towing submarines remained on patrol in their areas after slipping their X-craft. On 21st September Flag Officer, Submarines ordered *Seanymph* to shift area and patrol off Andöy in the hope of intercepting any enemy ships moving from Alten Fjord to Narvik after the X-craft attack. At about midday 22nd *Sceptre* received instructions to shift area and patrol off Kvalöy outside

Tromsö but unfortunately she arrived just too late to see *Lutzow* on her way south. The four remaining submarines were redisposed to cover the seaward side of Söröy, clear of the minefields. From 23rd to 27th they remained on patrol, trying to rendezvous with any returning X-craft, unharrassed by any German anti-submarine activity which indicated that the Germans had not appreciated how the X-craft had made the passage to Alten Fjord. An air raid on the Russian base of Polyarnoe in Kola Inlet on 24th suggests that the Germans believed the X-craft had made their passage unaided from there. On the nights of 27th and 28th the submarines searched off Söröy, where on 27th *Stubborn* found X-10 in O Fjord, and in the morning of 29th they separately started back for Lerwick, where they arrived between 3rd and 5th October. *Sceptre* and *Seanymph* remained on patrol until 4th October without incident and both were back in Lerwick by 7th.

So ended the first attack by British midget submarines and the first successful attempt to destroy or damage *Tirpitz*. Of the six X-craft which set out none returned home (incidentally the only operational X-craft to be lost) but their casualties were fortunately light. Three men were lost on passage in X-9 and X-8 was scuttled without casualty. In X-5, X-6 and X-7, all detailed to attack *Tirpitz*, six were lost and six were taken prisoner and came safely home after the war. X-10 was scuttled without loss on the way home.

The attack had been a tremendous success. For the loss of only nine men killed and six captured the battleship had been severely damaged, perhaps irreparably, and put out of action for six months and the morale of her crew undermined. Lieuts Cameron and Place were each awarded the Victoria Cross; Sub-Lts Aitken (X-7), Lorimer and Kendall (X-6) were each awarded the DSO and ERA Goddard (X-6) the Conspicuous Gallantry Medal. Lieut Hudspeth (X-10) and Lieut Duff (*Stubborn*) were awarded the DSC and the passage COs, Lieuts Terry-Lloyd (X-5), Wilson (X-6), Philip (X-7), Smart (X-8) and Sub-Lt Page (X-10) were all awarded the MBE.

In his final remarks in his Report on Operation Source, Rear-Admiral Barry wrote of Lieuts Henty-Creer, Cameron and Place and the crews of X-5, X-6 and X-7:

> 'It is clear that courage and enterprise of the very highest order in the close presence of the enemy was shown by these very gallant gentlemen, whose daring attack will surely go down to history as one of the most courageous acts of all time.'

Operational and passage crews of X-5 and X-6 pictured aboard HMS *Bonaventure*.
Right: X-5 (back row) Lt Terry-Lloyd (Pass CO), Mid Malcolm (Op), Lt Henty-Creer (Op CO), S/Lt Nelson (Op), (front row) Stoker Garrity (P), L/Sea Element (P), ERA Mortiboys (Op). */C. E. T. Warren*
Bottom right: X-6 (back row) Lt Wilson (Pass CO), Lt Cameron (Op CO), Lt Lorimer (Op), (front row) S/Lt Kendall (Op), ERA Goddard (Op), L/Sea McGregor (P), Stoker Oxley (P)./*C. E. T. Warren*

Operational and passage crews of X-7 and X-10 pictured aboard HMS *Bonaventure*. *Left:* X-7 (back row) S/Lt Aitken (Op), Lt Place (Op CO), Lt Whittham (Op), Lt Philip (Pass CO), (front row) L/Sea Magennis (P), Stoker Luck (P), ERA Whitley (Op)./*C. E. T. Warren*
Bottom left: X-10 (back row) Mid Harding (Op), Lt Hudspeth (Op CO), S/Lt Enzer (Op), S/Lt Page (Pass CO), (front row) ERA Tilley (Op), PO Brookes (P), ERA Fishleigh (P). /*C. E. T. Warren*

Top right: Admiral Sir Henry Moore, KCB, CVO, DSO on the quarterdeck of HMS *King George V*./*IWM*
Right: HMS *Furious* at sea in rough weather./*IWM*

Top: Bombing up Barracudas; note the Corsairs with long-range drop-tanks./*IWM*

Above: Hellcats ranged on the flight-deck of HMS *Emperor*. Astern are *Furious*, *Searcher*, *Pursuer* and *Jamaica*./*IWM*

Top right: Cdr S. T. C. Harrison briefing aircrews for Operation Tungsten./*IWM*

Right: HMS *Emperor*./*IWM*

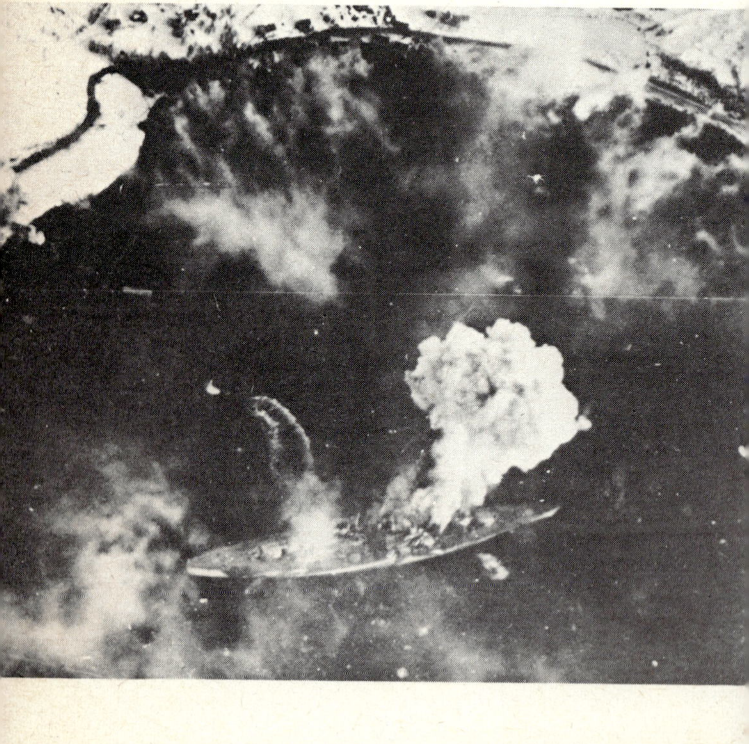

Left: HMS *Milne.*/*IWM*
Bottom left: An early hit on *Tirpitz* during Operation Tungsten. /*IWM*
Below: HMS *Formidable.*/*IWM*

Top: The crowded flight-deck of a fleet carrier; Corsairs in front, Barracudas behind./*IWM*

Above: A Seafire on the deck of HMS *Furious*; *Duke of York* on port bow./*IWM*

Right: Tirpitz photographed in July 1944 at her berth in Kaa Fjord. During the summer *Tirpitz* was moved from her earlier berth to one on the opposite side of the fjord./*MOD Crown Copyright*

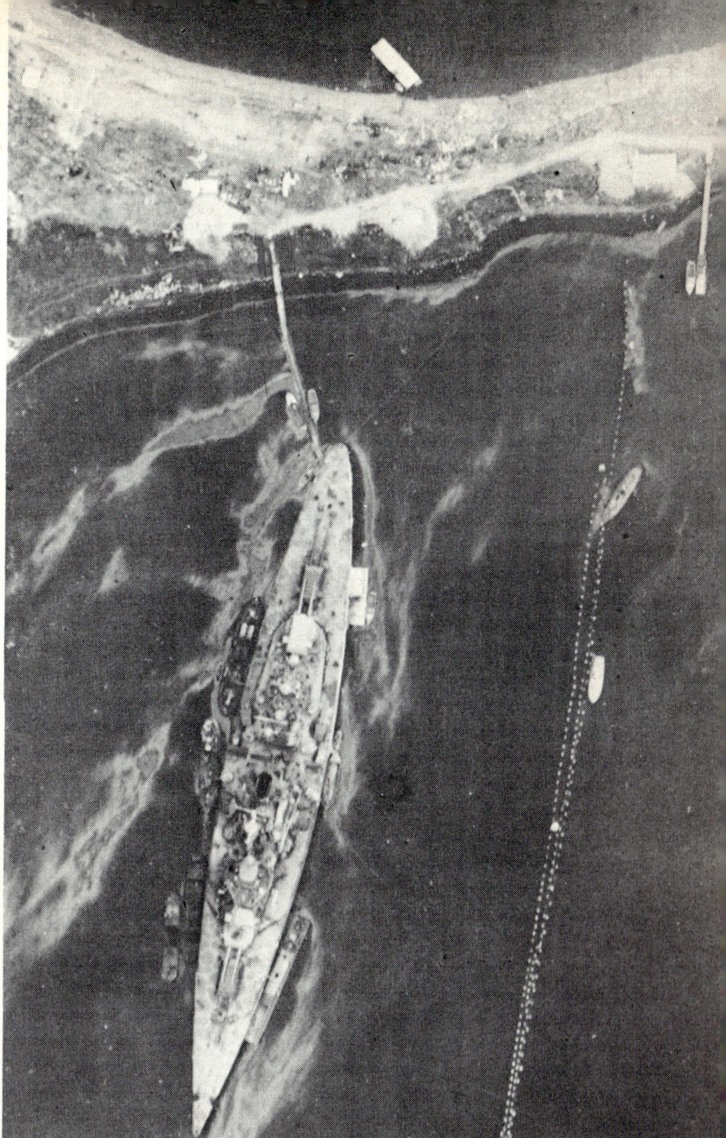

ROYAL NAVY

Top left: HMS *Nabob* torpedoed during Operation Goodwood. /*IWM*
Left: A Fairey Barracuda./*IWM*
Above: A Grumman Wildcat./*IWM*

Above: A Fairey Firefly./*IWM*

Top right: A Hellcat being sent 'round again' after making too high a landing approach./*IWM*

Right: A Chance-Vought Corsair./*IWM*

Top: Wing Commander 'Willy' Tait, DSO, DFC, RAF./*IWM*
Above: An Avro Lancaster of 617 squadron./*IWM*
Top right: *Tirpitz* at her moorings off Haakoy Island, Tromso. /*IWM*
Right: Photograph taken during the bombing of *Tirpitz* November 12th 1944, just before she blew up and capsized. /*MOD Crown Copyright*

Top: The propeller shaft of the capsized *Tirpitz.*/*IWM*
Above: Admiral von Freideburg and Admiral Kummetz after the surrender of Germany./*IWM*

CHAPTER FOUR

The Fleet Air Arm Attacks

Throughout the winter months of 1943–44 the Germans laboured in Kaa Fjord to repair *Tirpitz*, with special ship workers based on the repair ship *Neumark*. The naval staff considered how the defences had fallen short in their protection of the battleship and on 22nd November 1943 produced the following assessment.

1. The defensive measures were inadequate, and too little thought had been given to the possibility of submarine attack. The staff had a high opinion of British initiative in design and implementation of special attack methods if the target was considered worth while.

2. The anti-torpedo net booms should be opened only when absolutely necessary: all regular boat traffic should be outside the booms. There should be increased nets, obstructions in the fjord, constant A/S patrol and hydrophone watch, and counter-attacking vessels should always be in a state of immediate readiness.

3. The difficulty of defence when in an enemy country was appreciated. It was essential to keep changing the situation so that Resistance reports, which were known to have made possible the attack, would be less valuable: at least the ship should be moved irregularly for a day or so. (It was however a perpetual complaint that *Tirpitz* was kept so idle because of lack of fuel oil.)

4. The static life produced problems of monotony and low morale which must be overcome.

5. There was a requirement to use the experience of 'torpedo riders' off Trondheim as well as that of the Japanese and Italians to prepare countermeasures. German intelligence had known that X-craft had been built. (The Italians appear to have considered the chariot raid on Palermo in January 1943 to have been carried out by X-craft. Despite this and the intelligence knowledge of their

existence no specific warning seems to have been given to *Tirpitz*.)

6. There was a need for increased anti-aircraft cover.

A mild forewarning that this last might be an important recommendation was given on the night of 10–11th February 1944 when fifteen Russian aircraft, each carrying a 2,000lb bomb, set out with *Tirpitz* as their target. Only four of these located Kaa Fjord and none of them hit the ship, although one was credited with a near-miss.

By 15th March 1944 all possible repairs without dry-docking had been completed and *Tirpitz* spent a fortnight on trials, reaching a speed of 27knots. Her crew felt that they must now achieve a victory, if only to avenge *Scharnhorst* which had tried to attack convoy JW 55B and had been sunk by Admiral Sir Bruce Fraser, Commander-in-Chief Home Fleet, in *Duke of York* with his accompanying cruisers and destroyers on 26th December 1943. But *Tirpitz* had seen the British reconnaissance Spitfires and knew that they had observed her, and both sides knew that something must happen shortly. It was to happen early in the morning of 3rd April 1944.

Operation Tungsten

The Admiralty and Commander-in-Chief had decided that the Fleet Air Arm should attack *Tirpitz* early in April, as soon as the aircraft carrier *Victorious* had completed her post-refit trials and the date of 4th April was chosen. The attacking force was to be under the command of Vice-Admiral Sir Henry Moore and the aircraft carried out practice attacks against targets in Loch Eriboll.

The capital ships of the Home Fleet sailed on 30th March as Force I, ostensibly to cover convoy JW 58 which had left for Russia but also to link up with Force II, a group of escort carriers, which was already on its way. Force I consisted of *Duke of York* (C-in-C), *Anson* (V-A Moore), *Victorious*, and *Belfast*, with the destroyers *Onslaught*, *Javelin*, *Piorun*, *Sioux* and *Algonquin*, these going off to the Faeroes to refuel and being relieved by *Milne*, *Meteor*, *Matchless*, *Marne*, *Ursa* and *Undaunted*. Force II, consisting of *Royalist* (Rear-Admiral Bisset, RA Escort Carriers), *Searcher*, *Emperor*, *Pursuer*, *Fencer*, *Furious*, *Sheffield* and *Jamaica* with the destroyers *Virago*, *Verulam*, *Vigilant*, *Swift* and *Wakeful* and the oilers *Blue Ranger* and *Brown Ranger*, sailed a few hours later from Scapa Flow on a direct route for the rendezvous, en route being joined by the refuelled destroyers from the Faeroes. A stiff northerly wind gave the oilers some difficulty in maintaining their reputed speed of 13knots.

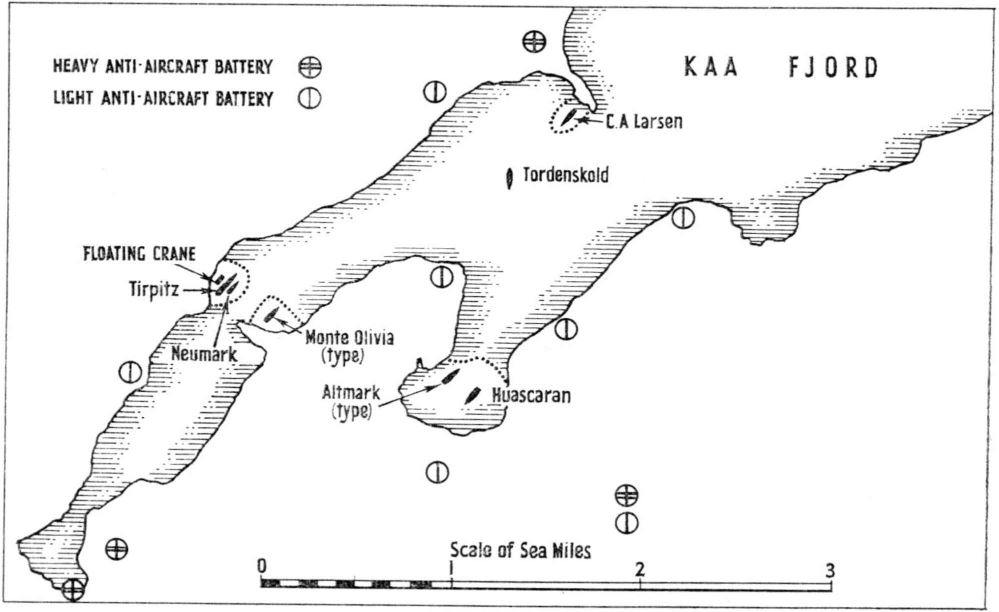

Fleet Air Arm attacks on the *Tirpitz*, 3rd April 1944, in Kaa Fjord. Map shows positions of ships and gun emplacements on 13th March 1944.

On the morning of 1st April Admiral Fraser decided that there was little likelihood of a serious attack being made on the convoy by surface forces and as the weather was ideal for flying the date of the attack on *Tirpitz* should be advanced by twenty-four hours and he accordingly made a signal at 1121 altering the rendezvous from 72° 30′ N. 13° 00′ E to a point 75mls south by west. This was received by Rear-Admiral Bissett at 1435 and he immediately increased to the maximum speed of Force II, 17knots, and detached the oilers with an escort of *Piorum* and *Javelin* to a point some 300mls north-west of Alten Fjord where they were to be ready to refuel destroyers as needed. On the following morning *Pursuer* had a breakdown of her steering gear at 0650 which nearly caused a collision as the force manoeuvred and was suddenly blinded by a snowstorm, but by 0725 *Pursuer* was back on course again. Forces I and II met during the afternoon of 2nd April and at 1620 Admiral Fraser with *Duke of York*, *Matchless* and *Marne* proceeded north-west while Vice-Admiral Moore led the remainder eastward to the flying-off position, some 120mls to the west of Alten Fjord. The Tungsten force was now regrouped into Force 7, *Anson*, *Victorious*, *Furious*, *Jamaica* and six destroyers, and Force 8, *Royalist*, *Sheffield*, and the four escort carriers, *Emperor*, *Searcher*, *Fencer* and *Pursuer* also with six destroyers.

By dawn on 3rd April the combined force was at position PP, 71° 30′ N. 19° 00′ E, for flying off in perfect weather and still undetected. An elaborate wireless organisation had been set up in Scapa Flow to simulate the continued presence of the fleet by using the correct types of transmitters to send dummy radio messages while radio silence was maintained at sea, and two days earlier *Victorious* had carefully refrained from sending a patrol to attack the routine German reconnaissance aircraft which had been on patrol out of sight to the eastward.

The air plan for the attack was complex. Two strikes were to be made by two wings of twenty-one Barracuda torpedo dive-bombers, No. 8 wing normally in *Furious* and No. 52 wing in *Victorious*, but to meet the requirements of the flying programme it was necessary to use both carriers simultaneously. In order that the wings should fly together one squadron from each wing had to be exchanged between the carriers, so for this operation 827 squadron was housed in *Victorious* in place of 831 squadron who went to *Furious*. To obtain the maximum effect on *Tirpitz* it was decided to use four types of bomb: eleven aircraft were each to carry three 500lb SAP, five aircraft one 1,600lb AP, and five aircraft either three 500lb MC or

600lb A/S bombs. Released from above 3,500ft the 1,600lb AP bombs were calculated to pierce the battleship's armoured deck, from 2,000ft the 500lb bombs should pierce the upper deck and do serious damage above the armoured deck, the 500lb MC bombs were primarily for effect against personnel manning the AA guns and were therefore carried in the first aircraft to attack in each strike, and the 600lb A/S bombs would have the same effect if they hit or if near misses should do underwater damage. In the actual attack nine aircraft of the first strike carried 500lb SAP and seven 1,600lb AP and in the second strike thirteen aircraft carried 500lb SAP and only three carried 1,600lb AP. Because of the light wind at take-off only two, not three, 600lb A/S bombs could be carried per Barracuda.

Victorious was also to fly off ten Corsairs with each strike to act as fighter escort for the Barracudas and because she was operating more aircraft than she was designed to do the first strike had to be parked on deck for some time prior to take off, an undesirable necessity as the deck was very wet and spray and sleet were freezing on it. Detailed briefing of all the air-crews had been carried out while at sea on 1st April.

At 0416 the first of the Corsairs of 1834 squadron took off from *Victorious*, followed eight minutes later by the Barracudas of 827 and 830 squadrons (No. 8 Wing) from the two fleet carriers. At the same time twenty Wildcats took off from *Searcher* and *Pursuer* and ten Hellcats from *Emperor* (800, 881 and 882 squadrons) while Seafires from *Furious* and Wildcats from *Fencer* formed a protective umbrella over the force. By 0437 the aircraft had formed up and headed 120° for their target.

As the strike was approaching her *Tirpitz* was weighing anchor before going to sea on more post-repair trials. The second anchor was coming in when it was seen that the smoke screen ashore was beginning and thirty-two aircraft were reported as heading south at a distance of 43mls. The alarm was sounded, guns manned and at 0528 the first aircraft were in sight while only a very thin smoke screen covered the fjord. No fire had been observed as the aircraft had flown over a destroyer and merchantman in Lange Fjord but flak began to interfere with the attackers some three miles from their target. As *Tirpitz* first sighted the aircraft they were beginning their attack. The Corsairs remained at 10,000ft to cover the Barracudas against counter-attack but the Wildcats and Hellcats came in low over the hills, straffing the battleship with 0·5 machine-gun fire as the Barracudas began their bombing dives at 0529. The attack was

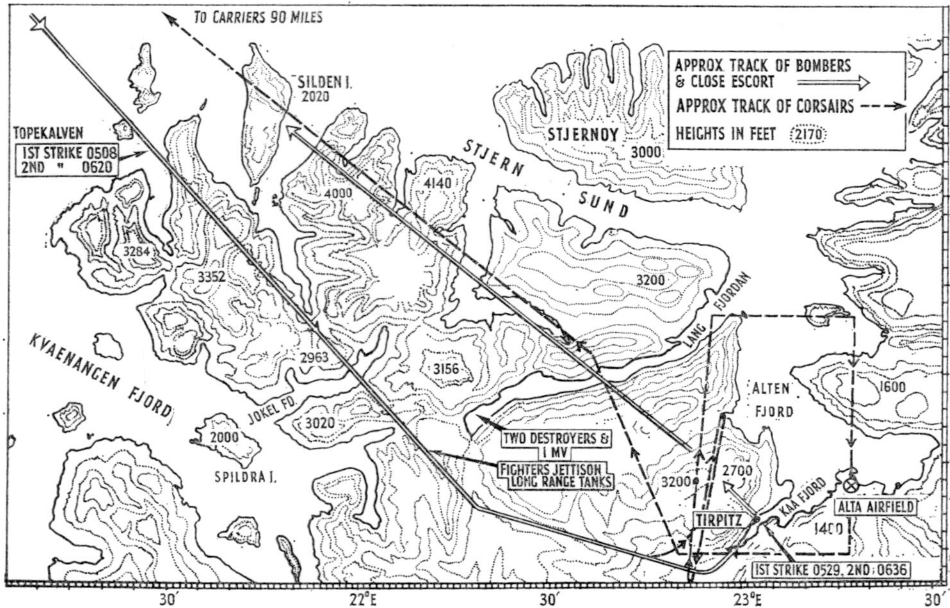

An air track chart of the Fleet Air Arm attack on the *Tirpitz* in Kaa Fjord on 3rd April 1944.

made in two columns along the fore-and-aft line of the target as practice had shown that errors of range exceeded errors of line. The bombs were meant to be dropped from a height above 3,000ft to ensure the penetration of the armoured deck but in their enthusiasm and determination to achieve accuracy most of the pilots dived much lower than this. The attack lasted exactly one minute. Six direct hits were claimed and three probable hits and the battleship's upper deck was left bloody with wounded men.

As the first strike were attacking the second strike were taking off: nineteen Barracudas from 829 and 831 squadrons* (No. 52 Wing), ten Corsairs from 1826 squadron, nineteen Wildcats from 896 and 898 squadrons and ten Hellcats from 804 squadron. At 0537 they formed up and made for *Tirpitz* whose smoke screen was visible when they were still forty miles from the target. This proved to be no deterrent. At 0635 the Hellcats again attacked the battleship's AA positions while the Wildcats sprayed the unprotected bridge and upper deck with bullets for a minute before the Barracudas came in to the attack. By 0637 it was again all over, eight definite and five probable hits being claimed, but the 1,600lb bomb which hit the bows failed to explode. The fighters followed the example of their predecessors by again gunning the German ships and shore installations as they presented themselves on the return flight. There was no interference from the German Air Force. By 0758 all the aircraft had landed back on their carriers except for two Barracudas shot down, one in each strike, and one damaged Hellcat deliberately ditched. British casualties were nine killed.

Vice-Admiral Moore had planned to repeat the attack on the next day but in view of the damage caused to *Tirpitz* and the fatigue and reaction of his air-crews after so successful an attack he revised his original intention and ordered a return to base. By 1630 6th April most of the force was back in Scapa Flow, with only *Searcher*, who had an engine defect, and the fleet oilers and their escorts remaining to come safely home some ten hours later.

The German administration had failed to heed the staff recommendation about improved AA defence. In just two minutes the Fleet Air Arm had ruined much of the six months of repair work and had done incalculable harm to the morale of the ship's company as it was about to recover after the X-craft attack. Although no damage was done to the main or auxiliary machinery the near misses had

* One Barracuda failed to start and one crashed immediately after take-off, killing its crew.

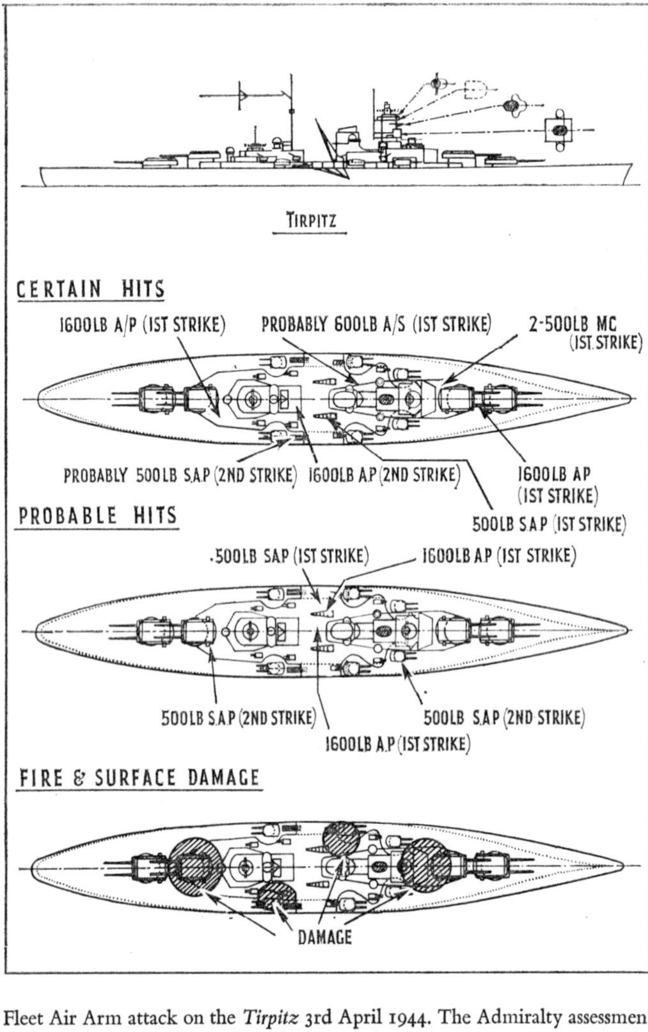

Fleet Air Arm attack on the *Tirpitz* 3rd April 1944. The Admiralty assessment of hits obtained (made on the 3rd May 1944).

caused flooding, the W/T aerials were again wrecked, the upper deck was a shambles with damage to the AA armament, and the casualty list was formidable. 122 men had been killed and 316 wounded including the captain, many of them by the machine gun fire from the fighters. It was not until 22nd of June that *Tirpitz* could recommence trials in Alten Fjord.

Operations Planet, Brawn, Tiger Claw and Mascot

A repeat of Operation Tungsten was given the codename Planet and planned for 26th April but was cancelled because of bad weather.

On 15th May Operation Brawn took place. Twenty-seven Barracudas from *Victorious* and *Furious* with twenty-eight Corsairs, four Seafires and four Wildcats took off for another attack on *Tirpitz*. Nearing the Norwegian coast they encountered 10/10ths cloud at 1,000ft and had no alternative but to return to their carriers, having lost one Barracuda on meteorological reconnaissance. A similar planned attack on 28th May—Operation Tiger Claw—was also abandoned because of weather and three days later the force attacked shipping further south off Ålesund.

Six weeks later, on 17th July, another attack was mounted by the Fleet Air Arm, Operation Mascot. The Germans had established an observation post on a mountain top nearby *Tirpitz* from which fire could be directed at approaching aircraft, particularly barrage fire from the 15in guns. Forty-four Barracudas, loaded with 1,000lb AP and 500lb bombs were escorted by eighteen Corsairs and a like number of Hellcats and twelve Fireflies as they flew from the aircraft carriers *Formidable*, *Indefatigable* and *Furious*. At 0204 *Tirpitz* received warning of the approach of a large formation of aircraft, AA crews closed up and within ten minutes the shore-based smoke screen was well established. By 0220 as the aircraft were beginning to attack the target was almost entirely obscured by smoke. A near miss was felt in *Tirpitz* at 0221 but by 0225 the battleship was totally obscured and no other bombs fell near. One Barracuda and one Corsair were lost but the airmen managed to sink a 500ton trawler on their way home.

Operations Goodwood I, II, III and IV

On 31st July and 1st August *Tirpitz* made her last sortie for exercises with the 4th Destroyer Flotilla. Three weeks later the Fleet Air Arm returned to the fray with a series of attacks under the operational codename 'Goodwood', using five aircraft carriers, *Indefatigable*,

Formidable, Furious, Nabob and *Trumpeter*. The first two attacks were carried out on 22nd August. Just after noon Barracudas and escorting Corsairs failed to repeat the success of 'Tungsten' as low cloud prevented them from reaching the target but Hellcats bombed through the cloud and claimed two hits. In the early evening a further six Hellcats from *Indefatigable* attacked *Tirpitz* and again claimed two hits with 500lb bombs. The morning sortie had also attacked other shipping and had damaged two small supply ships as well as *Tirpitz*'s sea-planes which were moored nearby.

Both sides were optimistic in their claims. In fact no hits were obtained by the Hellcats but the British losses were only one Barracuda and one Hellcat whereas the Germans had claimed no less than twelve aircraft to have been observed shot down. However the escort carrier *Nabob* was torpedoed by a U-boat but managed to return to harbour, while the CAP shot down two Blohm und Voss 138 flying boats that ventured too close to the carrier task force.

In the afternoon of 24th August Barracudas, Hellcats, Corsairs and Fireflies from *Indefatigable, Formidable* and *Furious* took off in the heaviest attack made by the Fleet Air Arm. The thirty-three Barracudas all carried 1,600lb AP bombs, the ten Hellcats each a 500lb bomb, and five of the twenty-four Corsairs carried 1,000lb AP bombs, the remainder with the ten Fireflies being detailed for anti-flak duties. At 1547 the German defences gave an aircraft alarm and the smoke screen was started. The aircraft approached from all directions at heights from 6,500ft to 10,000ft, diving low into the attack. This was a technique devised out of the lessons of 'Tungsten' which made the directing of AA fire very much more difficult for the gunnery control on board *Tirpitz*. Despite the smoke screen two hits were scored for the loss of two Hellcats and four Corsairs. A 500lb bomb landed straight on the top of 'B' turret dishing its top and temporarily damaging the elevating gear of the starboard gun and destroying the quadruple 2cm AA mounting on it. The other hit was to prove to be the Fleet Air Arm's greatest disappointment. A 1,600lb AP bomb hit just forward of the bridge on the port side and penetrated not only the upper deck but the armoured deck below, finally coming to rest in No. 4 Switch Room on the lower platform deck, having gone through 5¾ins of decking, mostly armoured steel. *It failed to explode* and when the Germans finally removed the explosive there was only 100lb instead of 215lb. Had this bomb exploded it would have wrecked the main fire control room and the switchboard room as well as causing serious flooding and *Tirpitz* would have been rendered useless if not actually sunk. Of this attack the German records state:

> 'The attack on 24th August 1944 was undoubtedly the heaviest and most determined so far. The English showed great skill and dexterity in flying. For the first time they dived with heavy bombs. During the dive bombing, fighter planes attacked the land batteries which, in comparison with earlier attacks, suffered heavy losses. The fact that an armour-piercing bomb of more than 1,540lbs did not explode must be considered an exceptional stroke of luck, as the effects of that explosion would have been immeasurable. Even incomplete smoke screening upsets the correctness of the enemy's aim and it has been decided from now on to use it in wind strengths up to 9 mts/sec. irrespective of possible gaps.'

The Germans also ordered a reduction in the required time of notice for smoke from 10 to 7 minutes.

Gales and fog alternated for the next five days until 29th August when another heavy attack of sixty aircraft was launched from *Formidable* and *Indefatigable*. Four of the seven Hellcats flew in with target indicators but the Germans had sufficient warning and the battleship was completely obscured by smoke. The aircraft bombed blindly and although they thought they had two hits in fact they had none. One Firefly and one Corsair were lost and the carrier force withdrew to cover convoy RA 59A briefly before returning to Scapa Flow.

So ended the Fleet Air Arm's attacks against *Tirpitz*. The effect had been very considerable and since the X-craft attack in September of the previous year the battleship had been rendered virtually useless. The cost had been seventeen aircraft and forty aircrew lost and one carrier damaged. But had German strategy and tactics not been bedevilled by the internecine feuding between the Navy and Göring's Luftwaffe, so that no fighter cover was ever provided to protect *Tirpitz*, the outcome might have been very different. When eventually fighters were allocated for this duty it was to be too late.

CHAPTER FIVE

Bomber Command, September—November 1944

As well as the attacks which had been carried out by the Fleet Air Arm other plans for sinking *Tirpitz* had been considered. In July a scheme had been put forward for the use of USAAF B-17 Flying Fortresses in a daylight raid with 1,600lb bombs but it had not been pursued. Although the Americans were keen to destroy so important a target there were obvious difficulties, not least that the Flying Fortress could only carry small bombs which had already proved somewhat ineffective. Another proposal for a high speed attack by Mosquito bombers, whose speed might enable them to surprise the smoke-screen defences, got as far as an operational codename of 'Servant' but never took place. In yet another scheme six Sunderland flying boats had been fitted to carry two chariots each, but this also remained untried. It was to be left to Bomber Command to resolve the problem.

Since the early raids by Stirlings and Halifaxes in 1942, and the even earlier raids by the Hampdens in the first year of the war, both the technique and technology of the Royal Air Force had increased enormously. The combination of the genius of Dr Barnes Wallis and the inspiring leadership of Wing Commander Guy Gibson, had created 617 squadron—the Dambusters. (When first ordered to form this squadron for special duty Gibson had thought the target was to be *Tirpitz* and was much relieved to learn otherwise!) Now, eighteen months later, the most determined and skilled squadron in Bomber Command, equipped with the most devastating bomb devised, was to attack *Tirpitz*. Not content with designing the skipping bombs for the Ruhr dams, Barnes Wallis had devised the 'Tallboy' bomb, 12,000lb in weight with over 5,000lb of high explosive, beautifully designed for accurate flight and great penetration. It was this combination which was to be sent against *Tirpitz*.

However in her fastness at Kaa Fjord *Tirpitz* was out of range for a round flight by a Lancaster loaded with a Tallboy bomb and it was therefore necessary for the bombers to land and refuel in Russia. Permission was readily obtained for them to use the facilities at Yagodnik, in marked contrast to the delayed agreement for the reconnaissance aircraft required for Operation Source a year previously. On 10th September thirty-three Lancasters of 617 and 9 squadrons, accompanied by two Liberators with spare parts and ground crew, took off from Lossiemouth under the command of Wing-Commander J. B. Tait, bound for Russia. Somehow or other they all arrived although the Yagodnik radio-navigation beacon was of the wrong type, the cloud level down below 1,000ft and the landscape monotonously and unidentifiably uniform, but two aircraft from 617 and four from 9 squadron made emergency landings in marshland and had to be abandoned.

For three days it poured with rain. Then, on 15th September, twenty-seven bombers took off for *Tirpitz*. Of these twenty-one carried the 12,000lb Tallboys, the other six each carried twelve 400lb JW Mk II Mines.* The bombers crossed the high peaks ninety miles distant from the battleship's berth at about 1100, but they were still five minutes short of the target when the smoke floats began operating. At about 12,000ft they levelled out for the attack, coming in in flights of six from the south-east. The shore batteries, flak ship and *Tirpitz* all opened fire, the battleship using her 15in guns for barrage fire as well as all her smaller weapons. Tait's bomber-aimer Daniels let go a Tallboy on a target rapidly disappearing beneath a smoke-screen, but he and others were virtually bombing blind. From another aircraft the aimer claimed to have seen Daniels hit *Tirpitz* but five bombers decided not to waste any bombs on a completely obscured target. Only sixteen out of the twenty-one Tallboys were dropped and the squadron flew back to Yagodnik before returning to England.†

The bombers had taken photographs during the attack and further reconnaissances were made shortly afterwards but it was not

* The JW Mine, the initials stood for Johnnie Walker, was a remarkable weapon. Dropped in the water near the target it sank to the bottom whereupon the ballast water with which it had been filled was automatically blown by compressed air and it came up hopefully under the target, exploding on contact. It was supposed to repeat this drill several times if it did not explode, drifting as wind and current dictated—hence its name.

† There were no aircraft lost in the raid but on the return from Yagodnik to Lossiemouth one Lancaster was lost, probably flying into a mountain because of a navigational error.

easy to assess the results and a hit on or near the stern seemed probable with some near misses. Later reports from the Norwegian Resistance stated that *Tirpitz* had been hit at the bows and this in fact was the truth although the British Cabinet were uncertain how serious was the extent of damage and had no guarantee that *Tirpitz* was seriously stricken. Actually the 12,000lb bomb hit *Tirpitz*'s bows about fifty feet back from the stem and went through the upper deck to emerge well below the waterline on the starboard side before exploding. The resultant damage was the flooding of the forward part of the ship and the shaking of much of the machinery, main and auxiliary. A German document found after the war could have set the minds of the British at rest:

> 'It was estimated that repairs, if they could be carried out without interruption, would take at least nine months. It was eventually decided at a conference on 23rd September 1944 at which the C-in-C and Naval Staff were present, that it was no longer possible to make the *Tirpitz* ready for sea and action again . . .'

The Germans decided to move *Tirpitz* to a shallow berth where she could not be sunk and after some careful hydrographic work she was moved under her own power on the night of 15th October and moored off Haakoy Island nearby to Tromsö. With *Tirpitz* went her AA batteries and anti-torpedo nets. Dredgers shifted spoil to fill in a hole under her berth so that, come what might, she could only sink a little way. Here in Tromsö, no longer a major war vessel, she was to be a floating battery helping to protect Germany's Norwegian flank.

But by moving from Kaa Fjord to Tromsö *Tirpitz* had come two hundred miles nearer Britain and it was now possible, just possible, for the bombers to reach her directly and return. The Lancasters of both 617 and 9 squadrons had their rear turrets removed, overload tanks from Wellington bombers slid inside the fuselage and the rear turrets then replaced, to give them a further three hundred gallons fuel capacity. To reduce weight the mid-upper turrets and the armour plating round the pilot's seat were removed.

On 28th October the bombers flew up to Lossiemouth to prepare for another attack. At midnight a weather-reporting Mosquito over Tromsö reported conditions favourable with the wind veering east and an hour later the Lancasters took off—thirty-two bombers each carrying a Tallboy bomb. They flew low over the water, crossed the Norwegian coast well to the south and turned left up the line of the

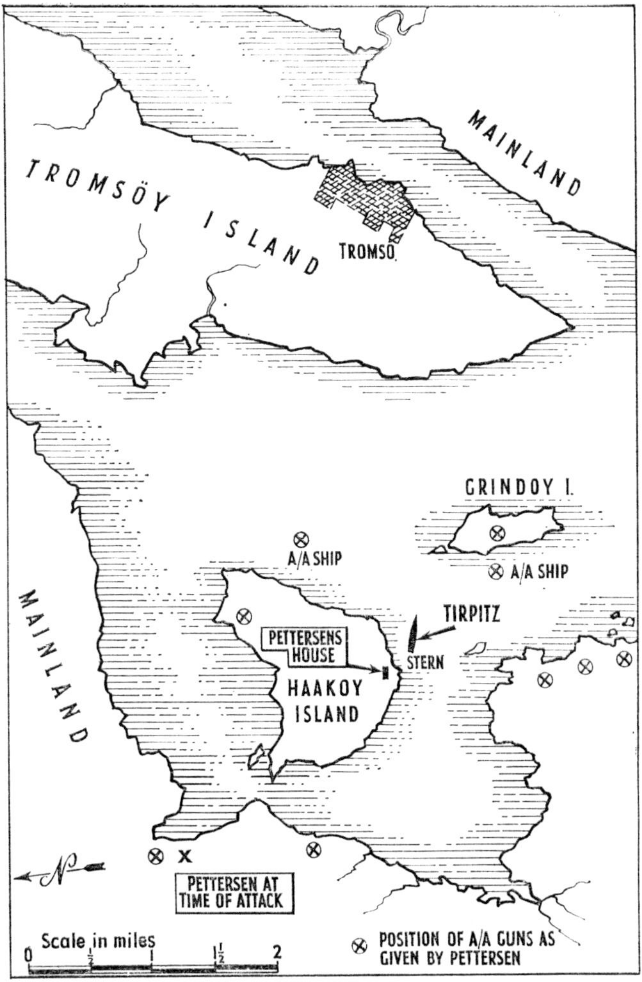

The sinking of the *Tirpitz* by Bomber Command, 12th November 1944. Position of *Tirpitz* and defences as reported by Pettersen at the time of the attack.

Swedish frontier to attack from inland. They were just half a minute too late. As they were approaching the forewarned *Tirpitz* at 0850 the wind shifted back to the west and cloud rolled in from the sea. Harrassed by heavy flak they tried to bomb through the breaks in the cloud. Not only would it have been dangerous to try and fly below the cloud which was wreathing the mountains but it would have been pointless since the bombs had to be dropped from a great height to penetrate the battleship's armoured deck. There were no hits but a near miss off the port quarter bent *Tirpitz*'s propeller shaft. One Lancaster, already flying with only three engines, was hit by a single gun sited on a small island. Carey, the pilot, kept it flying on two engines and made a forced landing in Sweden. The aircraft was a write-off but there were no casualties and all the others returned safely.

Early in the morning of 12th November the Lancasters took off again for their third and final raid against *Tirpitz*. Whatever the outcome of this attack there would be little chance of a fourth attempt since by 27th November the sun would be below the horizon even at mid-day and there would not be sufficient light to see the target. There was a heavy frost at the airfield and seven of 9 Squadron's Lancasters were so severely iced up that they could not take off in their overweight state; in all thirty-two aircraft took to the air at about 0300. The reached the rendezvous about 0935 low over Tornea Trask, a lake a hundred miles south-east of Tromsö, took up formation and then Tait led them north-west, climbing to 14,000ft to clear the mountains and gain height for the bombs. Radar picked them up as they gained height and the race was on, a race made even more tense than formerly by the knowledge that a German fighter squadron had recently been posted to Bardufoss. As the Lancasters came over the last mountain range they were met with intense ack-ack fire from *Tirpitz*, the other ships and shore batteries, but the battleship herself lay clearly visible. There was no cloud and no smoke-screen. *Tirpitz* indeed was trying to conceal herself by smoke which rose in the still air but the smoke pots brought down from Kaa Fjord although in position were not primed.

At 0941 Daniels, lying in the nose of Tait's Lancaster 'D for Dog', let go the first of the Tallboys, to hit *Tirpitz* for the second time. At Bardufoss, despite frantic calls for air cover, not one single fighter seems to have taken off; they sent a message to *Tirpitz* that there were British fighters over the airfield, but this was totally mistaken. The Germans should have had a killing amongst the Lancasters,

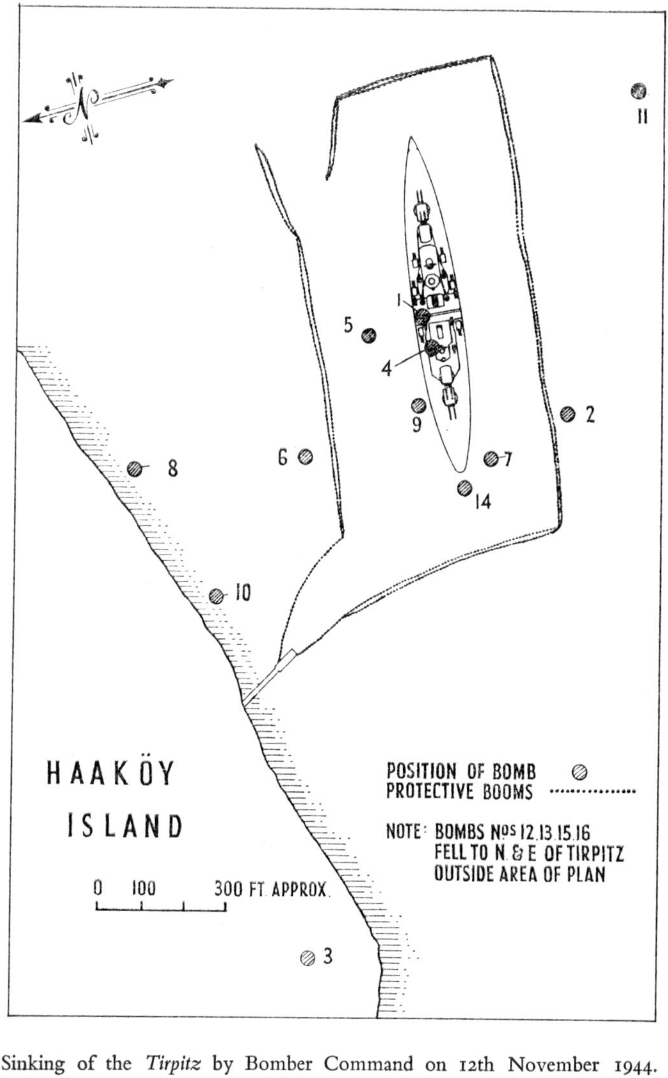

Sinking of the *Tirpitz* by Bomber Command on 12th November 1944. Approximate bomb plot compiled from photographs taken during the attack.

stripped as they were of their mid-upper turrets, but the bombers remained unmolested except for ack-ack fire. In the eight minutes after 0941 twenty-nine bombs were dropped with great precision from between 12,500 and 16,000ft.*

Two direct hits were achieved on the port side, one level with the bridge and the other alongside X-turret which seems to have started a fire. *Tirpitz* listed about 20° to port after the first hit and then further over after the second, aggravated by a number of near misses along the port side, until she was listing to almost 70°. At about 0950, just after the last bomb had fallen, there was a violent explosion and 'X' turret blew out completely. It was found some 40ft from where it would have been expected and appears to have been the result of an internal explosion, not a hit by a bomb. *Tirpitz* rolled over to port and capsized.

Although the order had been given to abandon ship *Tirpitz* capsized so suddenly that there was no time for the men on the lower decks to get clear and in the armoured conning tower, damaged on the starboard side in Operation Tungsten, the port door jammed as the ship heeled. Of the 1,700 men on board about 1,000 were drowned: eighty-seven were rescued by cutting holes in the ship's bottom to compartments where they had climbed. The bombers suffered no losses. The battle to sink the *Tirpitz* was finished.

* Two Lancasters from 9 squadron were late at the rendezvous and so returned without dropping their bombs. One Lancaster was fitted solely for photo-reconnaissance of the attack to allow as accurate an assessment of damage as possible, which proved unnecessary.

APPENDIX ONE

Chronological List of attacks against Tirpitz

1.	Autumn 1940	Bomber Command	Wilhelmshaven
2.	Autumn 1940	Bomber Command	Wilhelmshaven
3.	29th Jan. 1942	Bomber Command	Trondheim
4.	9th Mar. 1942	FAA	at sea
5.	31st Mar. 1942	Bomber Command	Trondheim
6.	28th Apr. 1942	Bomber Command	Trondheim
7.	29th Apr. 1942	Bomber Command	Trondheim
8.	29th Oct. to 1st Nov. 1942	Royal Navy and Norwegian Resistance (Operation 'Title')	Trondheim
9.	22nd Sept. 1943	Royal Navy ('Source')	Kaa Fjord
10.	11th Feb. 1944	Russian bombers?	Kaa Fjord
11.	3rd Apr. 1944	FAA ('Tungsten')	Kaa Fjord
12.	24th Apr. 1944	FAA ('Planet')	cancelled
13.	15th May 1944	FAA ('Brawn')	Kaa Fjord
14.	28th May 1944	FAA ('Tiger Claw')	cancelled
15.	17th July 1944	FAA ('Mascot')	Kaa Fjord
16.	22nd Aug. 1944	FAA ('Goodwood' I)	Kaa Fjord
17.	22nd Aug. 1944	FAA ('Goodwood' II)	Kaa Fjord
18.	24th Aug. 1944	FAA ('Goodwood' III)	Kaa Fjord
19.	29th Aug. 1944	FAA ('Goodwood' IV)	Kaa Fjord
20.	15th Sept. 1944	Bomber Command ('Paravane')	Kaa Fjord
21.	29th Oct. 1944	Bomber Command ('Obviate')	Tromsö
22.	12th Nov. 1944	Bomber Command ('Catechism')	Tromsö

Attacks by Bomber Command

Autumn 1940	Two attacks on battleship while fitting out by Handley-Page Hampdens carrying 2000lb AP bombs and 'M' Mines. No damage caused.
25th Jan. 1942	9 Handley-Page Halifaxes and 7 Short Stirlings. Failed to find target at Trondheim owing to cloud.
31st Mar. 1942	34 Halifaxes—1 aircraft sighted target. Bombs dropped 1—4000lb, instantaneous fuse 4— 500lb GP delayed fuse 0·1sec No damage caused. 5 aircraft lost
28th Apr. 1942	43 Avro Lancasters and Halifaxes Bombs dropped 20—4000lb, instantaneous fuse 20— 500lb GP, delayed fuse 0·1sec 10— 250lb GP, delayed fuse 0·1sec 44—1000lb Mk XIX mines with hydrostatic fuse set to 30ft. No damage. 5 aircraft lost
29th Apr. 1942	34 Lancasters and Halifaxes Bombs dropped 18—4000lb, instantaneous fuse 23— 500lb GP, delayed fuse 0·1sec 1— 250lb GP, delayed fuse 0·1sec 48—1000lb Mk XIX mines with hydrostatic fuse set to 30ft. No damage caused. 2 aircraft lost
15th Sept. 1944	27 Lancasters ('Paravane') Bombs dropped 16—12,000lb MC (Tallboy) delayed fuse 0·07sec 72— 400lb JW mines, contact fuse 1 hit on bow causing serious flooding. No aircraft lost
29th Oct. 1944	32 Lancasters ('Obviate') Bombs dropped 32—12,000lb MC (Tallboy) delayed fuse 0·07sec 1 near miss off port quarter causing flooding. 1 aircraft lost
12th Nov. 1944	32 Lancasters ('Catechism') Bombs dropped 29—12,000lb MC (Tallboy) delayed fuse 0·07sec 2 hits, 1 near miss to port caused flooding and severe

listing, followed by internal explosion of 'X magazine; *Tirpitz* capsized. No aircraft lost.

Attacks by Fleet Air Arm

9th Mar. 1942 HMS *Victorious* at sea with Home Fleet covering Convoy PQ 12. 12 Fairey Albacore torpedo bombers.

Bombs dropped 12—18in torpedoes, speed 40knots, depth setting 25ft, fitted with impact only pistol

No hits on target. 2 Albacores lost

Tirpitz fired 15cm 2 rounds long range barrage
16 rounds barrage
12 rounds nose fused
10·5cm 345 rounds
3·7cm 897 rounds
2cm 3,372 rounds

3rd April 1944 (Tungsten)

1st strike, No 8 TBR wing, 827 and 830 squadrons, 21 Barracudas

Bombs dropped 6—1,600lb AP, delayed fuse 0·08sec
24— 500lb SAP, delayed fuse 0·14sec
12— 500lb MC, instantaneous fuse
4— 600lb A/S hydrostatic fuse set 35ft

2nd strike, No 52 TBR wing, 829 and 831 squadrons 19 Barracudas

Bombs dropped 2—1,600lb AP, delayed fuse 0·08sec
36— 500lb SAP, delayed fuse 0·14sec
9— 500lb MC, instantaneous fuse
1— 600lb A/S hydrostatic fuse, set 35ft

Each strike escorted by 20 Wildcats, 10 Hellcats and 10 Corsairs.

1st strike achieved 10 hits, 2nd strike 5 hits. 8 hits were achieved with AP bombs, 7 with MC bombs and there were 2 near misses. 3 Barracudas were lost.

Damage caused was very heavy splinter damage to upper deck AA guns and aerials, casualties: 122 killed, 316 wounded.

Tirpitz fired 10·5cm 506 rounds
3·7cm 400 rounds
2cm 8,260 rounds

15th May 1944 (Brawn)

HMS *Victorious* and *Furious*

27 Barracudas (8 and 52 TBR wings) with 500lb SAP and MC and 600lb A/S bombs

28 Corsairs (1834 and 1836 squadrons)

4 Sea fires

4 Wildcats

Returned due to low cloud over Norwegian coast—no attack

17th July 1944 (Mascot)

HMS *Formidable, Indefatigable* and *Furious*

44 Barracudas (8 and 9 TBR wings)

18 Corsairs (1841 squadron)

12 Fireflies (1770 squadron)

18 Hellcats (1840 squadron)

Bombs dropped —1,600lb AP, delayed fuse 0·08sec
— 500lb

Barracudas bombed blind through the smoke screen; no hits, 1 near miss. 1 Barracuda, 1 Corsair lost.

Tirpitz fired 38cm 39 rounds
15cm 359 rounds
10·5cm 1,973 rounds
3·7cm 3,967 rounds
2cm 28,550 rounds

Tirpitz had fifteen minutes warning of the raid to start smoke screen and close up guns' crews. The AA fire was very heavy including 38cm (15in) barrage fire.

22nd Aug. 1944 (Goodwood I and II)

HMS *Indefatigable, Formidable, Furious, Nabob* and *Trumpeter*

32 Barracudas (820, 826, 827, 828 and 830 squadrons)

11 Fireflies (1770 squadron)

8 Seafires (887 squadron)
24 Corsairs (1841 and 1842 squadrons)
9 Hellcats (1840 squadron)
Bombs dropped 10—500lb SAP, delayed fuse 0·14sec
The Hellcats bombed through holes in the cloud, the Barracudas and Corsairs were unable to reach target.
6 Hellcats from *Indefatigable* with 8 Fireflies as escort attacked again in the evening (Goodwood II) with similar 500lb bombs.
No damage to *Tirpitz* but 2 Arados, 4 Blohm und Voss 138 and 1 Heinkel 115 destroyed, 2 B & V 138 shot down. 1 Barracuda, 1 Hellcat and 1 Seafire lost.

Tirpitz fired	Morning	Evening
38cm	62 rounds	13 rounds
15cm	363 rounds	124 rounds
10·5cm	1,300 rounds approx	750 rounds
3·7cm	1,600 rounds approx	1,538 rounds
2cm	15,000 rounds approx	15,800 rounds

24th Aug. 1944 (Goodwood III)
HMS *Indefatigable*, *Formidable* and *Furious*
33 Barracudas 1—1,600lb AP bomb
10 Hellcats 1— 500lb SAP bomb
5 Corsairs 1—1,000lb AP bomb
19 Corsairs, 10 Fireflies } escort and anti-flak
Bombs dropped 18—1,600lb AP, delayed fuse 0·08sec
5—1,000lb AP, delayed fuse 0·08sec
10— 500lb SAP, delayed fuse 0·14sec
2 hits, one by 1,600lb bomb which penetrated to keel but did not explode; little damage. 2 Hellcats, 4 Corsairs lost.
Tirpitz fired 38cm 72 rounds
15cm 510 rounds
10·5cm 30%, 3·7cm 20%, 2cm 40% } of the already considerably reduced stock.

29th Aug. 1944 (Goodwood IV)

HMS *Formidable* and *Indefatigable*

26 Barracudas	1—1,600lb AP bomb, delayed fuse 0·08sec
2 Corsairs	1—1,000lb AP bomb, delayed fuse 0·08sec
7 Hellcats	4 aircraft with target indicators 3 with 500lb MC bomb, instantaneous fuse

15 Corsairs } escort and anti-flak
10 Fireflies }

All bombs dropped, no hits, several near misses.

1 Corsair, 1 Firefly lost.

Tirpitz fired 38cm 54 rounds
15cm 161 rounds
10·5cm 22% } of remaining ammunition
3·7cm 9% }
2cm 18% }

APPENDIX TWO

Submarines taking part in Operation Source, 11th Sept.—5th Oct. 1943

Thrasher	Lieut Hezlet, DSC, RN
X-5	Lieut Henty-Creer, RNVR (Operational CO)
	Lieut Terry-Lloyd, SANF (Passage CO)
Truculent	Lieut Alexander, DSO, RN
X-6	Lieut Cameron, RNR
	Lieut Wilson, RNVR
Stubborn	Lieut Duff, RN
X-7	Lieut Place, DSC, RN
	Lieut Philip, SANF
Seanymph	Lieut Oakley, DSC, RN
X-8	Lieut McFarlane, RAN
	Lieut Smart, RNVR
Syrtis	Lieut Jupp, DSC, RN
X-9	Lieut Martin, RN
	S/Lt Kearon, RNVR
Sceptre	Lieut McIntosh, MBE, DSC, RN
X-10	Lieut Hudspeth, RANVR
	S/Lt Page, RNVR

APPENDIX THREE

British Ships taking part in Operation Tungsten, 3rd April 1944

Anson	Flag:	Vice-Admiral Sir Henry Moore, KCB, CVO, DSO
		Captain McCarthy, DSO
Victorious		Captain Denny, CB, CBE
Furious		Captain Philip, DSO, DSC
Searcher		Captain Davies
Emperor		Captain Hilken, DSO
Pursuer		Captain Graham, DSO, DSC
Fencer		Captain Bentinck, OBE
Royalist	Flag:	Rear-Admiral Bissett (RA Escort Carriers)
		Captain Eveleigh
Belfast		Captain Parham, DSO
Sheffield		Captain Addis, DSO
Jamaica		Captain Hughes-Hallett, DSO
Milne		Captain Campbell, DSO
Ursa		Commander Wyburd, DSC
Onslaught		Commander Pleydell-Bouverie
Piorun		Commander Dnienisiwicz, *VM* (Polish Navy)
Verulam		Lieut-Cdr Thomas, DSC
Undaunted		Lieut-Cdr Mackenzie, RNR
Meteor		Lieut-Cdr Jewitt
Vigilant		Lieut-Cdr Argles
Virago		Lieut-Cdr White
Swift		Lieut-Cdr Gower
Javelin		Lieut-Cdr Lewis, DSC
Wakeful		Lieut-Cdr Pound, DSC
Algonquin		Lieut-Cdr Piers, DSC, RCN
Sioux		Lieut-Cdr Boak, RCN

APPENDIX FOUR

Data for Tirpitz

Built by Wilhelmshaven Dockyard, laid down October 1936, launched 1st April 1939, completed November 1940, commissioned 25th January 1941.
Displacement standard 42,600tons, fully laden 50,000tons approx. Length 792ft pp. 822 oa. beam 118ft, draught 26ft, 33½ft fully laden. Performance: 3-shaft geared turbines supplied from six boiler-rooms, all boilers being forward of engine-rooms, S.H.P. 150,000 for a speed of 30knots with bursts of 165,000hp to give 31knots. Normal fuel capacity 5,000tons which could be increased; range 9,000mls at 19knots.

Armament: 8—38cm (15in) in four twin turrets, conventionally arranged two forward, two aft, max. elevation 35°, max. range 36,200m, 960 rounds
12—15cm (5·9in) in six twin turrets, three on each side amidships, max. elevation 35°, max. range 23,000m, 1,800 rounds
16—10·5cm (4·1in) QF AA in twin mountings, four each side amidships, max. elevation 80°, max. range 18,000m, 6,720 rounds
16—3·7cm AA in twin mountings, 32,000 rounds
Originally 16, ultimately 58—20mm, twin and quadruple mountings 90,000 rounds.
8—53·3cm (21in) Torpedo tubes in quadruple mountings; 24 torpedoes

Gunnery control: Three control positions for main and secondary armament with additional rangefinders. 10·5cm armament had four separate control directors with special gyro stabilisation.

Electrical supply: 8—500kw diesel generators
5—690kw turbo generators

Aircraft: 6 Arado 196 seaplanes launched from catapult abaft funnel

Armour: An armoured citadel protected the vital centre of the ship. The sides were of 320mm (12·6in) thick cemented armour plates from 8ft below the waterline up to the battery deck and thinner plating of 145mm (5·7in) thickness to the upper deck. The deck below the battery deck was armoured with 80mm (3·15in) non-cemented plating over the machinery spaces and 100mm (3·94in) over the magazines between the torpedo bulkheads; the sloping deck armour between the centre and the base of the side armour was 110mm (4·33in) and 120mm (4·72in) likewise. The citadel extended forward and aft with thinner plate and the upper deck generally was 50mm (1·97in) thick.

The 38cm gun turrets had 360mm thickness of armour on the face, 220mm on the sides and between 180 and 130mm on the top; the barbette armour was 220mm. The armour protection of the gunnery control towers was about the same. The 15cm turrets were protected by armour about one third the thickness of that of the main armament.

Complement: 2,400

APPENDIX FIVE

Ships' data German

Scharnhorst

Dimensions	32,000tons; 771×98×25ft
Performance	3-shaft geared turbines. Speed 31knots. Range 10,000mls at 18knots
Armament	9—11in (3×3), 12—5·9in (6×2), 14—4·1in (7×2), 16—37mm, 38—20mm, 6—21in TT (2×3), 4 Arado 196 seaplanes
Armour	Main belt 13in–3in; deck $4\frac{1}{2}$in–$3\frac{1}{2}$in; turrets 14in–4in
Complement	1,800

Lutzow
Admiral Scheer

Dimensions	12,100tons; 609×70×21ft
Performance	2-shaft diesels. Speed 26knots. Range 19,000mls at 19knots
Armament	6—11in (2×3), 8—5·9in (8×1), 6—4·1in AA (3×2), 8—37mm, 28—20mm, 8—21in TT (2×4), 2 Arado 196 seaplanes
Armour	Main belt 4in; deck 3–$1\frac{1}{2}$in; turrets $5\frac{1}{2}$–2in
Complement	1,150

Prinz Eugen
Hipper

Dimensions	10,000tons; 654×71×15ft
Performance	3-shaft geared turbines. Speed 32knots. Range 6,800mls at 18knots
Armament	8—8in (4×2), 12—4·7in AA (6×2), 12—37mm, 28—20mm, 12—21in TT (4×3), 3 Arado 196 seaplanes
Complement	1,600

Z.24, Z.27, Z.28, Z.29, Z.30, Z.31 ('*Narvik*' class)

Dimensions	2,600tons; 390× 40× 10ft
Performance	2-shaft geared turbines. Speed 38knots. Range 5,000 to 5,800mls at 19knots
Armament	5—5·9in (1×2+3×1), 4—37mm, 14—20mm, 8—21in TT (2×4)
Complement	321

Friedrich Eckholdt
Herman Schoemann
Erich Steinbrink
Friedrich Ihn
Richard Beitzen

Dimensions	2,200tons; 374× 37× 10ft
Performance	2-shaft geared turbines. Speed 30knots. Range 4,400mls at 19knots
Armament	5—5in (5×1), 4—37mm, 8—20mm, 8—21in TT (2×4)
Complement	315

Nymphe (ex Norwegian *Tordenskold*)
Thetis (ex Norwegian *Harald Haafrage*)

Dimensions	3,858tons; 307× 48× 17ft
Performance	Twin coal-fired triple expansion engines. Speed 17knots
Armour	Main belt 7–2in; deck 2in; (turrets 8–5in)
Armament	(2—8·2in, 6—4·7in, 6—3in, 2—3in AA)
	Originally built by Armstrongs in 1897 for coastal defence they were considerably refitted by the Germans as AA ships.

APPENDIX SIX

Ships' data British

King George V
Duke of York
Anson

Dimensions	35,000tons; 745×103×28ft
Performance	4-shaft geared turbines. Speed 29knots. Range 15,000mls at 10knots, 6,300/20, 3,200/27
Armament	10—14in (2×4, 1×2), 16—5·25in DP (8×2), 48—2pdr AA Additional 20mm and 40mm AA guns were added at various times up to about 60 in all.
Armour	Main belt 15in–4½in; deck 6in–1in; turrets 16in–9in
Complement	1,555

Renown

Dimensions	32,000tons; 794×102×27ft
Performance	4-shaft geared turbines. Speed 29knots. Range 3,650mls at 27knots
Armament	6—15in (3×2), 20—4·5 DP (10×2), 24—2pdr AA; additionally 4—2pdr and 62—20mm were added
Armour	Main belt 9in–3in; deck 4in–2½in; turrets 11in–7in
Complement	1,181

Indefatigable

Dimensions	26,000tons; 766×96×26ft
Performance	4-shaft geared turbines. Speed 32knots
Armament	16—4·5in DP (8×2), 38—20mm, 72 aircraft
Armour	Main belt 4½in; deck 3in–2½in
Complement	1,785

Victorious
Formidable

Dimensions	23,000tons; 753×96×24ft

Performance	3-shaft geared turbines. Speed 31knots
Armament	16—4·5in DP (8×2), 48—2pdr AA, 8—20mm, 36 aircraft
Armour	Main belt 4½in; deck 3–2½in
Complement	1,392

Furious

Dimensions	22,450tons; 786×90×24ft
Performance	4-shaft geared turbines. Speed 30knots. Range 3,500mls
Armament	12—4in AA (6×2), 24—2pdr, 33 aircraft
Armour	Main belt 3in–2in; deck 3in–1in
Complement	748 plus aircrew
	Originally designed as a battlecruiser with 2—18in guns as main armament, first commissioned with 1—18in aft and flight deck forward!

Pursuer
Fencer
Trumpeter
Emperor
Nabob

Dimensions	11,420tons; 492×70×23ft
Performance	1-shaft geared turbine. Speed 17knots
Armament	2—4in AA (2×1), *Pursuer* and *Fencer*: 8—40mm (4×2), 15—20mm (15×1), 18 aircraft *Trumpeter*, *Emperor* and *Nabob*: 16—40mm (8×2), 20—20mm, 24 aircraft
Complement	646

Berwick

Dimensions	9,750tons; 630×68×16ft
Performance	4-shaft geared turbines. Speed 31knots. Range 10,400mls at 12½knots, 2,300/max
Armament	8—8in (4×2), 8—4in AA (4×2), 8—2pdr (8×1) several 20mm, 4 Walrus seaplanes
Armour	Main belt 5in–3in; deck 1½in; turrets 4–3in
Complement	679

Sheffield

Dimensions	9,100tons; 591×62×17ft

Performance	4-shaft geared turbines. Speed 32knots. Range 7,000mls at 14knots
Armament	12—6in (4× 3), 8—4in AA (4× 2), 8—2pdr, 3 Walrus seaplanes, 6—21in TT (2× 3). Various 20mm were added and eventually X turret (3—6in) removed and 20—40mm added.
Armour	Main belt 4–3in; deck 2in; turrets 2–1in
Complement	700

Belfast

Dimensions	10,000tons; 613× 63× 17ft
Performance	4-shaft geared turbines. Speed 32knots. Range 8,000mls at 14knots
Armament	12—6in (4× 3), 12—4in AA (6× 2), 16—2pdr, 6—21in TT (2× 3), 3 Walrus seaplanes. 6—20mm added initially, later 4—4in AA were removed to allow for 20—2pdr and 5—40mm
Armour	Main belt 4½in; deck 2in; turrets 2—1½in
Complement	850

Jamaica
Kenya

Dimensions	8,000tons; 555× 62× 16ft
Performance	4-shaft geared turbines. Speed 33knots. Range 6,000mls at 13 knots
Armament	12—6in (4× 3), 8—4in AA (4× 2), 9—2pdr, 6—21in TT (2× 3) various 20mm and 40mm AA were added subsequently
Armour	Main belt 3¼in; deck 2in; turrets 2in
Complement	730

Royalist

Dimensions	5,770tons; 512× 50× 15ft
Performance	4-shaft geared turbines. Speed 33knots
Armament	8—5·25in DP (4× 2), 12—2pdr, 12—20mm, 6—21in TT (2× 3)
Armour	Main belt 3–2in; deck 2–½in; turrets 2–1in
Complement	535

Faulknor

Dimensions	1,475tons; 343× 34× 9ft

Performance	2-shaft geared turbines. Speed 35knots. Range 6,350mls at 15knots 4,290/20
Armament	5—4·7in (5× 1), 1—3in AA, 8—21in TT (2× 4)
Complement	175

Echo
Eclipse
Fury

Dimensions	1,375tons; 329× 33× 8ft
Performance	2-shaft geared turbine. Speed 35knots. Range 6,000mls at 15knots
Armament	4—4·7in (4× 1), 1—3in AA, 4—21in TT (1× 4)
Complement	145

Icarus
Intrepid

Dimensions	1,370tons; 323× 32× 8ft
Performance	2-shaft geared turbines. Speed 36knots. Range 5,530mls at 15knots, 2,950/20
Armament	4—4·7in, 8—0·5in AA, 10—21in TT (2× 5)
Complement	175

Ashanti
Bedouin
Eskimo
Punjabi

Dimensions	1,870tons; 377× 36× 9ft
Performance	2-shaft geared turbines. Speed 36knots. Range 5,700mls at 15knots, 3,200/20
Armament	8—4·7in (4× 2), 4—2pdr AA, 4—21in TT (1× 4)
Complement	190

Lookout
Marne
Matchless
Meteor
Milne

Dimensions	1,920tons; 362× 37× 10ft
Performance	2-shaft geared turbines. Speed 36knots. Range 5,500mls at 15knots, 2,250/25
Armament	6—4·7in (3× 2), DP, 4—2pdr, 8—21in TT (2× 4)
Complement	221

Onslow
Onslaught

Dimensions	1,540tons; 345×35×9ft
Performance	2-shaft geared turbines. Speed 37knots. Range 3,850mls at 20knots
Armament	4—4·7in (4×1), 4—2pdr, 8—20mm, 8—21in TT (2×4)
Complement	183

Javelin
Piorun

Dimensions	1,690tons; 356×36×9ft
Performance	2-shaft geared turbines. Speed 36knots. Range 5,500mls at 15knots 3,700/20
Armament	6—4·7in (3×2), 4—2pdr, 10—21in TT (2×5)
Complement	183

Ursa *Verulam*
Undaunted *Vigilant*
Swift *Wakeful*
Virago *Algonquin*
Sioux

Dimensions	1,710tons; 363×36×10ft
Performance	2-shaft geared turbines. Speed 37knots. Range 5,500mls at 15 knots, 3,700/20
Armament	4—4·7in (4×1), 2—40mm, 8—20mm, 8—21in TT (2×4)
Complement	180

Truculent
Thrasher

Dimensions	1,090/1,575tons; 275×26×15ft
Performance	2-shaft diesels/electric motors. Speed 15knots/9knots. Dived endurance with fully charged battery 9knots for 45mins, 2½knots for 36hrs. Diving depth 300ft
Armament	11—21in TT, 1—4in, 1—20mm
Complement	59

Seanymph *Sceptre*
Syrtis *Stubborn*

Dimensions	715/990tons; 217×24×11ft

Performance	2-shaft diesels/electric motors, 14/9knots Dived endurance with fully charged battery; 9knots for 45mins, $2\frac{1}{2}$knots for 36hrs. Diving depth 300ft
Armament	7—21in TT, 1—3in, 1—20mm
Complement	44

X-craft

Dimensions	35tons; $51\times 8\frac{1}{2}\times 7\frac{1}{2}$ft
Performance	Single screw diesel/electric motor. Speed $6\frac{1}{2}$/5knots. Range on surface 1,500mls at 4knots, dived with fully charged battery 80hrs at 2knots. Diving depth 300ft. Human endurance 10–14 days overall, 12hrs dived without ventilating.
Armament	Two side cargoes, each containing 2tons of Amatex, fitted with clock-work time fuses up to 36hrs delay
Complement	Passage crew—1 officer, 1 seaman, 1 stoker Operational crew—3 officers (1 qualified diver), 1 ERA

It must be appreciated that the length of time that a submarine can remain dived depends both on its battery capacity and on the oxygen for the crew. After 24hrs without a reasonable chance to ventilate the submarine the air will be foul and the crew will begin to be thick-headed; 36hrs is about the maximum. The performance of the battery deteriorates as its charge is used and a fully discharged battery will need about 12hrs of charging with both engines initially.

Chariot

Dimensions	$1\frac{1}{2}$tons; 25ft long× 21in diameter
Performance	Single screw electric motor. Range 18mls at 3knots
Armament	600lb TNT detachable warhead with clockwork time fuse
Complement	2 men in underwater diving dress with oxygen breathing apparatus. Safe operating depth 35ft—below that unpredictable due to effects of pressure and liability to oxygen poisoning and unconsciousness

APPENDIX SEVEN

Aircraft data British

Albacore	Torpedo bomber/reconnaissance Speed 155knots max. Range 650mls with 1,500lb bombs or 1—18in torpedo. Crew 2/3. Armament 1—0·303 MG
Barracuda	Torpedo bomber/reconnaissance Speed 210knots at 2,000ft max, 149knots at 5,000ft cruising. Range 535–730mls, 1,000mls with extra fuel. Bomb load, 1,500lb or 1—18in torpedo. Crew 2/3. Armament 2—0·303 MG
Firefly I	Fighter Speed 278knots at 17,000ft max, 187knots at 15,000ft cruising. Range 500mls/980mls with drop tanks. Performance 9·6mins to 15,000ft. Crew 2. Armament 4—20mm
Seafire	Fighter Speed 307knots at 12,000ft max, 170knots at 12,000ft cruising. Range 405mls/630mls with drop tanks. Performance 2mins to 5,000ft. Crew 1. Armament 2—20mm, 4—0·303 MG
Corsair	Fighter-bomber Speed 352knots at 20,000ft max, 158knots at 1,500ft cruising. Range 957mls/1,350mls with drop tanks. Performance 7·3mins to 20,000ft. Crew 1. Armament 6—0·5 MG. Bomb load 1,000lb
Hellcat	Fighter-bomber Speed 325knots at 18,000ft max, 138knots at 1,500ft cruising. Range 1,030mls/1,380mls with drop tanks.

Performance 7mins to 20,000ft. Crew 1. Armament 6—0·5 MG. Bomb load 500lb

Wildcat	Fighter Speed 283knots at 10,500ft max, 142knots at 1,500ft cruising. Range 564mls/1138mls with drop tanks. Performance 7·5mins to 20,000ft. Crew 1. Armament 4—0·5 MG

Note: American fighters had a lesser range but a much increased economical speed when flown at height.

Hampden	Bomber Length 53ft. Span 69ft Speed 265mls. Range 1,100mls. Bomb load 4,000lb Crew 6. Armament 6—0.303 MG
Stirling	Bomber Length 87ft. Span 99ft Speed 280mph. Range 3,000mls. Bomb load 18,000lb Crew 7. Armament 8—0·303 MG
Halifax	Bomber Length 71ft. Span 104ft Speed 270mph. Range 3,000mls. Bomb load 14,500lb Crew 7. Armament 9—0·303 MG
Lancaster	Bomber Length 69ft. Span 102ft Speed 275mph. Range 3,000mls. Bomb load 18,000lb (normal) Crew 7. Armament 10—0·303 MG The Lancaster was the only bomber which could carry the 12,000lb Tallboy and the 22,000lb Grand Slam bombs.

The range of bombers was considerably reduced when carrying a very heavy bomb load due to the need to reduce the weight of fuel carried. The critical factor was the all-up weight at take-off and the power which the engines could develop.

APPENDIX EIGHT

Aircraft data German

Arado 196	Single engine reconnaissance seaplane Speed 169knots max at sea level, 152knots cruising at 6,000ft Range 500mls. Crew 2. Armament 2—20mm, 3—7·9mm
Blohm und Voss 138	Triple engined reconnaissance/bomber flying boat Speed 152knots max, at sea level, 126knots cruising Range 2,710mls max., 2170mls with two torpedoes Crew 6. Armament 1—15/20mm, 1—20mm, 1—13mm
Heinkel 115	Twin engined torpedo-bomber seaplane Speed 161knots max at sea level, 141knots cruising at 1,000ft Range 1,400mls with one torpedo Crew 3. Armament 1—15mm, 4—7·9mm

APPENDIX NINE

German Defences of Kaa Fjord, September 1943

Across the entrance of Kaa Fjord, from Auskarneset on the north side to Jemmeluftneset on the south side was stretched a wide-meshed anti-submarine net to a depth of 48 metres. There was a gap 400 metres wide at the extreme southern end which, since the summer of

1943, could be closed by a moveable boom of loosely interlocked wire network suspended by buoys to a depth of 10 metres and secured to the bank at Jemmeluftneset; owing to the continuous traffic passing to and from Alta and Bossekop this gap was only closed in the event of a submarine alarm at Altenfjord or its approaches and was protected by depth charge throwers.

A small boat, either an A/S vessel or patrol boat fitted with hydrophone apparatus was constantly stationed some 600 metres ESE of the gap to check all ships passing through.

The net enclosure at Barbrudalen, where *Tirpitz* lay, consisted of a double air-torpedo net to a depth of 15 metres and a secondary net of 36 metres. A 20-metre gap was left at the side nearest the mouth of the fjord, i.e. on the battleship's port bow, which could be closed by a baffle to which was attached a net with a depth of between 11 and 36 metres. Whenever this gap was left open at night a special boat was put on watch to guard it and watch was also kept from *Tirpitz*, the hydrophones being continuously manned. (It was fortuitous that owing to a breakdown in the telephone system this gap had to be left open all through the night of 21st–22nd September to permit boat traffic from *Tirpitz* to Bossekop. The guard boat and hydrophone watch were secured at 0600, an hour before the X-craft made their attacks.)

Identical net defences protected the *Scharnhorst* anchorage at Auskarneset, with a 10-metre gap in the north-west edge.

Stjern Sund and Varg Sund were both guarded by patrol boats.

Anti-aircraft armament around the anchorage consisted of 4—4in and 22—20/40mm at Auskarneset, 4—4in and 12—20/40mm at the head of the fjord; 8—20/40mm at the point separating Barbrudalen from the bay to the east, 4—20mm at the head of each bay, and single and twin mountings of 20 and 40mm guns along the shores of the fjord, as well as the *Nymphe* at anchor in the middle.

APPENDIX TEN

The Fate of X-5, 22/23rd September 1943

What exactly happened to X-5 (Lieut Henty-Creer) is uncertain, but at 0843/22 the craft was briefly sighted on the surface some 650yds on the starboard bow of *Tirpitz*, which opened fire with 5·9in, 37 and 20mm guns and claimed to have obtained several hits. The craft submerged and five depth-charges were dropped shortly afterwards.

On 12th October a signal was sent to the German Naval Staff reporting that:

i) Because of the current, heavy silting and depth of water, the search for the third craft (X-5) had been abandoned. Numerous hits with gunfire, a pattern of depth-charges dropped at the spot where it had been seen to disappear, the limited resistance of the craft against depth-charge explosions and the steady seepage of oil to the surface, all made its destruction appear certain.

ii) The after part of the first craft (X-6) had been raised and beached alongside that of the other craft (X-7).

iii) No further salvage operations were intended.

It was always assumed by both British and German authorities that X-5 had been sunk as a result of shelling and depth-charging, but Lieut Henty-Creer's family were not convinced of this and after the war his mother and sister spent three months in the area of Alten Fjord trying to discover further details. They met Captain Sarilla, an experienced arctic skipper, and were given the following statement which he had attested before the local magistrate.

> The 23/9 1943, about 8 o'clock in the morning—the day after the British submarine attack on *Tirpitz* had taken place in Kaa Fjord—from the window in my home in Bossekop I became aware of something ranging up from the sea by Bossekopberget—which I presumed was the periscope of a submarine in the underwater position. It moved rather fast in the direction of Krakenes (the other side of the fjord). The sea was quite calm with a glassy surface and I could clearly see a foam-stripe on the water after the

periscope. I stood and followed the periscope till it was about in the middle of the fjord and I could not see it any more because of the distance. I think three to four minutes, five at most, passed from the time I became aware of the periscope by Bossekopberget till I lost sight of it out in the fjord. By this occasion a few other persons were present in our house, who also saw what I have related, but I cannot remember who they were.

When the periscope of the submarine passed the area near my house some German soldiers who worked by a shore house near my home became aware of the periscope. They pointed at it and shouted to each other 'British submarine'. A couple of them then ran to the telephone room in the store house, probably to report to their superiors. However I did not see that anything was done by the Germans to destroy the submarine.

It has to be mentioned that I once, during the world war 1914–18, while out fishing saw a German submarine passing in underwater position with periscope above the water and because of this I could with certainty say that what I saw move from Bossenkopberget towards Krakenes on the morning of 23/9 was a periscope of a submarine passing in the underwater position.

Signed Mathis Aleksandersen Sarilla

The Henty-Creers were also given verbal reports by two other Norwegians, one of whom claimed to have sighted a periscope off Talvik at about 1130/23 and the other to have seen a flat topped object like a submarine entering a deserted bay of Stjernoy Island at about 1800. If these reports are to be believed these sightings can only have been X-5 escaping from Kaa Fjord, since Bossekopberget is well beyond the Brattholm Islands where X-10 had lain up for repairs and anyhow X-10 had already left Stjernoy at 1100/23.

Although it is possible that X-5 had laid her charges and was withdrawing when she broke surface and was attacked, the evidence suggests otherwise:

i) If X-5 had made a successful penetration and withdrawal of the nets without being detected this would have had to have been before 0712 when X-6 was first identified and in an hour and a half X-5 should have been more than 650yds clear of *Tirpitz*.

ii) If X-5's charges had been laid they should have been countermined at 0812 but no third explosion was observed.

iii) By choice Lieut Henty-Creer would have laid his charges under *Tirpitz*'s propellors (statement made to me by his family) but the damage was only commensurate with the single charge laid there by X-7.

It seems most likely that what happened was something like this. X-5 was delayed in the approach more than X-6 and X-7, both of which were uncomfortably near the 0800 deadline when they dropped the charges, and Henty-Creer was forced to plan for an attack after 0900. He may have heard the hand-grenades dropped around X-6 at 0723 but most certainly the explosions at 0812 would have told him that one or two charges had been laid. The effect of underwater explosions is unpredictable, especially in confined waters, and X-5 may have been damaged at 0812 or subsequently by the depth-charges which were being dropped at random in the fjord. The experiences of the other craft show that the compass and periscope were the two most vulnerable pieces of equipment and X-5 may well have been both lost and blind when breaking surface at 0843 trying to discover what was the actual situation.

If X-5 survived the shelling and depth-charging the craft was undoubtedly damaged and would most probably have spent the day on the bottom of the fjord, slowly leaking oil as the Germans reported, trying to make repairs and to plan for an escape in darkness. The flagrant exposure of the periscope reported next day by Captain Sarilla suggests that the compasses were still useless and that Henty-Creer was forced to con the craft visually out of Kaa Fjord. If the subsequent reports are true then he succeeded but what happened thereafter will probably never be known, although he had expressed his intention of making for Kola Inlet in Russia if he failed to rendezvous with a British submarine.

(I am indebted to Mr Lawson of the Naval Historical Branch for the translation of the German signal relating to salvage and to Mrs and Miss Henty-Creer for the information which they have given me and for the translation of Captain Sarilla's statement. I am responsible for the analysis of evidence and the possible reconstruction of X-5's movements.)

Bibliography

The Tirpitz	J. Brennecke
The Tirpitz	D. Woodward
Sink the Tirpitz	L. Peillard
Above Us the Waves	C. E. T. Warren & J. Benson
Against All Odds	W. Gallagher
The Shetland Bus	D. Howarth
The Dam Busters	P. Brickhill
The War at Sea	S. W. Roskill
The Second World War	Sir Winston Churchill

Technical

Janes Fighting Ships	
Warships of World War II	Lenton & Colledge
German Warships of World War II	J. C. Taylor
British Battleships	O. Parkes
British Destroyers	E. March
Schlachtschiffe und Schlachtkreuzer	S. Breyer
K. S. Bismarck	Profile Publication

Index

LES JUIFS DANS LE CORAN

ESPACES libres

MEIR M. BAR-ASHER

LES JUIFS DANS LE CORAN

Albin Michel

ESPACES *libres*

Histoire

Collections « Présences du judaïsme » dirigées par Menorah/F.S.J.U.

Collection « Présences du judaïsme poche » Mireille Hadas-Lebel

À la mémoire de mes chères sœurs,
Hadassa et Sima.

Préface

À l'heure où la question de l'attitude de l'islam envers les juifs occupe souvent le devant de la scène médiatique, un ouvrage comme celui-ci est indispensable. Entre ceux qui défendent – parfois sans l'avoir lu – la thèse d'un Coran « antisémite » et ceux qui, à l'aide de quelques versets coraniques choisis, entendent démontrer à leurs ouailles le caractère « perfide » des juifs, les discours passionnels s'affrontent, aux dépens d'une approche objective. Si l'islam ne se réduit pas au Coran, ce dernier n'en reste pas moins la pierre fondatrice. Encore faut-il, d'une part, être en mesure de le lire sérieusement, c'est-à-dire en le prenant en compte dans sa totalité et sa complexité, ainsi que d'en définir le contexte ; d'autre part savoir déterminer selon quelles modalités les diverses formes de l'islam classique et moderne puisent à ce fonds coranique pour élaborer, selon les circonstances historiques de chaque époque, un discours sur les juifs et le judaïsme.

La présence massive, dans le Coran, d'éléments appartenant ou issus du judaïsme intrigue orientalistes, islamologues et arabisants depuis près de deux siècles. De l'étude d'Abraham Geiger, *Was hat Mohammed aus dem Judenthume aufgenommen ?*, parue dans la première moitié du XIXe siècle, jusqu'à l'ouvrage de Gabriel Said Reynolds, *The Qur'an and the Bible : Text and Commentary* (2018) en passant par de grands savants comme Ignaz Goldziher, David Sidersky, Shlomo Dov Goitein, Patricia Crone-Michael Cook, Uri Rubin, Michael Lecker, Sydney Griffith et beaucoup d'autres, la recherche critique, fondée sur de rigoureuses méthodes historiques et philologiques, n'a cessé d'ouvrir des pistes prometteuses, de susciter des débats passionnants, de démontrer l'extrême complexité des problématiques.

De quelle(s) forme(s) de judaïsme parle-t-on ? Quels courants et quels corpus religieux ont pu influencer le Coran ? Tout aussi féconde paraît la piste dite « judéo-chrétienne », c'est-à-dire la religion de juifs restés fidèles aux croyances et pratiques juives, comme la circoncision, la célébration du sabbat, l'interdiction de la consommation du porc, etc., mais croyant en même temps à Jésus comme Christ et Sauveur de la Fin des temps. Là encore, de H. J. Schoeps et M. P. Roncaglia à C. Sogovia en passant par Sh. Pines et G. Rizzardi, les études sont nombreuses. Récemment, dans le volume d'hommage à Patricia Crone, Guy G. Stroumsa en présente une érudite historiographie et Dominique Bernard, dans sa somme imposante, *Les Disciples juifs de Jésus du Ier siècle à Mahomet*, parue à Paris en 2017, montre la présence active des ébionites / nazaréens jusqu'aux premiers siècles de l'hégire et au sein de la communauté musulmane.

Les tenants et les aboutissants, les implications et les pistes d'investigation de ces problématiques sont considérables. Les premières questions que celles-ci posent concernent rien de moins que la religion de Muhammad lui-même. Quel a été le milieu religieux de sa naissance et de son éducation ? À quelle(s) tradition(s) s'est abreuvée sa spiritualité ? Contrairement à ce que soutiendra plus tard l'apologétique musulmane, l'Arabie préislamique n'était pas celle de « l'ère de l'ignorance » et de l'idolâtrie ni l'islam le commencement du monothéisme arabe. Probablement l'idolâtrie n'y existait plus depuis de longs siècles, sauf peut-être chez quelques bédouins non sédentarisés.

À part de nombreuses preuves épigraphiques, archéologiques et historiques, surtout en dehors du *Hijâz*, comme l'ont montré les nombreuses études de savants tels Frédéric Imbert, Christian Robin ou encore Jan Retsö, les attestations textuelles les plus évidentes se trouvent dans le Coran lui-même : la présence massive des figures de l'Ancien et du Nouveau Testament, le caractère allusif des récits bibliques qui montre que l'auditoire les connaissait bien, sinon ces allusions seraient restées complètement inintelligibles, l'onomastique des personnages bibliques issue de celle des christianismes orientaux de culture syro-palestinienne, les racines hébraïques, araméennes et syriaques de termes techniques aussi importants que *qur'ân* (Coran), *sûra* (chapitre du Coran), *âya* (verset coranique) ou *zakât* (aumône) et *salât* (prière canonique) ou encore *hajj* (grand pèlerinage à La Mecque) ou *ʿumra* (petit pèlerinage à La Mecque), etc.

Dans le présent ouvrage, Meir M. Bar-Asher relève magistralement le défi de faire la synthèse des études antérieures tout en proposant de nouvelles interrogations pertinentes. Il est sans doute actuellement un des savants les plus indiqués pour ce genre de travail. Grand connaisseur de l'islam et du judaïsme, maîtrisant parfaitement les langues concernées, fin analyste de la pensée et de la spiritualité dans les deux religions, historien et philologue, il a la grande vertu de transmettre son savoir sur des sujets fort difficiles de manière limpide et accessible. Je suis en plus particulièrement heureux, en tant que spécialiste du shîʿisme, de constater qu'il consacre un chapitre important à cette branche de l'islam, le « parent pauvre » des études islamologiques (malgré quelques évolutions positives notables ces dernières années). Cet ouvrage est d'une utilité extrême aussi bien pour le chercheur confirmé et l'étudiant que le simple lecteur curieux et cultivé.

Mohammad Ali AMIR-MOEZZI,
École pratique des hautes études (Sorbonne)

INTRODUCTION

Le présent livre doit sa naissance à une conférence que j'ai donnée à Paris en 2015 sur le thème « L'islam et la Torah d'Israël à travers le Coran et le Hadîth », à l'invitation de mon ami Tony Lévy, chercheur émérite du CNRS spécialiste de l'histoire des mathématiques. Le professeur Mireille Hadas-Lebel, directrice de la collection « Présences du judaïsme poche », qui assistait à la conférence, m'a invité à élargir cette réflexion aux dimensions d'un livre. Je leur en suis reconnaissant ; ce sont eux qui m'ont convaincu d'écrire le présent ouvrage. De manière plus large, le contenu de ce livre est tiré de deux séminaires que j'ai animés, le premier à l'Institut européen d'études juives Paideia à Stockholm de 2007 à 2017 ; le second à Pilsen, en République tchèque, en 2012, tous deux consacrés aux points de contact et aux frictions entre islam et judaïsme. Les échanges fructueux qui se sont fait jour avec mes collègues et mes élèves, aussi bien au cours de ces deux séminaires qu'à l'occasion d'autres conférences que j'ai pu donner sur ces thèmes au fil des ans, m'ont permis de mieux comprendre ce problème complexe, et j'espère que ce livre me donnera l'occasion d'en faire profiter le lecteur. Je tiens à rendre hommage à Shmuel Trigano, avec lequel j'ai animé un colloque à Paris en 2005 sur le thème « Le judaïsme et les origines de l'islam ». Je tiens encore à remercier Julien Darmon pour l'important travail d'enrichissement et de lecture critique qui a permis à ce livre de prendre sa forme définitive.

Le présent ouvrage entend approcher la nature des affinités entre islam et judaïsme ; et pour cela, il est indispensable d'en revenir aux sources, c'est-à-dire à ce qui se joue dans le Coran lui-même. Pour autant, dans la mesure du possible, on recourra également à la littérature religieuse islamique qui puise son inspiration dans le Coran, puisque aussi bien il n'est ni faisable ni juste de considérer le Coran isolément de la littérature qu'il a engendrée : la tradition orale attribuée au prophète de l'islam ou Hadîth, les commentaires du Coran, la littérature islamique de polémique contre le judaïsme, etc. Il en va d'ailleurs de même dans le judaïsme, où Torah écrite et Torah orale sont inextricablement mêlées. Bien souvent, il est impossible de comprendre le texte et le contexte coraniques sans recourir à la tradition post-coranique. À tout le moins, cette tradition orale nous permet-elle de saisir comment, à différentes époques, les musulmans ont compris le Coran. C'est pourquoi tous les chapitres de ce livre font appel, à des degrés divers, à ces sources post-coraniques.

Les deux derniers, en particulier, appellent des explications complémentaires. Le chapitre v, consacré aux « fondements coraniques du statut juridique des juifs sous domination islamique », aurait à première vue pu ne pas être inclus dans cet ouvrage, dans la mesure où il porte sur des évolutions théologico-politiques qui se sont produites après la clôture du corpus coranique. Pour autant, son inclusion se justifie par le fait que ce processus, pour n'être pas « coranique » en soi, s'appuie sur des versets coraniques pour élaborer le statut juridique des juifs ainsi que d'autres minorités religieuses. Il en va de même pour le chapitre vi, consacré à « La place du judaïsme et des juifs dans le shîʿisme duodécimain » : il s'agit de développements certes tardifs en islam, mais qui font appels à des notions qui sont bel et bien traitées dans le Coran lui-même. Ce chapitre de clôture nous permettra également de ne pas restreindre notre regard au point de vue sunnite majoritaire, mais de l'élargir à un monde shîʿite qui, pour minoritaire qu'il soit, n'en est pas moins puissant. On estime que les diverses traditions shîʿites comptent cent cinquante millions de fidèles, ce qui représente un dixième de la population musulmane mondiale. Au sein du shî'isme, la branche duodécimaine est aujourd'hui nettement majoritaire.

Nous avons tenté de rendre compte du rapport coranique aux juifs dans toutes ses nuances, les plus lumineuses comme les plus sombres. Dans le Coran, il est très souvent fait mention des juifs, de leur religion et de leurs Écritures saintes. De nombreux épisodes bibliques fort connus sont relatés dans le Coran de manière très détaillée, certains d'entre eux le sont même plusieurs fois, entre autres : l'histoire des Patriarches, la servitude des fils d'Israël au pays de Pharaon, la sortie d'Égypte, l'arrivée et l'installation en Terre sainte, le don de la Torah. On y trouve encore des références à divers miracles survenus dans le désert aux enfants d'Israël : la colonne de nuée qui les accompagnait, la manne, les cailles tombées du ciel, l'eau jaillie du rocher pour étancher la soif du peuple.

Certaines figures bibliques avec les récits qui les concernent sont citées plusieurs fois : comme Abraham et sa famille, Loth et les siens ainsi que Moïse et la souffrance des fils d'Israël en Égypte, ou incidemment les éclaireurs envoyés par Moïse avant l'entrée en Terre promise, David et Salomon, Jonas (Yûnus), appelé aussi *Dhû l-nûn* (« l'homme au poisson »), Job (Ayyûb) et bien d'autres.

Les voix des héros bibliques ne sont pas seules à se faire entendre dans le Coran. La foi, la loi et le droit public et privé sont extrêmement présents et tous imprégnés par la Bible ainsi que d'autres sources juives dont on parlera plus loin. Revenons d'abord sur l'étendue et la profondeur des liens unissant le Coran à la Bible et au judaïsme post-biblique. La question a certes été souvent débattue par les chercheurs. On présentera ici le contexte historique et culturel dans lequel apparaît l'islam, en décrivant de manière détaillée le judaïsme professé par les juifs en Arabie à l'époque où Muhammad commence sa carrière prophétique, d'abord pendant douze ans à La Mecque, sa ville natale (610-622), puis à Yathrib, appelée plus tard al-Madîna (Médine), comme le rapporte la tradition musulmane. Muhammad aurait connu les juifs surtout à Médine et dans ses environs où il aurait été actif pendant les dix dernières années de sa vie (622-632). À leur contact, il aurait appris leur religion et leur histoire.

Après avoir présenté l'arrière-plan historique de la rencontre entre Juifs et Arabes – et plus tard entre juifs et musulmans – des centaines d'années avant l'apparition de l'islam tel qu'il nous est connu par des sources arabes essentiellement, ce livre s'efforcera de retracer l'image des juifs et du judaïsme qui se dégage du Coran.

On examinera tout d'abord la terminologie et

les divers noms par lesquels les juifs sont désignés dans le Coran. Nous dégagerons les caractéristiques de chacun de ces noms et ce qu'ils reflètent du regard porté sur les juifs et leur religion. Nous retiendrons en particulier trois appellations : *banû isrâ'îl* (« fils d'Israël »), *al-yahûd* (« juifs ») et *ahl al-kitâb* (« le peuple du Livre »).

Nous relèverons ensuite les aspects divers et contradictoires sous lesquels les juifs et leur religion sont dépeints dans le Coran. D'un côté des déclarations positives : Israël est présenté comme le peuple élu que Dieu a comblé de bienfaits en le tirant de l'esclavage en Égypte, lui faisant don de la Torah, suscitant en son sein des prophètes, le guidant vers la Terre promise et la lui accordant. D'un autre côté, un peuple infidèle à l'Alliance, qui retombe dans l'idolâtrie et falsifie la Torah que Dieu lui a donnée et tue les prophètes qui lui ont été envoyés pour le remettre dans le droit chemin ; un peuple qui, pour avoir trahi son alliance avec Dieu, mérite que l'on s'abstienne d'alliance avec lui. « Ô vous qui croyez ! Ne prenez pas les juifs et les chrétiens comme affiliés ; ils sont affiliés les uns avec les autres » (5 : 51*).

Ce petit livre entend donner à lire combien les deux religions sont inextricablement liées, à la fois

* Toutes les références sous la forme XX : XX, sans autre mention, renvoient aux sourates et aux versets du Coran.

proches et distantes, entre lesquelles l'amitié et la haine se conjuguent sans cesse. Ces ambivalences, faites d'accueil et de rejet simultanés, orientent le rapport fondamental de l'islam au judaïsme et, par là, aux juifs. Nous examinerons les raisons de cette ambiguïté de la relation aux juifs et au judaïsme qui revêt plusieurs aspects. Elle est également sensible dans l'attitude complexe du Coran envers la Bible : d'un côté, celle-ci est présentée comme un texte révélé par Dieu à l'espèce humaine et donc comme un livre susceptible d'authentifier la révélation faite à Muhammad dans le Coran puisqu'elle émane de la même source divine. D'un autre côté, selon le Coran, le Livre donné aux juifs aurait perdu de sa valeur car ils l'auraient sciemment altéré, entre autres raisons pour en retirer toute référence à la future apparition de Muhammad et de la nouvelle religion qu'il apporterait au monde. Il va de soi que la falsification de la Bible la rend inférieure au Coran, qui est considéré comme la parole divine authentique. En d'autres termes, les juifs sont aussi bien le « peuple du Livre » (*ahl al-kitâb*) qu'un « âne chargé de livres » (62 : 5), c'est-à-dire un peuple qui porte sur ses épaules un héritage immense mais dont il ignore tout et qu'en réalité il ne mérite pas.

L'ambiguïté du Coran face à l'héritage biblique – et postbiblique – apparaît aussi dans les lois coraniques. Tout ce qui concerne la prière, le jeûne, les règles alimentaires, la pureté et l'impureté a un lien très évident avec la Bible et les sources postbibliques. Cependant, on observe par ailleurs de nombreuses lois qui marquent une volonté délibérée de s'écarter du judaïsme. Entre les exemples les plus frappants nous pouvons mentionner le changement d'orientation de la prière (*qibla*) vers La Mecque plutôt que vers Jérusalem, le jeûne (*sawm*) et les lois alimentaires ou bien la fixation du calendrier, sur lesquels nous reviendrons.

Le lien entre le Coran et la Bible est signalé depuis le début de la recherche islamologique dont le pionnier fut Abraham Geiger, par ailleurs surtout connu comme l'un des chefs du mouvement réformé juif en Allemagne. Dès 1833, il publie à Bonn son étude pionnière *Was hat Mohammed aus dem Judenthume aufgenommen ?* (« Qu'est-ce que Muhammad a reçu du judaïsme ? »). Il est suivi par un grand nombre de chercheurs. Je ne saurais citer ici tous ceux qui ont consacré d'importantes études aux liens entre judaïsme et islam et me limiterai aux plus marquants. Josef Horovitz dans son livre *Koranische Untersuchungen* (« Études coraniques »), paru à Berlin et Leipzig en 1926, relève les nombreux points de contact entre le Coran et les sources bibliques et postbibliques. Heinrich Speyer, *Die biblischen Erzählungen im Qoran* (« Les récits bibliques dans le Coran »), paru à Gräfenhainichen en 1931, cite les nombreux parallèles entre les récits du Coran et de la Bible ou de la littérature talmudique. Dans la même veine, on peut citer David Sidersky, *Les Origines des légendes musulmanes dans le Coran et dans les vies des prophètes* (Paris, 1933).

Plus près de nous, les nombreux articles de Sidney Griffith et tout particulièrement son livre *The Bible in Arabic : The Scriptures of the « People of the Book » in the Language of Islam* (Princeton, 2013), ainsi que les œuvres d'Uri Rubin et spécialement son livre *Between Bible and Qur'an* (Princeton, 1999). On doit une contribution importante au livre de Jacqueline Chabbi, *Le Coran décrypté. Figures bibliques en Arabie* (Paris, 2008). On trouvera aussi une étude générale chez Daniel Sibony, *Coran et Bible en questions et réponses* (Paris, 2017) et tout récemment l'œuvre de Gabriel S. Reynolds, *The Qur'an and the Bible : Text and Commentary* (New Haven, 2018). Ce ne sont là que quelques titres pris parmi la floraison d'études publiées dans les deux siècles passés.

Les traductions coraniques employées dans ce volume sont celles de Denise Masson, *Le Coran. Introduction, traduction et notes* (Paris, 1967 ; quelquefois avec de légers changements).

Plutôt qu'une translittération précise des termes

arabes avec points diacritiques, nous avons adopté une transcription simplifiée pour faciliter la lecture du lecteur non spécialiste, tandis que l'arabisant reconnaîtra facilement les termes. À l'intention du premier, quelques remarques sur la prononciation. Le ' indique la *hamza*, qui correspond à un arrêt glottal (un peu comme dans « hein ? ») et le ' note le 'ayn, lettre gutturale caractéristique de l'arabe et d'autres langues sémitiques ; le *th* correspond au *th* anglais du mot *thing* et le *dh* au *th* anglais du mot *this* ; le *kh* correspond au *ch* allemand (comme dans le mot allemand « Buch ») et le *gh* au *r* dit « grasseyé » français ; le *q* est un *k* prononcé au fond de la gorge. Le *s*, enfin, est toujours dur, comme dans « poisson », jamais comme dans « poison ». Il n'existe que trois voyelles en arabe, *a*, *i* et *u* (toujours prononcé « ou »), qui peuvent être courtes ou longues ; elles sont alors notées *â*, *î* et *û*.

Pour des raisons de simplicité toujours, les dates sont données uniquement selon le calendrier grégorien, sans mention de leur équivalence selon le calendrier dit « de l'hégire ».

I

LE CADRE HISTORIQUE

Les premiers contacts entre Juifs et Arabes eurent lieu presque mille ans avant l'avènement de l'islam en Arabie, en particulier dans le sud de la péninsule. Avant leur irruption fulgurante sur la scène de l'histoire universelle, les Arabes entretenaient déjà des liens avec les Juifs, mais nous en savons peu de chose. Comme le dit si bien Gordon Newby, ce qui a été écrit au sujet des Juifs en Arabie préislamique consiste en « beaucoup de fantasmes, beaucoup de polémiques et peu de ce que l'on pourrait appeler l'histoire[1] ». De fait, la majorité de nos informations provient de sources musulmanes rédigées à partir du VIIIe siècle, c'est-à-dire bien après l'avènement de l'islam.

La façon dont des Juifs en sont venus à s'installer en Arabie n'est pas clairement établie par les sources historiques. Elle n'est connue, dans sa plus grande part, qu'à travers des légendes qui font remonter la présence juive au VIe siècle avant notre ère : selon une légende juive yéménite, les premiers habitants juifs seraient arrivés quarante-deux ans avant la destruction du premier Temple (– 586). Lorsque, à la chute de Babylone, Ezra appela le peuple à revenir au pays d'Israël et à participer à la reconstruction du Temple, ils refusèrent car ils avaient prévu que le Second serait aussi détruit. En réponse, dit la légende, Ezra les aurait maudits, les vouant à la misère physique et spirituelle[2].

Les juifs yéménites lient traditionnellement l'époque de leur installation dans la région à l'épisode biblique de Salomon et de la reine de Saba, dont le Coran se fait l'écho dans la sourate 27 (« Les fourmis »). Le pays de Saba est généralement situé de part et d'autre de l'embouchure de la mer Rouge, soit entre le Yémen et l'Éthiopie actuels. Selon les légendes musulmanes, la reine de Saba, appelée Bilqîs, se serait convertie au judaïsme avec un grand nombre de dignitaires de sa cour avant d'épouser Salomon. Puis, lorsque le couple royal aurait donné naissance à un fils, Salomon aurait dépêché au royaume de Saba des maîtres juifs de Terre sainte afin qu'ils dispensent au prince une bonne éducation juive. Ces éducateurs seraient ainsi les premiers habitants juifs du Yémen. Que cette légende et les nombreuses autres datant cette implantation juive de l'époque biblique soient véridiques ou non, on ne peut, par ailleurs, nier que des liens commerciaux aient existé entre le sud de l'Arabie et la Terre sainte plusieurs siècles avant notre ère, comme le confirme une inscription sabéenne découverte au Yémen en 2008. Selon une autre tradition, les juifs seraient arrivés dans la péninsule Arabique et plus particulièrement dans la région du Hijâz sous l'autorité de Nabonide, le dernier souverain babylonien (de – 556 à – 539). Pénétrant dans la région du Hijâz, Nabonide soumit les habitants du lieu et s'installa à Tema'. Il raconte lui-même la conquête : « Je me suis caché loin de ma ville de Babylone [sur] la route vers Tema', Dadanu, Padakku, Khibrâ, Yadikhu et aussi loin que Yatribu ; dix ans j'étais parmi eux [et] dans ma ville je ne suis pas entré[3]. »

La majorité des villes mentionnées dans les propos de Nabonide sont des localités importantes dont nous savons par les sources musulmanes qu'elles abritaient des juifs dans la période préislamique avant qu'ils ne soient expulsés par Muhammad : Yatribu se réfère à Yathrib (la future Médine) ; Khibra à Khaybar ; Padakku à Fadak ; Tema' à Tayma' et Dadanu à Dedan (aujourd'hui al-'Ulâ). Les chercheurs supposent que son armée comptait de nombreux juifs, qu'on peut considérer comme les premiers habitants juifs du nord et de l'ouest de l'Arabie. Même s'il n'est guère possible de voir dans ce témoignage partiel l'attestation claire des débuts de l'implantation juive en Arabie, on sait que la présence juive s'est considérablement accrue quelques siècles plus tard dans la région du Hijâz, le berceau de l'islam, vraisemblablement en raison d'une arrivée massive de juifs après la destruction du Second Temple en l'an 70 de notre ère.

Un royaume juif en Arabie

Dans l'histoire fragmentaire de la présence juive en Arabie, l'épisode du royaume de Himyar reste l'un des plus importants. Les chercheurs s'accordent à dire que les origines de ce royaume situé dans l'angle sud-ouest de la péninsule datent de – 110. En 275, Himyar annexe Saba, se rend maître de l'Hadramaout et unifie pour la première fois le sud de l'Arabie en un seul royaume après plus de mille ans de morcellement politique et culturel. Cent ans plus tard, en 370, Himyar adopte le monothéisme dans sa version juive. Entre le IVᵉ et le VIᵉ siècle, les Himyarites étendent leur influence sur le centre et l'est de l'Arabie, atteignant Yamâma et les alentours de La Mecque. Les émissaires de Himyar créent des liens avec les tribus arabes dans ces contrées et lancent des expéditions militaires contre d'autres tribus. Au Vᵉ siècle, les Himyarites désignent comme roi Hujr Âkil al-Murâr de la tribu de Kinda en Arabie du Sud, dont l'autorité s'étend par la suite aussi à d'autres tribus de la région. Sa descendance se maintient sur le trône jusqu'à la fin du VIe siècle.

Le royaume de Himyar innove non seulement par son expansion mais aussi par sa conception même de l'État : alors que tous les États anciens dans le sud de l'Arabie assoient leur pouvoir et affirment leur identité par l'exercice d'un culte divin, Himyar réussit à s'unifier grâce à sa loyauté envers son souverain. C'est ainsi que le Yémen connaît, au Ve siècle déjà, un peuple avec un pouvoir centralisé, une même langue – le sabéen, langue de la même famille que les langues éthiopiennes mais très éloignée de l'arabe – et une écriture commune, le sud-arabique, appelé en arabe *musnad*.

Au IVe siècle de notre ère, les dirigeants de l'Éthiopie (appelée alors Aksoum) s'étaient convertis au christianisme et s'étaient rapprochés de Byzance. C'est à la même époque, et peut-être en réponse à cette adoption de la foi chrétienne, que les dirigeants de Himyar s'étaient convertis au judaïsme. Cette région à l'embouchure de la mer Rouge est le lieu d'une guerre par procuration entre les Empires byzantin et perse, l'Éthiopie chrétienne étant alliée de Byzance et Himyar étant soutenu par les Perses[4]. Au VIe siècle, les

Éthiopiens manœuvrent pour renverser le roi juif et le remplacer par un chrétien ; ils finissent par l'emporter pour une brève période (518-522). La diffusion du judaïsme à Himyar s'accroît considérablement aux ve et vi^e^ siècles et le processus de conversion au judaïsme connaît son apogée sous le règne de Yûsuf Dhû Nuwâs (522-525). Pendant ses trois années d'exercice du pouvoir, celui-ci persécute les chrétiens, ordonnant en particulier le massacre de la cité chrétienne de Najran en 523, resté dans les annales – les commentateurs s'accordent d'ailleurs pour voir une allusion à cet épisode dans le Coran (85 : 4). Deux ans plus tard, aidés par Byzance, les Éthiopiens envahissent Himyar et font tomber Dhû Nuwâs. Ils nomment comme dirigeant l'un des leurs (qui sera aussitôt renversé par un autre Éthiopien appelé Abraha), laissent une garnison sur place et rentrent en Éthiopie.

L'historien byzantin Procope de Césarée, évoquant le règne de Justinien (527-565), soit la période qui précède l'avènement de Muhammad, relate ces événements et signale en passant la présence de nombreux juifs dans le sud de l'Arabie :

> À l'époque de cette guerre, Hellestheaus, roi des Éthiopiens de confession chrétienne et parmi l'un des plus pratiquants de cette foi, apprit que d'une part de nombreux juifs et d'autre part des adeptes

de l'ancienne foi que les hommes d'aujourd'hui nomment hellénique [c'est-à-dire le paganisme hellénistique] parmi les Homérites [autrement dit les Himyarites] du continent opposé, usaient de machinations contre les chrétiens sans commune mesure. Après avoir réuni une flotte de vaisseaux et une armée, il marcha contre eux ; vainqueur au combat, il tua le roi et la plupart des Homérites[5].

Entre l'Arabie et la Terre sainte

Les liens entre le royaume de Himyar et les juifs de Palestine sont attestés aussi bien par l'archéologie que par les sources arabes. Au XXe siècle, on a découvert des inscriptions concernant les juifs de Himyar qui témoignent de ce que, longtemps avant les débuts de l'islam, vivaient en Arabie des tribus juives ou arabes converties au judaïsme. À ce jour, la salle des tombes himyarites, datant du IIIe siècle de notre ère et située dans la nécropole monumentale de Beit She'arim au sud-est du mont Carmel en Israël, constitue la découverte archéologique la plus importante mais aussi la plus ancienne dans ce domaine. H. Z. Hirschberg fut le premier à relever le grand intérêt de ces sépultures dans son livre *Israël en Arabie* (*Israël ba-'Arav*). Il pense que les défunts himyarites n'auraient pas été transportés de Himyar sur deux mille kilomètres et que des membres de cette communauté étaient plutôt venus s'installer dans une des localités du sud-est de la Terre sainte[6]. Les hypothèses d'Hirschberg sont étayées par la découverte récente à Tso'ar, au sud de la mer Morte, d'inscriptions sur des tombes juives himyarites datant de 470 et 477 de notre ère. Elles sont écrites en un mélange d'arabe, d'araméen et de sabéen. Sur l'une d'entre elles, il est cependant signalé que le défunt avait été transféré depuis Zafâr, capitale de Himyar (à cent trente kilomètres au sud de San'â'), jusqu'à Tso'ar pour y être enterré.

Hirschberg suppose que la majorité des juifs, en particulier ceux des contrées éloignées des centres historiques de Palestine et de Babylonie et situées le long de la *Via odorifera*, la route de l'encens, se consacrait au commerce, ainsi que le confirment les sources littéraires comme la poésie arabe antéislamique, écrite pendant le VIe siècle. Parmi les poètes arabes mentionnant les juifs himyarites, on peut citer Imru' l-Qays (v. 500-550 de notre ère), prince du royaume de Kinda, converti au judaïsme pendant la période préislamique et vassal de Himyar[7]. D'autres poètes arabes célèbres ont rappelé dans leurs vers que les juifs du sud du Yémen produisaient et vendaient du vin dans la région de l'Hadramaout ; on a d'ailleurs repêché des amphores de vin datant du Ier siècle de notre ère lors de fouilles sous-marines à Qâni' (l'actuel Bi'r 'Alî), ville située sur la côte sud du Yémen.

Les études archéologiques nous apprennent que les juifs du royaume de Himyar étaient organisés en une communauté dotée de toutes les institutions habituelles de la diaspora juive. On a trouvé dans la région les vestiges de nombreuses synagogues ainsi que de bains rituels*. Le bain rituel exhumé à Zafâr par le chercheur Paul Yule correspond aux exigences de la Loi juive exprimées dans les sources rabbiniques quant aux dimensions et à la forme des bains rituels ou encore à la provenance de l'eau[8]. On a aussi repéré des cimetières exclusivement réservés aux juifs, conformément aux exigences de la Loi. Néanmoins, malgré tous ces témoignages archéologiques, nous ne sommes pas en mesure de dire quelle forme de judaïsme pratiquaient les juifs de Himyar : se rattachaient-ils au judaïsme rabbinique de Palestine ou de Babylonie ? Pratiquaient-ils un judaïsme plus sectaire, de type judéo-chrétien, proto-karaïte ? L'état actuel de la recherche livre quelques pistes (cf. Robin éd., *Le Judaïsme de l'Arabie antique*), mais ne nous permet pas de répondre définitivement à ces questions.

---

* En hébreu *miqva'ot* (sg. *miqveh*). Selon la Loi juive, une femme mariée doit se plonger dans un bain rituel une semaine après son cycle menstruel avant de reprendre les relations intimes avec son époux.

La présence juive dans le Hijâz aux débuts de l'islam

L'installation de juifs dans le Hijâz a commencé, comme on vient de le voir, des siècles avant le début de l'islam. Ils se sont établis à Yathrib (la future Médine) ainsi qu'au nord de la ville, dans la région du Wâdi al-Qurâ (« la vallée des villages ») par où passait l'antique voie caravanière reliant Yathrib au nord-ouest de l'Arabie. Cette vallée s'étend sur environ deux cents kilomètres, tout le long des oasis depuis l'implantation de Khaybar, au nord-est de Yathrib, jusqu'à Taymâ', notamment l'oasis de Fadak. Yathrib, de loin la ville la plus importante de la région, se trouvait au nord-ouest d'une constellation d'implantations – villes et villages – entrecoupées de grands espaces ouverts, de palmeraies, de champs et de marchés.

Les juifs de Yathrib auraient été répartis en trois tribus : les Banû Nadîr, les Banû Qurayza et les Banû Qaynuqâ'. Grâce à une terre fertile riche en ruisseaux dans le Wâdi al-Qurâ et à Yathrib, les juifs, très actifs dans l'agriculture, pouvaient cultiver la vigne, fabriquer et exporter des olives et surtout des dattes. Pourtant, selon l'étude de Michael Lecker, ils tiraient leur principale subsistance non pas de l'agriculture, mais du commerce, tout comme leurs coreligionnaires du royaume de

Himyar : en effet, les quatre places de marché que comptait Yathrib avant l'avènement de l'islam témoignent d'une activité commerciale particulièrement intense. De plus, les tribus de Nadîr et de Qurayza possédaient en ville des forteresses et des demeures fortifiées qu'elles n'auraient jamais pu faire construire avec les seuls revenus agricoles. De nombreux juifs, en particulier ceux de la tribu de Qaynuqâ', travaillaient et commercialisaient l'orfèvrerie. Les trois tribus faisaient également commerce d'armes et d'armures[9].

Dans les sources musulmanes, les tribus de Nadîr et de Qurayza sont appelées *al-kâhinân* (les deux tribus des *cohanim* ou prêtres) ou encore *Banû Hârûn* (fils d'Aaron), car elles disaient descendre du grand prêtre Aaron, frère de Moïse. Les *cohanim,* dont le rôle dans le service du Temple était primordial, étaient soumis aux règles de pureté les plus strictes, comme le souligne avec force détails la Bible (en particulier le Lévitique et Ézéchiel) et, à sa suite, la littérature talmudique. Shlomo D. Goitein, dans son ouvrage *Jews and Arabs*, fait remarquer que l'existence de villes peuplées uniquement de *cohanim* était extrêmement répandue encore des siècles après la destruction du Second Temple. Les *cohanim* espéraient ainsi, à l'aide de leurs communautés fermées, respecter plus facilement leurs règles de pureté exigeantes. Goitein en conclut que « tout porte à croire qu'il faille accepter le témoignage des écrivains musulmans attestant que Yathrib, la ville où Muhammad menait sa mission, était à l'origine une ville de prêtres, de *cohanim,* qui s'y trouvaient encore à l'époque du Prophète[10] ».

Il ajoute que, selon certains *midrashim* du Talmud, après la destruction du Temple, les *cohanim* choisirent de s'établir dans la péninsule Arabique. Un texte syriaque, *Ketâba de-Himyarayâ* (« Le livre des Himyarites »), signale en outre que des *cohanim* originaires de Tibériade en Terre sainte étaient au service du roi de Himyar, ce qui constitue une preuve indéniable de la relation entre les juifs d'Arabie et la Terre sainte[11]. Ce témoignage pourrait permettre de trancher la question souvent débattue de l'origine ethnique des juifs d'Arabie : il s'agirait de Judéens d'origine et pas seulement de convertis – puisqu'un converti ne peut jamais devenir *cohen.* Néanmoins, on ne peut nier qu'il y ait eu aussi un grand nombre de conversions au judaïsme en Arabie et les chercheurs s'accordent tous en ce sens pour ce qui est des juifs de Himyar.

Le Coran et les sources postcoraniques se font l'écho du rayonnement intellectuel des juifs de Yathrib et de ses environs. Le Coran fait très souvent mention de ces *rabbâniyyûn* (« rabbins ») et de ces *ahbâr* (« docteurs ») « qui rendaient la justice, conformément au Livre de Dieu dont la garde leur était confiée » (5 : 44 ainsi que

5 : 63 et 9 : 31, 34). Ces sages juifs lisent la Torah à leurs fidèles et reçoivent leur estime grâce à leurs grandes connaissances. De plus, les juifs et les chrétiens sont présentés comme « le peuple du Livre » offrant à Muhammad la possibilité de renforcer sa foi : « Si tu es dans le doute au sujet de notre Révélation, interroge ceux qui ont lu le Livre avant toi » (10 : 94). Il nous faut ajouter que les sources musulmanes mentionnent à de nombreuses reprises la maison d'études juives (*bayt al-midrâs*, en hébreu *beit ha-midrash*) qui se trouvait dans la ville basse de Yathrib (*al-sâfila*) où étudiaient aussi quelques païens de la ville. On raconte que les femmes de Yathrib envoyaient leurs enfants grandir dans des familles juives « car les juifs sont des hommes de savoir et du Livre[12] ». On dénombre plusieurs *ansâr* (« partisans » de Muhammad, c'est-à-dire des musulmans natifs de Yathrib) qui auraient étudié dans ces maisons d'études, notamment Zayd b. Thâbit, scribe de Muhammad et plus tard chef de la commission que désignera le calife 'Uthmân (mort en 656) pour fixer le texte officiel du Coran, comme le soutient la Tradition[13]. Toutefois, nous ne savons presque rien de la nature du judaïsme de cette communauté, ni de celle de Himyar ni d'ailleurs des autres communautés de l'Arabie.

Parmi les orientalistes et les islamologues, une question a été souvent débattue : les juifs du Hijâz antéislamique étaient-ils des bédouins passant leur vie à batailler, à l'instar des Arabes de la région ? Ou jouissaient-ils d'une vie tranquille comme citadins ou villageois ? Cette question recoupe celle de l'origine ethnique des juifs. Israël Friedländer, qui avait adopté les vues spéculatives de l'historien juif allemand Heinrich Graetz, dépeint les juifs du Hijâz comme des nomades : « les fils du désert, des hommes d'épée, des soldats et des combattants[14] ». Hartwig Hirschfeld, de son côté, considère que cette description n'a aucun fondement et qu'elle ne correspond nullement à ce qu'en rapportent les sources musulmanes : les juifs étaient des hommes pacifiques, agriculteurs, artisans et commerçants habitant Yathrib et les localités avoisinantes au nord tout le long du Wâdi al-Qurâ. Même si parmi eux se trouvaient des guerriers, la majorité de la population n'a jamais pris part aux guerres. La vie des juifs de la région ne fut pas émaillée d'actes de bravoure[15].

Quel judaïsme Muhammad a-t-il connu en Arabie ?

Il en va des juifs du Hijâz comme des juifs de Himyar : nous ne disposons d'aucune source nous permettant de savoir quel judaïsme ils pratiquaient effectivement. A-t-on affaire à un groupe religieux homogène ou à un ensemble de courants voire de sectes dont les pratiques et les croyances s'infiltreront dans l'islam en formation ? Le premier témoignage fiable de l'existence d'une communauté juive dans le Hijâz pratiquant un judaïsme talmudique date du xe siècle ; il s'agit des fragments de questions halakhiques adressées aux directeurs des académies talmudiques babyloniennes (*geonim*) Rav Sherira Gaon (mort en 1006) et Rav Hai Gaon (mort en 1038) découverts dans la Geniza du Caire. Le voyageur Benjamin de Tudèle nous fournit deux siècles plus tard un autre témoignage allant dans le même sens. Ces sources ont été écrites plusieurs siècles après l'avènement de l'islam et ne nous apprennent rien sur les communautés juives de la région aux époques antérieures.

Le Coran lui-même fait allusion en divers passage à la fragmentation des opinions parmi les juifs : « Nous avons donné le Livre à Moïse, mais ce Livre a été l'objet de discussions. Si une Parole de ton Seigneur n'était pas intervenue auparavant, une décision concernant leurs différends aurait été prise. Ils se trouvent dans un profond embarras au sujet de ce Livre » (11 : 110) ; ou encore « Ce Coran raconte aux fils d'Israël la plus grande partie des choses sur lesquelles ils ne sont pas d'accord » (27 : 76). Cependant, les témoignages dans le Coran adoptent un ton bien général. Il est donc difficile d'en tirer des conclusions précises sur les courants et les sectes juives de la péninsule Arabique qui se seraient séparés du judaïsme rabbinique. Cette question a préoccupé de nombreux chercheurs. De nombreuses hypothèses ont fleuri mais il semble que, encore aujourd'hui, l'incertitude demeure toujours vivace.

Certains pensent que le Coran fait allusion à un courant antirabbinique prépondérant en Irak et en Perse pendant les deux premiers siècles de l'islam. Goitein, quant à lui, envisage que le judaïsme contre lequel le Coran polémique est un judaïsme karaïte – ou plutôt proto-karaïte, car le karaïsme n'apparaît que bien après l'avènement de l'islam[16]. Goitein pense que l'empreinte karaïte se manifeste entre autres dans l'estime portée à la Torah écrite et aux réserves émises envers les ajouts postbibliques, dénoncés comme « falsifications », attitude semblable à celle des karaïtes. D'autres chercheurs, comme Chaim Rabin dans son article « Islam and the Qumran Sect[17] » et – de manière plus détaillée – Naphtali Wieder dans son livre *The Judean Scrolls and Karaism*, défendent la thèse d'une influence des sectes du désert de Judée sur l'islam.

Autre hypothèse très partagée : le Coran se fait l'écho des conceptions judéo-chrétiennes des ébionites et même celui des elkasaïtes, développement gnostique tardif du précédent. Un grand nombre de recherches récentes conçoivent le judaïsme coranique comme une survivance du judéo-christianisme. C'est l'esprit du livre de Holger Michael Zellentin, *The Qur'ān's Legal Culture. The Didascalia Apostolorum as a Point of Departure*[18]. L'auteur soutient qu'une majorité significative de préceptes et d'épisodes narratifs concernant les fils d'Israël et Jésus dans le Coran entre en résonance avec ceux énoncés dans la *Didascalie des Apôtres* et les homélies pseudo-clémentines. La *Didascalie des Apôtres*, texte juridique chrétien aux accents juifs, a survécu partiellement en grec, entièrement dans une traduction latine mais aussi dans une version syriaque réalisée après l'an 683 de notre ère. Les homélies pseudo-clémentines, texte judéo-chrétien écrit en grec au IVe siècle, sont parvenues jusqu'à nous dans des versions plus tardives en latin, syriaque et arabe. Bien que Zellentin prenne soin de préciser qu'il n'existe aucune relation d'interdépendance directe entre tous ces textes, en particulier entre la *Didascalie* et le Coran, il est impossible de ne pas s'étonner de leurs similitudes. En effet, Zellentin remarque que la *Didascalie* et le Coran présentent un point de vue commun mêlant foi et loi. D'ailleurs, selon lui, les parties juridiques du Coran qui se lisent dans les sourates médinoises ne peuvent s'expliquer uniquement par leur relation à des sources purement juives comme le Talmud et que, parmi toutes les sources qui influencent le

Coran, la *Didascalie* reste la première. Auparavant, les chercheurs tendaient à expliquer les éléments bibliques du Coran en établissant des comparaisons avec la littérature talmudique. Aujourd'hui, la recherche sur l'environnement chrétien syriaque des premiers musulmans met en lumière d'autres parallèles. Ainsi, on peut légitimement penser aux écrits des Pères de l'Église syriaque datant de plusieurs siècles avant l'avènement de l'islam comme sources des épisodes bibliques du Coran. Ce point de vue a été défendu, entre autres, dans la thèse encore inédite de Joseph Witztum, *The Syriac Milieu of the Quran : The Recasting of the Biblical Narratives*[19].

Cependant, nous pensons que ses arguments demeurent trop spéculatifs et la question du judaïsme coranique reste encore une énigme loin d'être élucidée. Il n'est pas inutile non plus de rappeler que certains rares chercheurs ont tendance à émettre des doutes sur l'existence même de communautés juives en Arabie avant les débuts de l'islam. Il existe toute une école dite « révisionniste » ou « hypercritique » qui, disqualifiant a priori les sources musulmanes comme des constructions tardives, propose des hypothèses radicales sur les premières décennies de l'islam. Ainsi, Moshe Sharon, l'un des défenseurs de cette thèse « révisionniste », considère notamment que le Coran n'apparaît que plus d'un demi-siècle après Muhammad, et pense que les musulmans n'auraient acquis la connaissance des juifs et de leur religion qu'après la conquête de la Syrie et de l'Irak. Ils ont alors décrit les juifs des époques antérieures à l'image de ceux des VIIIe et IXe siècles[20]. Nous ne suivrons pas cette ligne dans cet ouvrage.

Des poètes juifs arabes avant l'islam

Nous connaissons très peu de biographies de juifs vivant dans le Hijâz avant l'avènement de l'islam. On peut néanmoins citer le plus connu d'entre eux, à savoir le poète al-Samaw'al (Shemu'el) b. 'Adiyâ', au VIe siècle de notre ère, dont la loyauté est louée dans la littérature arabe classique. Ses rares poèmes parvenus jusqu'à nous laissent la part belle à l'ambiguïté. Ainsi, son poème le plus célèbre, *lâmiya* (du nom de sa rime en *lâm*), ne diffère en rien des poèmes des Arabes païens. Al-Samaw'al y loue les vertus morales et sociales des Arabes à l'époque antéislamique. Connues sous le terme de *muruwwa* (« virilité »), ces vertus comprennent la protection de ceux qui sont dans le besoin, l'hospitalité, le courage au combat, etc. – toutes ces attitudes étant considérées comme les principes de base de la morale sociale des Arabes avant et après l'avènement de l'islam. En revanche, le texte du poème ne fait aucune allusion à une vision du monde juive ou à des éléments issus de sources juives.

Toutefois, on a attribué à al-Samaw'al d'autres poèmes où son judaïsme se manifeste par des motifs bibliques comme, par exemple, la prophétie concernant la royauté davidique. Cependant l'authenticité de ces poèmes est douteuse, en particulier les vers contenant des allusions à la Bible, lesquels ne figurent pas dans toutes les versions du *Dîwân* (Recueil poétique) d'al-Samaw'al, voire n'apparaissent dans aucune. Hirschberg examine longuement un poème attribué à al-Samaw'al riche de motifs juifs, découvert à la Geniza du Caire[21], tandis que l'œuvre d'autres poètes juifs de cette période de transition entre la période préislamique que les musulmans appellent Jâhiliyya (l'ère d'« ignorance ») et l'islam possède ce même caractère arabe païen dénué d'éléments juifs évidents : ainsi celle de Ka'b al-Ahbâr, de la tribu de Qurayza, sans doute le plus célèbre des sages juifs convertis à l'islam à l'époque de Muhammad, ou encore celle de l'obscure poétesse juive Sarah, elle aussi de la tribu de Qurayza. Une autre poétesse juive de Yathrib, 'Asmâ' bint Marwân, sera assassinée par un des disciples de Muhammad, accusée d'avoir composé des poèmes dénigrant le prophète de l'islam[22].

Il faut toutefois noter que toutes nos informations concernant les juifs du Hijâz proviennent de sources musulmanes, dont la plus grande partie a été rassemblée longtemps après les événements qu'elles sont censées relater. De fait, ces sources datent d'une époque où il n'existe déjà plus aucune communauté juive dans la majorité des régions où ils étaient si présents dans le passé. En d'autres termes, nous sommes confrontés à un double problème méthodologique : premièrement, la description des juifs et de leur religion se fait uniquement à partir de sources extérieures ; deuxièmement, aucune de ces sources n'est contemporaine de ces communautés juives. Étant postérieures de plusieurs siècles, elles ne peuvent être exemptes d'accents polémiques. Elles décrivent en réalité les juifs tels que les musulmans les percevaient après s'être détachés d'eux et leur être devenus hostiles. Certains auxiliaires médinois du Prophète, connus pour leur attachement aux juifs et pour avoir été même influencés par eux, étaient maintenant tournés en dérision. Les appellations « juif, fils de juif » ou « savant (*habr*) juif » qu'ils reçoivent semblent loin d'être élogieuses.

Par conséquent, en l'absence d'autres sources, obligation nous est faite d'analyser les sources musulmanes et en particulier le Coran pour dresser le tableau du judaïsme aux temps de l'avènement de l'islam et des siècles qui suivirent. En effet, ces sources sont remplies d'allusions aux juifs pendant la vie de Muhammad ainsi qu'aux époques antérieures. Goitein aimait rappeler le problème posé par ces sources musulmanes : selon lui, le Coran « constitue l'unique source pour la recherche sur la religion juive dans l'entourage de Muhammad ainsi que le regard que ce dernier portait sur elle. Or, en ce qui concerne la mission du Prophète à La Mecque, la tradition n'a gardé aucune information digne de confiance[23] ».

Les Arabes et la Palestine avant l'islam

En retour, il est important de prendre conscience que, contrairement à l'image romantique d'un peuple arabe bédouin enfermé dans son désert, à l'écart de la civilisation, le monde arabe antéislamique entretient des liens importants avec les régions situées au nord-ouest de la péninsule Arabique proprement dite, autrement dit avec ce qu'ils appellent *al-Shâm* et qui sont alors les provinces byzantines de Palestine, de Phénicie et de Syrie. Les historiens arabes ont notamment conservé la trace d'anciens récits qui voient Muhammad effectuer des voyages commerciaux dans la région avant la révélation coranique.

De manière plus générale, les Arabes d'avant l'islam eux-mêmes font une nette différence entre les « Arabes du Sud », perçus comme autochtones dans la péninsule, et les « Arabes du Nord », qui diront plus tard descendre d'Ismaël et auxquels se rattache la tribu de Muhammad, les Quraysh. Il existe d'ailleurs à l'époque deux royaumes arabes au nord de la péninsule : les Ghassanides, dans le sud de la Syrie, vassaux des Byzantins, et les Lakhmides, dans le sud de la Mésopotamie, vassaux des Perses[24].

La langue arabe elle-même, si consubstantielle au Coran, est évocatrice de cette situation civilisationnelle au moins aussi proche du monde syro-palestinien que de l'Arabie du Sud. Avant le Coran, l'arabe est la langue certes des bédouins, mais aussi des royaumes arabes cités plus haut ; il appartient à la même sous-famille de langues sémitiques que l'hébreu et l'araméen, tandis que les langues sud-arabiques appartiennent à une branche assez éloignée, dans le même groupe que les langues éthiopiennes. De plus, le Coran sera écrit dans un arabe beaucoup plus pétri d'influences hébraïques et araméennes que l'arabe classique. Enfin, pour l'écrire, les musulmans choisiront d'adapter un alphabet dérivé de l'écriture nabatéenne (du nom des prédécesseurs des Ghassanides) ou bien du syriaque, en introduisant des points diacritiques pour noter les sons propres à l'arabe, plutôt que de reprendre l'écriture sud-arabique qui aurait été mieux adaptée – mais sans le prestige culturel et religieux.

La première communauté musulmane et les juifs de Médine

Quand Muhammad trouve refuge à Yathrib en 622, fuyant les persécutions que lui et son petit cercle de fidèles subissent à La Mecque – c'est la *hijra*, qui marquera par la suite le début du calendrier islamique –, il trouve donc sur place des communautés juives bien implantées. C'est dans cette ville, qu'on appellera par la suite Médine (en arabe *al-Madîna*, « la Cité », exact équivalent de l'hébreu postbiblique *medina*), que se construit le premier État islamique et que Muhammad s'impose non seulement comme un prédicateur religieux, mais encore comme un chef politique. L'un des gestes fondateurs de cet *islâm* politique, au sens étymologique de « pacification », consiste à instituer le Prophète comme « juge de paix » dans le cas où naîtraient des conflits entre les différentes composantes de la société médinoise : les musulmans mecquois « émigrés » à Médine, appelés les *Muhâjirûn*, les tribus arabes médinoises Aws et Khazraj, converties à l'islam et appelées les « partisans », *al-Ansâr*, et les principales tribus juives Qurayza, Qaynuqâʿ et Nadîr (ainsi que d'autres, comme les ʿAwf). Ces groupes se lient par un « Pacte de bonne entente et de soutien mutuel », qu'on désignera par la suite sous le nom de Constitution de Médine. Celle-ci énonce notamment que les tribus juives « forment avec les Croyants [i. e. les musulmans] une seule communauté, *umma* ».

Les années 622-632 sont décisives pour la construction de l'islam et serviront de référent symbolique pour toute l'histoire musulmane. Au cours de cette décennie, Muhammad construit un État, crée une société musulmane et livre un certain nombre de batailles décisives contre ses adversaires mecquois : les batailles de Badr (624), de Uhud (625) et celle dite « de la Tranchée » (*al-Khandaq*) (627). La tradition musulmane relate qu'en ces trois occasions, l'une ou l'autre des tribus juives a violé le pacte d'entraide et a trahi le Prophète, ce qui justifie les représailles menées contre elles. Les Qurayza, en particulier, sont accusés d'avoir tenté de prendre à revers les armées médinoises lors de la bataille de la Tranchée. Muhammad remet leur sort aux mains de leurs anciens alliés, les Aws, qui les jugent « conformément aux règlements de la guerre codifiés dans la Torah » : les hommes pubères sont exécutés et les femmes et les enfants sont réduits en esclavage[25].

Cette dégradation des relations entre juifs et musulmans à Médine est évoquée ailleurs dans le Coran, sous la forme d'allusions aux revers de fortune subis par les tribus juives. Si aucune des trois grandes tribus juives qui vivaient à Médine et dans ses environs n'est nommée expressément dans le Coran, la tradition exégétique s'accorde néanmoins à voir dans divers versets une allusion à ces tribus. Par exemple, nous lisons dans le verset 2 : 109 : « Un grand nombre des gens du Livre (*ahl al-kitâb*) voudraient – bien que la Vérité se soit manifestée à eux – vous faire revenir à l'incrédulité après que vous avez eu la foi. » Ou bien, au début de la sourate 59 : « C'est lui qui, dès le premier rassemblement, a chassé de leurs demeures ceux qui, parmi les gens du Livre, étaient incrédules. Vous ne pensiez pas qu'ils partiraient, et ils s'imaginaient que leurs forteresses les défendraient contre Dieu. Mais Dieu les a saisis par où ils ne s'y attendaient pas... » Ces versets sont compris par les commentateurs musulmans comme rapportant l'expulsion et l'exil de la tribu de Nadîr. Dans la suite de la sourate, les exégètes musulmans retrouvent le destin de la tribu de Qaynuqâʿ à travers ces allusions : « ceux qui, peu de temps avant eux, ont goûté les conséquences de leur conduite. Ils subirent un douloureux châtiment » (59 : 15).

Ces commentateurs perçoivent aussi dans divers versets coraniques les épisodes de vie de la tribu de Qurayza jusqu'au cataclysme final. Ainsi, la sourate 8 est consacrée à la description des prises de guerre après la bataille de Badr marquant le succès des musulmans sur les polythéistes mecquois. Cependant, selon les exégètes, elle contiendrait aussi la justification de la guerre contre la tribu de Qurayza, arguant du fait qu'ils avaient trahi leur alliance avec le Prophète : « ceux d'entre eux avec qui tu [Muhammad] as conclu un pacte, et qui, ensuite, ont toujours violé leur engagement ; ceux qui ne craignent pas Dieu » (8 : 56). La sourate 33 au verset 26 rappelle comment Muhammad expulse les membres de la tribu de leurs fortins et aux versets 60-61 quels sont les préparatifs de la guerre contre eux : « Maudits en quelque lieu où ils se trouveront, ils seront capturés et tués ». Toutefois, le Coran ne décrit pas les massacres qu'ils ont subis. Il ne fait que de brèves allusions au sort subi par les juifs médinois tandis que la littérature historique musulmane et les œuvres de la *sîra* (« biographie » du Prophète) – comme celle très connue de Muhammad Ibn Ishâq (mort en 768) remaniée par 'Abd al-Mâlik Ibn Hishâm (mort en 834) – rapportent en détail leur expulsion et leur exil forcé et tout particulièrement le massacre de la tribu de Qurayza[26].

La dernière grande bataille entre Muhammad et des tribus juives est celle de Khaybar, en 628, quelque temps avant la prise de La Mecque. Cette ville, située à 150 kilomètres au nord de Médine, était essentiellement peuplée par des juifs. Les armées musulmanes attaquent la ville en représailles de la trahison des Banû Nadîr, liés à la cité. La ville est prise mais les habitants ne sont pas massacrés : ils sont soumis, les premiers, au paiement de la *jizya*, l'impôt des populations non musulmanes conquises. C'est en 642, après la mort de Muhammad, que son successeur 'Umar déportera les juifs de Khaybar en Syrie, dans le cadre de l'expulsion générale des non-musulmans du Hijâz. Cette expulsion relève cependant sans doute plus de l'idéologie que des faits, puisqu'au XIIe siècle encore le voyageur juif Benjamin de Tudèle dira avoir rencontré à Khaybar et Tayma' les communautés juives locales. Dans l'imaginaire musulman, Khaybar deviendra cependant synonyme de la dernière bataille du Prophète contre les traîtres juifs, imaginaire qui sera réactivé dans le discours islamiste antijuif du XXIe siècle.

Ces épisodes, qui sont des éléments essentiels de la mémoire musulmane, ne nous sont cependant pas connus par la tradition juive, qui ignore tout des communautés juives dans la péninsule Arabique. Cette asymétrie mémorielle entre les traditions juive et musulmane nourrit jusqu'à aujourd'hui beaucoup de malentendus.

Le sort tragique des juifs de Khaybar ainsi que celui de leurs frères de Médine a fait de Khaybar le symbole d'une catastrophe. La propagande antijuive menée aujourd'hui par des cercles islamistes radicaux vise à réactiver la mémoire de cette peur, tout en lui restituant sa réalité historique ; que l'on songe aux slogans scandés par les activistes du Hamas ou d'autres groupes islamistes : *Khaybar Khaybar yâ yahûd, jaysh Muhammad sa-ya'ûd*, « Khaybar Khaybar, ô juifs, l'armée de Muhammad est de retour ! ». L'invocation du nom de Khaybar a une portée idéologique : elle vise à « approfondir la dimension historique du combat » entre judaïsme et islam[27].

II

LA REPRÉSENTATION DU JUDAÏSME ET DES JUIFS DANS LE CORAN

Le Coran se présente à nous aujourd'hui sous la forme d'un livre découpé en chapitres appelés « sourates » et en versets, mais il ne se lit pas comme un récit, à la différence de la Torah et des autres livres bibliques. L'ordre des sourates est arbitraire, globalement des plus longues aux plus courtes, et non pas chronologique ou thématique. En outre, la structure même des sourates est venue dans un deuxième temps : pendant quasiment toute la vie prophétique de Muhammad, le Coran est un ensemble de versets ou de groupes de versets disparates, révélés au gré des circonstances, et c'est seulement dans les derniers mois de sa vie que Muhammad a ordonné qu'ils soient rassemblés. Tout cela rend l'interprétation du Coran malaisée : si certaines sourates, comme la douzième, *Yûsuf*, se lisent comme des récits, nombre d'entre elles, par exemple la troisième, *Âl 'Imrân*, semblent à la première lecture beaucoup plus décousues. L'interprétation précise des versets ne dépend de ce fait pas tant de leur place dans la sourate que dans les circonstances originelles de leur révélation (*asbâb al-nuzûl*) que le Coran lui-même n'indique pas et que les commentateurs tentent de reconstituer à partir de la tradition orale.

On a évoqué à la fin du chapitre précédent la *hijra*, l'émigration de Muhammad à Médine. Cet épisode marque une césure invisible dans le Coran lui-même, au sein duquel les chercheurs contemporains comme les commentateurs classiques distinguent les sourates et versets « mecquois » des « médinois ». Les premiers, reçus à l'époque où Muhammad est un prédicateur quasi seul qui s'adresse à une foule indifférente voire hostile, sont essentiellement de teneur eschatologique, théologique et morale ; les seconds, énoncés dans le contexte sociopolitique d'un islam en construction et bientôt triomphant, font la part belle aux prescriptions légales et à la polémique contre les juifs, les chrétiens et autres groupes qui refusent de rejoindre la communauté naissante.

Les diverses dénominations données aux juifs dans le Coran

Le Coran se sert de trois termes distincts pour désigner les juifs, chacun d'entre eux mettant l'accent sur un aspect différent. Le plus courant, *banû Isrâ'îl* (« fils d'Israël »), désigne les descendants d'Israël à l'époque biblique ; en de rares occasions, il s'emploie pour les juifs contemporains de Muhammad. Dans la majorité des cas, l'emploi de « fils d'Israël » se révèle ambivalent. Il est parfois utilisé de manière très favorable : les « fils d'Israël » sont le peuple élu (2 : 47 et 2 : 122) que Dieu a délivré de la servitude en le faisant sortir d'Égypte et entrer en Terre sainte (5 : 21). Toutefois, l'expression sert aussi à désigner péjorativement les Hébreux quand ils commettent des fautes : les « fils d'Israël » brisent l'alliance avec Dieu (5 : 13) en se prosternant devant le Veau d'or. Ils sont aussi appelés « fils d'Israël » quand on les accuse de tuer les prophètes*.

L'appellation *al-yahûd* (« les juifs ») ou encore la locution *alladhîna hâdû* (« ceux qui sont devenus juifs » ou « ceux qui pratiquent le judaïsme ») désignent le plus souvent les juifs aux époques

* Tous ces éléments mentionnés ici brièvement seront traités en détails ci-dessous.

postbibliques et surtout les juifs que Muhammad a connus à La Mecque et à Médine. Ces termes revêtent dans la majorité des cas une connotation clairement péjorative. Ainsi, par exemple, ceux qui sont accusés d'avoir falsifié la Torah sont désignés comme juifs (4 : 46). Sont aussi appelés juifs ceux qui, à l'instar des chrétiens, croient que Dieu a engendré un fils appelé 'Uzayr (9 : 30*). Bien évidemment, est-il écrit, il faut se garder de devenir leurs alliés, tout comme il convient de s'écarter des chrétiens (5 : 51).

La troisième expression *ahl al-kitâb* (« le peuple du Livre ») ne désigne pas uniquement les juifs mais aussi les chrétiens, qui détiennent des Écritures sacrées révélées. Le Coran désigne la Bible principalement de deux façons : *al-Kitâb* (« le Livre ») et *al-Tawrât* – terme qui désigne, au-delà de la Torah au sens strict ou Pentateuque, la Bible hébraïque tout entière et parfois même les sources juives postbibliques. Le texte coranique évoque également *al-Zabûr* (c'est-à-dire les Psaumes) comme un livre saint indépendant révélé à David : « Nous avons préféré certains prophètes à d'autres et nous avons donné *al-Zabûr* à David » (17 : 55). Le Coran mentionne égale-

* Sur cette accusation, inconnue des sources juives préislamiques, que l'islam attribue aux juifs et sur la figure de 'Uzayr, voir ci-dessous, pp. 88-95.

ment, de manière vague, « les livres [ou les feuillets] d'Abraham et de Moïse » (*suhuf Ibrâhîm wa-Mûsâ*, 87 : 19) ou tout simplement « les premiers livres [ou feuillets] » (*al-suhuf al-ûlâ*, 20 : 133[1]). Cependant, on ne sait pas ici de quels écrits il s'agit : peut-être cette expression ne fait-elle allusion qu'aux propos de ces deux prophètes (ainsi que d'autres) mentionnés dans le Coran.

Outre ces appellations par lesquelles sont désignés les anciens Hébreux et les juifs contemporains de Muhammad, on trouve divers termes qui leur sont appliqués. Ils sont parfois traités de *kâfirûn* (pluriel de *kâfir*, « mécréant »). Certains versets coraniques évoquent ainsi la colère divine contre les pécheurs – ce qui se réfère souvent, d'après les commentateurs, aux juifs et aux chrétiens. Tel est notamment le cas du verset qui conclut la première sourate du Coran (*al-fâtiha*) : « Dirige-nous dans le chemin droit : le chemin de ceux que tu as comblés de bienfaits ; non pas le chemin de ceux qui encourent ta colère ni celui des égarés. » Comme on peut le voir, le Coran s'exprime ici en termes généraux sans désigner de groupes spécifiques, mais dès les premiers commentaires il apparaît clairement que « ceux que tu as comblés de bienfaits » sont les premiers musulmans ; « ceux qui encourent ta colère » sont les juifs, et « les égarés » sont les chrétiens. C'est notamment ainsi que les qualifie Tabarî (m. en 923), l'un des plus grands exégètes du Coran[2].

Les enfants d'Israël, peuple élu

L'image des juifs et du judaïsme qui se dégage du Coran est donc très contrastée suivant qu'il s'agit des Hébreux de la Bible ou des contemporains du début de l'islam. Les versets où Dieu répand ses louanges sur les enfants d'Israël se répartissent en trois catégories : la vision des enfants d'Israël comme peuple élu ; la sortie d'Égypte et l'arrivée en Terre promise ; et l'Alliance et le don de la Torah, vue comme une source qui confirme l'islam. Nous verrons plus loin qu'il faut apporter des nuances à ces appréciations positives.

L'idée de l'élection d'Israël revient souvent dans le Coran. Tantôt cela concerne le peuple tout entier, tantôt seulement quelques personnalités ou quelques familles comme celle d'Abraham, de 'Imrân (c'est-à-dire 'Amram, père d'Aaron, de Moïse et de Myriam) ou encore certains prophètes. L'idée s'exprime par une série de verbes de sens proche comme *istafâ*, *faddala*, *ijtabâ*, *ikhtâra*, mais parfois, comme dans la Bible, sans terminologie particulière. Dans certains versets, l'idée d'élection se dégage par elle-même de la grâce de Dieu envers Israël et des nombreux bienfaits que

Dieu répand sur eux : « Nous avions donné aux fils d'Israël le Livre (*al-kitâb*), la Sagesse (*al-hukm*) et la Prophétie (*al-nubuwwa*). Nous les avions pourvus d'excellentes nourritures. Nous les avions élevés au-dessus des mondes » (45 : 16) et dans un autre verset : « Ô mon peuple ! Souvenez-vous de la grâce de Dieu à votre égard, quand il a suscité parmi vous des prophètes ; quand il a suscité pour vous des rois ! Il vous a accordé ce qu'il n'avait donné à nul autre parmi les mondes » (5 : 20).

Dans le premier verset, l'élection est exprimée par le verbe *faddala*, qui signifie « préférer » : les enfants d'Israël sont « préférés » aux autres peuples ou « élevés » au-dessus d'eux, comme traduit Denise Masson. Dans le deuxième verset au contraire, le vocabulaire de l'élection est absent et l'idée se dégage qu'Israël a reçu des bienfaits qui n'ont pas été accordés à d'autres.

L'idée d'élection est presque toujours mentionnée dans un contexte polémique : elle sert même parfois de point de départ au débat. Naturellement, cette tendance se retrouve autour d'autres sujets de dissension entre l'islam et les religions sœurs et rivales, judaïsme et christianisme. Quelques versets présentent l'élection comme un fait « historique », par exemple dans la sourate 2 verset 47, repris au verset 122 : « Ô fils d'Israël ! Souvenez-vous des bienfaits dont je vous ai comblés. Je vous ai préférés à tous les mondes. » On note une dimension polémique dans ces deux versets 47 et 122 où apparaît la notion d'élection. Entre les deux intervient toute une série de rappels historiques. À la suite du premier verset, la sortie d'Égypte, la traversée de la mer Rouge à pied sec et la noyade de Pharaon et de sa suite (quelques versets mentionnent même toute son armée, par exemple 44 : 24 : « Voici une armée qui sera noyée »). À cela s'ajoutent plusieurs miracles cités dans la Bible, pour la plupart survenus pendant la marche des enfants d'Israël dans le désert : la manne et les cailles tombées du ciel (2 : 57 ; 7 : 160), les douze sources apparues au moment où le peuple se plaignait à Moïse du manque d'eau (2 : 60). Il est aussi fait allusion à des rencontres de Dieu avec Moïse durant quarante nuits dont le peuple profita pour construire le Veau d'or (2 : 51). On trouve aussi une référence à la révélation au Sinaï (2 : 63), à la vache rousse (2 : 67-73*), etc.

L'impression qui se dégage clairement des passages du Coran contenant des références à l'élection d'Israël est qu'il s'agit d'une élection *conditionnelle* : depuis la sortie d'Égypte jusqu'à l'entrée dans « la Terre sainte que Dieu vous a destinée » (5 : 21), le peuple apparaît comme vindicatif et ingrat, conformément d'ailleurs à ce qu'en disent les livres de l'Exode et des Nombres.

---

* Pour l'histoire de la vache rousse, voir pp. 148-151.

Cependant, à rebours du texte mosaïque et des livres des Prophètes, qui ne cessent de rappeler que les châtiments divins ne sauraient remettre en cause la fidélité inconditionnelle de Dieu envers Israël, dans le Coran la conduite du peuple justifie qu'il soit déchu de l'élection. Bien plus, le rappel de l'élection donne lieu à des réprimandes au souvenir des bienfaits divins à son égard. C'est le ton de la remontrance qui domine. Elle s'exprime particulièrement avec véhémence dans les passages qui suivent les deux versets mentionnés plus hauts : « Redoutez un Jour : où nul ne sera récompensé pour autrui, où nulle intercession ne sera acceptée, où nulle compensation ne sera admise, où personne ne sera secouru » (2 : 48 ; cf. aussi 2 : 123).

Cette mise en garde peut s'interpréter – et de fait, elle l'a été – comme un avertissement selon lequel l'élection n'est pas assurée pour toujours. Au contraire, elle peut être donnée à d'autres, en particulier aux musulmans : « Pour que les peuples du Livre sachent qu'ils ne peuvent en rien disposer de la grâce de Dieu. Oui, la grâce est dans la main de Dieu ; il la donne à qui il veut. Dieu est le Maître de la grâce incommensurable » (57 : 29). Le mot traduit ici par « grâce », *fadl*, peut aussi inclure la notion d'élection[3]. Cette idée est largement développée par de nombreux commentateurs à propos du verset : « Nous les avons choisis, sciemment (*ikhtarnâhum 'alâ 'ilm*) parmi tous les peuples de l'univers » (44 : 31). Ici, l'idée d'élection conclut le récit de la sortie d'Égypte. Il y est même dit que le choix divin s'est exercé « sciemment » (*'alâ 'ilm)* ; mais malgré cela, l'élection reste un don temporaire et conditionnel.

Tabarî affine cette idée d'élection conditionnelle. Selon lui, les circonstances justifiant l'élection d'Israël, à savoir l'existence de nombreux prophètes en son sein, ne sont plus d'actualité ; il ajoute un autre argument tiré d'une tradition exégétique qu'il cite à propos du verset 2 : 47 : « Cette idée [c'est-à-dire l'élection des enfants d'Israël] dépend de leur observance des commandements divins ; mais certains d'entre eux ont été punis [ils ont été transformés en singes*] et ils sont devenus les plus détestables des créatures, et c'est aux musulmans que Dieu a dit : "Vous formez la meilleure Communauté suscitée pour les hommes" » (3 : 110[4]).

Cette exégèse de Tabari qui justifie le transfert de l'élection d'Israël par ses péchés est très connue aussi dans la polémique chrétienne contre les juifs. Le christianisme a lui aussi expliqué l'abandon d'Israël par Dieu en raison des péchés du peuple. Pour le remplacer, Dieu a choisi « le petit reste

---

* Sur le motif de la transformation des juifs en singes, voir aussi ci-dessous, p. 102 et p. 103 note 26.

d'Israël[5] », c'est-à-dire les chrétiens, ceux qui ont suivi Jésus, et qui constituent le *Verus Israël*[6], le « véritable Israël ». L'attitude musulmane ne diffère pas fondamentalement de la position chrétienne ; nous verrons que cette idée est récurrente dans le Coran. Dans le dernier chapitre, l'on pourra constater qu'elle caractérise encore davantage la vision shî'ite.

Les éloges que l'on trouve dans le Coran à propos des enfants d'Israël doivent donc être situés dans un contexte plus large d'où il ressort clairement que l'élection d'Israël est une notion ambigüe. Le verset suivant par exemple, particulièrement polémique envers les juifs et les chrétiens, conteste l'idée d'élection et en fait la rejette :

> Les juifs et les chrétiens ont dit : « Nous sommes les fils de Dieu et ses préférés. » Dis : « Pourquoi, alors, vous punit-Il pour vos péchés ? Non !... vous êtes des mortels, comptés parmi ses créatures. Il pardonne à qui Il veut ; Il punit qui Il veut. » La royauté des cieux et de la terre et de ce qui est entre les deux appartient à Dieu. Le retour final se fera vers Lui (5 : 18).

Dans un important article intitulé « L'idée de l'élection dans l'islam ancien », Haggai Ben-Shammaï fait deux observations à propos de ce verset. D'une part, il renferme une polémique explicite contre l'idée d'élection au sens littéral que l'on rencontre dans le judaïsme et dans l'interprétation chrétienne qui en est donnée. L'expérience historique prouve que cette élection est caduque, car une telle élection ou une proximité particulière dépend de toute façon de l'arbitraire divin. D'autre part, la prétention attribuée aux juifs dans ce verset coranique s'appuie sur quelques versets bibliques et peut-être sur des expressions liturgiques forgées à l'époque de la Mishna et du Talmud, mais que le verset du Coran attribue aussi aux chrétiens. Le Coran élève contre les juifs un vieil argument déjà entendu chez les chrétiens au Iᵉʳ siècle, selon lequel la situation historique des juifs invalide leur prétention[7].

Il faut noter cependant que les commentateurs du Coran font aussi, par cohérence, du comportement moral des musulmans une condition de leur élection. Commentant le verset « Vous formez la meilleure Communauté suscitée pour les hommes » (3 : 110), Tabarî nous rappelle la continuation de ce verset : « Vous ordonnez ce qui convenable, vous interdisez ce qui est blâmable, vous croyez en Dieu. » Ces paroles peuvent être interprétées comme se référant à la communauté (ou la nation, *Umma*) musulmane en général, mais aussi, selon certaines exégèses traditionnelles citées par Tabarî, comme une condition pour la validité de l'élection. Autrement dit, c'est seulement si la *Umma* musulmane observe ce qu'ordonne Dieu dans ce verset (« ordonner ce qui convenable, interdire ce qui est blâmable et croire en Dieu ») que l'élection sera effective. L'élection n'est pas donc une grâce éternelle qui va de soi[8] ; Le comportement du peuple ou des individus et des groupes en son sein peut susciter l'élection ou son rejet.

Plus encore, il existe dans l'islam shî'ite une tendance à attribuer l'élection, non à l'ensemble des musulmans, mais aux seul shî'ites, c'est-à-dire à ceux qui reconnaissent les Imâms comme seuls héritiers légitimes de Muhammad. Ainsi, le célèbre exégète shî'ite 'Alî ibn Ibrâhîm al-Qummî (fin du IXe-début du Xe siècle) affirme que ce verset ne saurait s'appliquer à l'ensemble des musulmans, puisqu'il se trouve parmi eux des pécheurs notoires qui ont commis des crimes comme l'assassinat des Imâms. Le verset ne saurait donc s'appliquer qu'à un groupe sélectionné, les Imâms shî'ites eux-mêmes, perçus comme totalement exempts de péchés. Pour asseoir cette exégèse, la tradition shî'ite impose une autre lecture du verset 3 : 110 : Non pas « Vous formez la meilleure *Umma* » mais : « Vous formez les meilleurs Imâms (*A'imma*) suscités pour les hommes[9] ».

La critique que l'islam sunnite adresse aux autres religions est ainsi reprise par les shî'ites à l'intérieur de l'islam même, contre les sunnites. Ce ne sont donc pas seulement les juifs qui ne sauraient être le peuple élu. L'élection est exclusive : les seuls bénéficiaires en sont une communauté restreinte d'élus à l'intérieur du shî'isme ou, à la rigueur, l'ensemble des shî'ites.

L'Alliance de Dieu avec le peuple d'Israël

On trouve aussi dans le Coran des échos des passages bibliques évoquant l'Alliance de Dieu avec le peuple d'Israël, laquelle est une marque d'élection. Cette Alliance appelée dans le Coran *mîthâq* ou *'ahd* est une composante centrale du rôle historique attribué par Dieu à Israël. C'est l'histoire d'une promesse en plusieurs étapes : libération de l'esclavage, choix divin, conclusion de l'Alliance, conduite vers la Terre promise et installation des tribus. De même que l'élection, l'Alliance est un contrat synallagmatique entre Dieu et le peuple élu :

> Ô fils d'Israël ! [...]. Soyez fidèles à mon alliance ; je serai fidèle à votre alliance. – Craignez moi ! – Croyez à ce que j'ai révélé, confirmant ce que vous avez déjà reçu. Ne soyez pas les premiers à ne

> pas croire ; ne troquez pas mes Signes à vil prix. Craignez-moi ! Ne dissimulez pas la Vérité en la revêtant du mensonge, Ne cachez pas la Vérité, alors que vous savez (2 : 40).

L'Alliance dont il est question ici et dans d'autres versets est celle qui a été conclue entre les enfants d'Israël après la sortie d'Égypte. Dieu a alors suscité parmi eux « douze chefs » (*naqîb*, 5 : 12) – qui semblent correspondre aux chefs des douze tribus d'Israël (Nombres 7 : 2) – et leur a envoyé des prophètes (5 : 70). La conclusion de l'Alliance aurait eu lieu au Sinaï, mais ce nom n'est pas mentionné ; on trouve seulement le terme *tûr* (« montagne »), emprunté à l'araméen, dans le verset : « Nous avons contracté une alliance avec vous ; nous vous avons élevé le Mont (*al-Tûr*) au-dessus de vous : "Prenez avec fermeté la loi que nous vous avons donnée […]" » (2 : 63).*

Cette image de Dieu plaçant la montagne au-dessus de la tête des enfants d'Israël rassemblés à son pied, tout comme l'affirmation qu'ils doivent accepter la Torah « avec fermeté » ou « avec force » (*bi-quwwa*) reviennent à d'autres reprises dans le Coran. Comme l'ont souligné de nombreux chercheurs, le parallèle est clair avec un

* Voir aussi les versets 2 : 93 et 4 : 154.

célèbre *midrash* que l'on trouve notamment dans le Talmud de Babylone* :

> « Ils se tinrent au pied de la montagne » (Exode 19 : 17) : Dieu leur imposa la Torah en menaçant de renverser sur eux la montagne comme une cuve en leur disant : « Si vous acceptez la Torah, tant mieux, sinon ce lieu sera votre tombeau » (Talmud de Babylone, traité *Shabbat* 88a).

La mention est dans le Coran très allusive, mais elle fait l'objet de développement chez certains exégètes, dans la continuité de ce midrash[10]. L'Alliance divine, liée à l'élection, est elle aussi une grâce conditionnelle. Dès le début, elle est accompagnée d'une série de mises en garde : « Ne soyez pas les premiers à ne pas croire ; ne troquez pas (mes Signes à vil prix) » (2 : 40). Le Coran ne laisse aucun doute à ses destinataires sur le fait que cette Alliance est conclue avec un peuple destiné à la transgresser : toute mention de l'Alliance est en effet accompagnée du rappel de sa violation. Par exemple, après la sortie d'Égypte, lorsque Dieu exige des enfants d'Israël qu'ils Le servent Lui seul, qu'ils traitent

* Il n'est sans doute pas inutile de rappeler que le Talmud de Babylone est achevé entre la fin du Ve siècle et le début du VIe, soit plus d'un siècle avant les débuts de l'islam.

leurs parents, leurs proches, leurs orphelins avec respect et compassion, qu'ils ne répandent pas de sang innocent et ne chassent pas de leur sein ceux qui vivent avec eux, il est immédiatement ajouté que les enfants d'Israël n'ont pas su répondre à ces exigences morales et leur ont tourné le dos « à l'exception d'un petit nombre d'entre vous » (2 : 83). Et le Coran ajoute des paroles très dures :

> « Mais voilà comment vous vous comportez ensuite : vous vous entretuez ; vous expulsez de leurs maisons certains d'entre vous ; vous vous liguez contre eux pour leur causer du tort et commettre des crimes » (2 : 85).

Dans ces versets, on ne trouve pas la moindre référence au contexte. Si ces versets évoquent une réalité historique, on ne voit pas laquelle. Quand donc les Hébreux ont-ils chassé des personnes qui vivaient parmi eux ? Mais là où le Coran ne dit rien, l'exégèse apporte un éclaircissement : selon divers commentateurs, ce verset peu clair ne renvoie pas à la période biblique mais aux deux tribus juives de Nadîr et Qurayza qui vivaient à Yathrib et qui, dès avant l'islam, étaient alliées aux tribus arabes locales de Aws et Khazraj[11]. Comme ces dernières se livraient combat, chacune des deux tribus juives dut voler au secours de ses alliés arabes et c'est ainsi que les juifs se retrouvèrent engagés dans une lutte fratricide. Dès que le pouvoir de Muhammad se fut affermi à Médine, il se retourna contre elles pour leur perte*.

Cette approche exégétique est un bon exemple de l'actualisation du message coranique : des versets qui décrivent la lutte des Hébreux contre leurs ennemis à l'époque biblique – en l'occurrence Pharaon et son armée – sont reliés à la lutte de Muhammad contre les tribus juives de Médine et ses environs.

De l'Égypte à la Terre sainte

L'élection d'Israël et l'alliance contractée avec Dieu apparaissent dans le Coran, conformément à ce que dit la Bible, comme les deux fondements du statut élevé attribué au peuple d'Israël. L'amour de Dieu pour les enfants d'Israël s'exprime par sa protection alors qu'ils étaient sous le joug de Pharaon, par les plaies d'Égypte, par la libération des Hébreux. Tous ces sujets sont évoqués à plusieurs reprises dans le Coran, par exemple en 7 : 103-162 ; 26 : 10-67 et 28 : 6-41. Le don de la terre est présenté comme la réalisa-

---

* Voir *supra*, pp. 53-57.

tion de la promesse divine : « Nous avons donné en héritage aux gens qui avaient été opprimés les contrées orientales et les contrées occidentales et la terre que nous avions bénie. Ainsi s'accomplit la très belle promesse (*kalima**) de ton Seigneur envers les fils d'Israël, parce qu'ils ont été patients » (7 : 137).

La conquête de Canaan et l'installation dans le pays que le Coran qualifie de « Terre sainte » (*al-ard al-muqaddasa*) sont aussi évoquées dans divers passages où l'on reconnaît des réminiscences du livre des Nombres et de Josué :

> Lorsque Moïse dit à son peuple : « Ô mon peuple ! Souvenez-vous de la grâce de Dieu à votre égard, quand il a suscité parmi vous des prophètes ; quand il a suscité pour vous des rois ! Il vous a accordé ce qu'il n'avait donné à nul autre parmi les mondes ! Ô mon peuple ! Entrez dans la Terre sainte que Dieu vous a destinée ; évitez de retourner sur vos pas, car vous vous retrouveriez ayant tout perdu. » Ils dirent : « Ô Moïse ! Un peuple d'hommes très forts réside en ce pays. Nous n'y entrerons pas, tant qu'ils ne seront pas sortis. S'ils en sortent, nous y

* Littéralement : « parole ». Et cf. Josué, 1 : 3-4 : « Tout lieu que foulera la plante de vos pieds, je vous le donne, comme je l'ai déclaré à Moïse. Depuis le désert et le Liban jusqu'au grand fleuve, l'Euphrate ; et jusqu'à la Grande Mer, vers le soleil couchant, tel sera votre territoire. »

entrerons. » Deux hommes d'entre eux qui craignaient Dieu, et auxquels Dieu avait accordé sa faveur, dirent : « Franchissez ses frontières, vous vaincrez dès que vous serez entrés, Confiez-vous à Dieu, si vous êtes croyants. » Ils dirent : « Ô Moise ! Nous n'y entrerons certainement pas tant qu'ils seront là. Mets-toi en marche, toi et ton Seigneur ; combattez tous deux. Quant à nous, nous restons ici » (5 : 20-25).

Comme en d'autres occurrences, les versets cités ici mêlent l'éloge à la réprobation. Le jugement positif tient à ce qu'Israël est le peuple d'où sont issus des prophètes et des rois et qu'il a de ce fait mérité de conquérir la terre qui lui était destinée. La réprobation tient à sa rébellion, à son peu de foi, tels qu'ils s'expriment dans sa discussion avec Moïse. Dans le groupe d'explorateurs envoyés pour inspecter le pays, deux personnages font exception et sont décrits dans le Coran – de même que dans la Bible – comme des hommes de foi. Leurs noms ne sont pas mentionnés, ce qui est une pratique fréquente dans le texte du Coran (voir *infra* chap. 4). Le lecteur familier de la Torah identifie sans mal dans ces personnages anonymes Josué fils de Noun et Caleb fils de Jéphoné, les héros de cet épisode biblique (Nombres 13-14).

Quelques siècles après Muhammad, les commentateurs classiques du Coran éprouveront pourtant des difficultés à identifier cette « Terre sainte » : certains croiront y voir « le mont Sinaï et ses environs », d'autres « le Shâm », c'est-à-dire la Syrie-Palestine, d'autres « Jéricho », d'autres encore « Damas et la Palestine[12] ». Dans d'autres passages où il est question de la conquête de Canaan, Dieu ordonne aux Hébreux de pénétrer dans une ville dont le nom n'est pas donné : « Entrez dans cette cité ; mangez de ses produits à satiété, partout où vous voudrez ; franchissez-en la porte en prospérant et dites : "pardon" » (2 : 58). Des exégètes du Coran proposent là aussi de l'identifier à Jérusalem ou à Jéricho. Parfois le texte se limite à mentionner la porte de la ville par laquelle entrera le peuple (4 : 154).

La Torah comme confirmation du Coran

Le rappel des bienfaits divins envers le peuple d'Israël amène à des déclarations positives concernant sa sagesse, ses prophètes et bien entendu le don de la Torah descendue du ciel, qui sera développé plus loin. De toute façon, l'attitude du Coran envers les juifs (et les chrétiens) reste complexe : bien qu'il se méfie des Écritures saintes détenues par eux, il considère qu'ils valident son propre message. Ce point de vue s'exprime clairement dans le verset déjà cité : « Si tu es dans le doute au sujet de notre Révélation, interroge ceux qui ont lu le Livre avant toi » (10 : 94). Selon l'interprétation habituelle, ce verset s'adresse au Prophète afin de lui montrer que s'il s'élève en lui un doute quant à la Révélation qu'il reçoit, il peut toujours consulter les gens du Livre, c'est-à-dire les juifs et les chrétiens. Ce qu'ils lui enseigneront à partir de leurs Écritures l'aidera à affermir sa propre prophétie : « Celui auquel une preuve de son Seigneur a été donnée peut-il rester en doute ? D'autant plus qu'un témoin venu de la part de son Seigneur lui communique ceci et qu'avant lui le Livre de Moïse était déjà un guide et une miséricorde » (11 : 17). Bien plus, les Écritures des juifs et des chrétiens, telles que les présente le Coran, contiendraient des références à Muhammad et aux principes de la religion qu'il annonce : « Le prophète des Gentils que ces gens-là trouvent mentionné chez eux dans la Torah et l'Évangile » (7 : 157).

Bien que ce bref aperçu soit loin d'épuiser toutes les déclarations positives du Coran sur les juifs et leur religion, il donne une idée des éléments qui ont été retenus dans le texte et ses exégèses. Cela ne doit pas faire oublier les jugements négatifs qui s'y trouvent aussi.

Des fils indociles et rebelles

Les critiques violentes dirigées par le Coran contre les Hébreux de la Bible puis contre les juifs y occupent une place plus importante que les jugements positifs. Ce sont des « fils indociles et rebelles », des « transgresseurs de l'alliance divine », des adorateurs du Veau d'or coupables aussi d'autres crimes d'idolâtrie, des falsificateurs de la Torah, des assassins des prophètes, des usuriers, etc.

Le Coran reprend l'image biblique des Hébreux sortant d'Égypte comme un peuple rebelle, pécheur et ingrat. Bien que Dieu les ait libérés de l'esclavage, les ait conduits vers la Terre promise et ait conclu une alliance avec eux, les Hébreux auraient répondu au moment où Dieu s'apprêtait à leur donner la Torah : *sami'nâ wa-'aṣaynâ* (« Nous avons écouté, et nous avons désobéi ») (2 : 93). On reconnaît là l'écho de la célèbre réponse « Nous écouterons et nous ferons », *we-shama'nu we-'asinu* (Deutéronome 5 : 23) ; mais le Coran opère un jeu de mots, transformant *'asinu*, « nous ferons », en *'aṣaynâ*, « nous avons désobéi », en remplaçant simplement le *s* שׂ\س par un ṣ צ\س·de sonorité proche. Mais qui en inverse totalement le sens. C'est sans doute une des raisons pour lesquelles les Hébreux sont accusés par le Coran d'avoir intentionnellement modifié le message divin*.

La rébellion des Hébreux s'exprime par la rupture de l'Alliance, ce qui justifie la déception de Dieu à leur égard : « Nous les avons punis parce qu'ils ont rompu leur alliance, parce qu'ils n'ont pas cru aux Signes de Dieu, parce qu'ils ont tué injustement les prophètes, et parce qu'ils ont dit : "Nos cœurs sont incirconcis" » (4 : 155). Comme souvent dans le Coran, la mention d'un péché commis par les Hébreux appelle le souvenir de plusieurs autres. À cela s'ajoute l'accusation réitérée dans le Coran selon laquelle les juifs ont falsifié l'Écriture et encouru de ce fait la malédiction de Dieu qui a endurci leur cœur : « Mais ils ont rompu leur alliance, nous les avons maudits et nous avons endurci leurs cœurs. Ils altèrent le sens des paroles révélées ; ils oublient une partie de ce qui leur a été rappelé » (5 : 13).

Dans le feu de la polémique, la rupture de l'Alliance par les Hébreux est reportée sur les juifs tout au long de leur histoire : « Les pires des êtres devant Dieu sont vraiment ceux qui sont incrédules ; ceux qui ne croient pas, ceux d'entre eux avec qui tu as conclu un pacte et qui, ensuite,

---

* Le verset le plus connu à ce sujet est : « Certains juifs altèrent le sens des paroles révélées… Ils tordent leur langue et ils attaquent la religion… » (4 : 46).

ont toujours violé leurs engagements ; ceux qui ne craignent pas Dieu » (8 : 55-56). Ces paroles sont proférées en termes généraux, sans se référer à des individus ou des groupes précis ; pour autant, il faut noter que la majorité des commentateurs classiques, suivant leur méthode habituelle qui consiste à reconstituer le contexte des versets coraniques, y voient non pas une critique visant des pécheurs ou des juifs en général, mais une attaque contre des juifs bien précis, ceux de l'une ou l'autre des tribus de Médine mentionnées plus haut[13].

Ce point est très important : aucun texte, a fortiori un texte religieux souvent difficile comme le Coran, ne se donne à lire de manière absolue, et le sens qu'on en retire dépend beaucoup du contexte que l'on prête à ses versets. Certaines phrases à fort potentiel polémique prises isolément se voient ainsi « neutralisées » quand elles sont ramenées à un contexte historique précis ; à l'inverse, des versets dont l'interprétation traditionnelle a toujours cherché à éclaircir le contexte deviennent « explosifs » quand ils sont sciemment décontextualisés pour être brandis contre les juifs et les chrétiens d'aujourd'hui. Les polémistes antimusulmans, quand ils appellent à la « suppression » ou à l'« obsolescence théologique » de certains versets du Coran, font en réalité le jeu des islamistes en accréditant l'idée que le Coran aurait un sens univoque et clair.

Idolâtres et adorateurs du Veau d'or

La rupture de l'Alliance par les Hébreux est une accusation d'ordre général dont les ramifications sont les divers péchés égrenés comme une litanie : refus des signes envoyés par Dieu, falsification des paroles révélées aux prophètes, massacre des prophètes, etc. Mais la faute la plus grave est l'idolâtrie, preuve tangible du rejet du monothéisme par les Hébreux puis, après eux, les juifs. La fabrication et le culte du Veau d'or, le péché le plus grave, pour lequel Dieu menace d'exterminer le peuple infidèle selon l'Exode (32 : 10), est rappelé à maintes reprises dans le Coran comme le pire qui soit :

> Dieu dit : « Oui, après ton départ, nous avons éprouvé ton peuple, le Sâmirî les a égarés. » Moïse revint vers son peuple, courroucé et affligé. Il dit : « Ô mon peuple ! Votre Seigneur ne vous a-t-il pas fait une belle promesse ? L'alliance vous a-t-elle paru trop longue ? Ou bien avez-vous désiré que tombe sur vous la colère de votre Seigneur puisque vous avez trahi votre engagement envers moi ? » Ils répondirent : « Nous n'avons pas manqué de nous-

> mêmes à l'engagement pris envers toi ; mais nous avons été contraints de transporter des charges de parures appartenant à ce peuple : nous les avons jetées ; c'est ainsi que le Sâmirî les a lancées ; puis il a fait sortir pour eux un veau, un corps mugissant. » Ils dirent alors : « Voici votre dieu et le dieu de Moïse ! Il a donc oublié […] » (20 : 85-88).

Le récit coranique ressemble en bien des points à l'épisode biblique du Veau d'or (Exode 32 : 1-6). Sa particularité réside dans l'intervention du « Samaritain » (*al-Sâmirî*), totalement absent du texte biblique. Les Samaritains, qui tirent leur nom de la ville de Samarie et de sa région, située entre la Judée et la Galilée, sont un peuple rival des Juifs. Aujourd'hui quasiment disparus, ils affirment être les authentiques descendants du peuple d'Israël, ne reconnaissent que la Torah, qu'ils écrivent dans un alphabet propre dérivé de l'ancien alphabet hébreu, et affirment que Dieu a choisi le mont Garizim plutôt que Jérusalem comme lieu de son Temple. Les juifs les considèrent pour leur part comme des imposteurs étrangers, importés en Terre sainte par les Assyriens. Avant cela, le royaume d'Israël s'était scindé, après le règne de Salomon, en deux royaumes, celui de Judée et celui du Nord, dont la capitale était Sichem (traditionnellement identifiée à la ville actuelle de Naplouse). Le Livre des Rois raconte que pour détourner les pèlerins de Jérusalem, le roi du Nord, Jéroboam, avait institué deux Veaux d'or offerts à l'adoration des fidèles. La rivalité entre les Juifs et les Samaritains est postbiblique, puisqu'elle se joue essentiellement entre le retour des captifs de Babylone et l'époque des Hasmonéens. Comme le dit I. Goldziher cité par Blachère dans une note de sa traduction du Coran, « cet épisode du Samaritain instituant le culte du Veau d'or, comme l'a bien montré Goldziher, est destiné à retrouver dans un péché ancien l'origine de la scission survenue entre la communauté samaritaine et Israël[14] ».

Quoi qu'il en soit, l'épisode du Veau d'or sert à souligner l'idolâtrie des Hébreux et à remettre en cause leur attachement au monothéisme.

La figure de 'Uzayr

L'autre grave accusation d'idôlatrie faite au peuple d'Israël se retrouve dans un célèbre verset où il est présenté comme adorant un certain 'Uzayr, qu'il croit fils de Dieu :

> Les juifs ont dit : « 'Uzayr est le fils de Dieu. » Les chrétiens ont dit : « Le Messie est le fils de Dieu. » Telle est la parole qui sort de leurs bouches ; ils

> répètent ce que les incrédules disaient avant eux. Que Dieu les anéantisse ! Ils sont tellement stupides ! (9 : 30).

Que signifie le nom 'Uzayr ? Parmi les commentateurs du Coran, certains proposent de le considérer comme une déformation du mot biblique *'Azazel* (Lévitique 16 : 8-10, qui se réfère probablement à un démon) ou du nom de la divinité égyptienne Osiris. Cependant, l'opinion la plus couramment admise chez les auteurs musulmans est que 'Uzayr serait un diminutif arabe du nom de 'Ezra ou Esdras ; dans la tradition musulmane, *'Uzayr al-warrâq* est la traduction exacte de 'Ezra le scribe, *'Ezra ha-sofer*, ainsi qu'il est appelé dans la Bible (Néhémie 12 : 36) et dans les sources juives postbibliques[15]. Que l'appellation coranique se réfère au 'Ezra biblique ou à un autre personnage, aucune source juive ne corrobore l'accusation coranique en vertu de laquelle les juifs auraient tenu 'Uzayr pour le fils de Dieu. En cela, cette calomnie diffère des nombreuses autres accusations polémiques puisqu'elle n'a pas de précédent dans littérature antijuive d'avant l'islam. De manière générale, le fait que cet argument soit rapporté dans le Coran en même temps que la croyance des chrétiens dans la filiation divine de Jésus met en relief l'intention polémique du verset de présenter le judaïsme et le christianisme comme des monothéismes pervertis. La juxtaposition de ce verset aux versets polémiques dirigés contre le judaïsme et le christianisme rend plus évident encore son caractère polémique.

Cependant, il est possible que l'origine de cette croyance, comme l'a suggéré G. D. Newby dans son étude sur l'histoire des juifs en Arabie à l'époque antéislamique, soit à chercher dans l'identification de 'Uzayr avec le personnage de Hénoch, dont il est dit dans la Bible : « Hénoch marcha avec Dieu, puis il disparut, car Dieu l'avait enlevé » (Genèse 5 : 24). Le cas singulier d'Hénoch, enlevé mystérieusement comme Élie (II Rois 2 : 11), lui a conféré une place particulière dans la tradition juive. La littérature juive postbiblique, aussi bien dans les textes dit « apocryphes » que dans les textes mystiques (Premier, Deuxième et Troisième Livres d'Hénoch), atteste de la croyance selon laquelle Hénoch aurait été enlevé vivant au ciel et aurait été métamorphosé en un ange suprême appelé Métatron. Ce Métatron, figure quasi divine (appelé dans certains textes « le petit YHWH »), aurait notamment été celui qui aurait dicté la Torah à Moïse au Sinaï. Newby affirme que, parmi les juifs d'Arabie, certains auraient vu en 'Uzayr/'Ezra un avatar d'Hénoch. Si de telles croyances au sujet d'Hénoch se sont projetées sur le personnage de 'Uzayr, cela pourrait expliquer l'accusation du Coran contre les juifs, bien que, pour l'instant, cette explication reste une simple hypothèse. Dans la mesure où cette angélologie mystique juive ancienne a aussi pu influencer les doctrines chrétiennes du Christ cosmique dès l'origine[16], il s'agit d'une piste à creuser.

Quoi qu'il en soit, le commentaire islamique du verset en question insiste sur le fait que cette croyance n'est pas partagée par tous les juifs. Certains exégètes ont limité la portée de l'accusation et considèrent qu'elle est dirigée contre une croyance appartenant à un passé reculé, puisqu'ils ont remarqué qu'on ne trouve plus semblable blasphème chez les juifs de leur temps. D'autres soutiennent que cette idée n'a jamais appartenu qu'à un petit groupe parmi les juifs. Selon d'autres encore, un seul juif aurait affiché cette croyance, un certain dénommé Finhâs. Ce genre de commentaires se trouve surtout dans l'exégèse médiévale du Coran, par exemple dans les écrits de Tabarî et de Qurtubî.

La relation qu'entretiennent les sources musulmanes avec 'Uzayr est équivoque. D'une part, il est considéré comme l'un des prophètes du peuple d'Israël, comme cela apparaît clairement par exemple dans les « Récits des prophètes » d'al-Tha'labî (m. en 1035), et il est rapporté à son sujet qu'il a joué un rôle central dans l'enseignement de la Bible au peuple juif après son retour de l'exil babylonien. Selon les sources musulmanes, lorsque les juifs revinrent de l'exil en Babylone, ils avaient perdu la Torah, « et leurs cœurs l'avaient oubliée ». ‘Uzayr pleurait et se lamentait sur cette perte. D'après une version du récit, alors que ‘Uzayr était plongé dans son deuil, lui apparut un ange sous la forme d'un homme qui lui demanda la raison de son affliction et de ses pleurs. ‘Uzayr lui raconta que c'était la perte de la Torah qui le désolait et l'endeuillait. L'ange lui demanda de jeûner, de purifier ses vêtements et de venir le rencontrer le lendemain au même endroit. Le lendemain, l'ange arriva. Il lui donna à boire d'un récipient qu'il tenait en main (selon une autre version, une lumière céleste se répandit sur lui) et ainsi, la Torah s'éveilla à nouveau dans sa mémoire et il la mit par écrit pour les enfants d'Israël. Désormais, ‘Uzayr pouvait enseigner la Torah à son peuple[17].

On trouve différentes versions de cette histoire dans de nombreuses sources musulmanes, par exemple dans le monumental livre d'histoire de Tabarî, qui dresse un portrait positif de ‘Uzayr comme le résurrecteur de l'enseignement de Moïse. D'après Tabarî, c'est peut-être ce rôle joué par ‘Uzayr dans la redécouverte de la Bible perdue qui expliquerait l'admiration que lui porta son peuple au point que certains commencèrent à le considérer comme le fils de Dieu. Ces notions sont bien connues de la littérature rabbinique, qui raconte notamment que ʻEzra, au retour des exilés de Babylonie, a reconstitué le texte de la Torah à partir de trois exemplaires anciens (Talmud de Jérusalem, traité *Ta'anit* 4 : 2), ou encore que c'est lui qui a institué qu'elle soit désormais écrite en caractères « assyriens » (l'hébreu carré actuel) plutôt que dans l'alphabet paléo-hébraïque (Talmud de Babylone, traité *Sanhédrin* 21b-22a).

Le rapport de ʻUzayr avec la redécouverte de la Torah servit aussi de base à la création de son image négative. Des auteurs musulmans, à commencer par ʻAlî b. Ahmad Ibn Hazm l'Andalou (m. en 1064), ont vu dans ʻEzra le responsable principal de la déformation et de la falsification de la Bible. Dans un ouvrage polémique dirigé contre le poète, talmudiste et vizir de l'émir de Grenade al-Samaw'al Ibn al-Naghrîla, dit Samuel ha-Nagîd, son éminent compatriote, Ibn Hazm écrit notamment :

> Et eux [les juifs] reconnaissent que ʻEzra, qui leur a copié la Bible lorsqu'il s'en est rappelé après qu'elle s'était perdue, n'était qu'un scribe (*warrâq*) et non pas un prophète. Cependant une partie de leur peuple dit qu'il est fils de Dieu, et ceux-là se sont perdus et ont disparu[18]...

À partir de là, Ibn Hazm commence à présenter ʻEzra comme un homme méchant, un scélérat qui a délibérément falsifié le Livre saint. L'opinion d'Ibn Hazm eut une grande influence sur l'obscurcissement du personnage de 'Uzayr/'Ezra et, dans une grande mesure, sur le rejet ou l'oubli de l'image positive que donnaient de lui les sources plus anciennes.

Un autre personnage médiéval important qui prit part à la tentative de présenter 'Ezra comme le plus grand des falsificateurs de la Bible fut le juif converti à l'islam al-Samaw'al al-Maghribî (m. en 1175) dans son ouvrage *Ifḥâm al-yahûd* (« Réduction des juifs au silence »). Al-Maghribî – qui ne reprend pas à son compte l'identification établie entre le 'Uzayr coranique et le 'Ezra biblique – insiste sur la notion de falsification par 'Ezra, qui transparaît par exemple dans le caractère licencieux de la généalogie du roi David. Dans le même esprit que la critique biblique moderne, qui tend à déceler dans ces récits la main d'un écrivain appartenant à des cercles opposés à la cour des rois de Judée, al-Maghribî affirme que les histoires bibliques concernant les rapports licencieux de Loth et ses filles et surtout les récits de Juda et Tamar ont été délibérément introduits dans la Torah par 'Ezra, prêtre de la tribu de Lévi, afin de porter atteinte à la maison de David (issu de la tribu de Juda) et de leur légitimité à la royauté. Comme preuve de ce qu'il avance, al-Maghribî ajoute que « au temps du deuxième temple, le gouvernement appartenait aux prêtres de la maison d'Aaron (Hârûn) et non aux souverains de la maison de David[19] ». Il fait là référence à la dynastie hasmonéenne, qui régna après la révolte des Maccabées contre les rois séleucides (de – 140 à – 37).

Au-delà de la polémique antijuive, les arguments d'al-Maghribî, qu'on retrouve aussi chez Ibn Hazm, sont révélateurs d'une grande différence de sensibilité entre auteurs musulmans et juifs. Alors que pour un musulman le fait que la Torah attribue à des prophètes des comportements peu glorieux est la marque de la falsification de son texte par les juifs, et révélateur de leur perversité, pour les auteurs juifs au contraire le fait que ces épisodes figurent dans le texte biblique est la preuve que ce dernier n'a pas été altéré : si quelqu'un s'était aventuré à « corriger » la Torah, il aurait sans nul doute escamoté ces passages peu flatteurs. C'est l'argument que le talmudiste Salomon ben Adret (1235-1310) oppose à Ibn Hazm[20].

Falsificateurs de la Torah

Dans la relation que le Coran, ainsi que dans les sources musulmanes postcoraniques, entretient avec la Bible réside une ambivalence : d'une part, l'islam considère la Bible comme l'un des textes saints que Dieu a révélé aux hommes avant d'offrir le Coran aux Arabes et plus largement à l'humanité tout entière. C'est pourquoi le Coran, et les musulmans après lui, recourent à la Bible pour prouver la véracité du Coran – tout comme le christianisme l'avait fait avant lui. Nombre des versets de la Bible sont d'ailleurs interprétés comme étant des prédictions de la venue future de Muhammad et de la victoire de l'islam. Un exemple parmi beaucoup d'autres est le verset « Car un enfant nous est né, un fils nous a été donné, la souveraineté repose sur son épaule… » (Isaïe 9 : 5), verset bien connu des exégèses juive et chrétienne qui le considèrent comme l'annonce de l'avènement du Messie. Cette interprétation, basée sur le sens littéral, n'a pas échappé aux érudits musulmans qui y voient une allusion à la mission prophétique de Muhammad. Ils appuient leur interprétation sur les mots « la souveraineté repose sur son épaule… ». Le mot « souveraineté » (*misra* en hébreu, de la racine *s-r-y*, « avoir autorité ») a été traduit en arabe par différents termes désignant le pouvoir (*sultân*, *ri'âsa*), et les savants musulmans perçurent le verset biblique comme parlant du « Sceau de la prophétie » qui, selon la croyance musulmane, figurait littéralement sur l'épaule de Muhammad. Ils insistèrent ainsi sur le fait que le verset ne pouvait absolument pas faire allusion à Jésus dont l'épaule ne portait pas un tel signe, mais uniquement à Muhammad dont le corps était, dit-on, marqué par le Sceau sacré.

D'autre part, l'islam a contesté dès sa naissance l'intégrité du texte biblique tel que nous le connaissons. Le Coran accuse les juifs d'avoir tendancieusement falsifié (*tahrîf*) ce dernier et d'avoir modifié (*tabdîl*) l'ordre de ces versets : « Certains juifs altèrent le sens des paroles révélées… » (entre autres 4 : 46) ; « Malheur à ceux qui écrivent le Livre de leurs mains, et qui disent, ensuite, pour retirer un faible prix : "Ceci vient de Dieu" ! » (2 : 79). Le but des falsifications et des modifications que la tradition musulmane imputa essentiellement à 'Uzayr/'Ezra, comme on l'a vu, était donc d'éradiquer de la Bible tous les témoignages en rapport avec la venue future de Muhammad : la description du personnage, de ses qualités, et de la victoire de la religion qu'il était destiné à apporter à l'humanité, etc.

Cette ambivalence envers la Bible est présente dès le texte coranique ; elle a déterminé la relation de l'islam au texte biblique tout le long de son histoire. Cette ambiguïté est peut-être aussi l'une des raisons pour lesquelles le Coran ne contient presque aucune citation littérale de la Bible. L'une des caractéristiques frappantes du Coran réside dans le fait que, s'il paraphrase très fréquemment des récits bibliques, il ne cite pratiquement jamais littéralement un verset de la Bible. La seule citation littérale d'un verset biblique est la suivante : « Nous avons écrit dans les Psaumes... : "En vérité, mes serviteurs justes hériteront de la terre" » (21 : 105), alors que le verset des Psaumes est légèrement différent : « Les justes posséderont la terre et l'habiteront éternellement » (Psaumes 37 : 29). Cet exemple montre que le Coran s'intéresse à ce qu'il saisit du contenu de la Bible et non à sa formulation. Autrement dit, le fait que la Bible soit considérée comme falsifiée est une raison suffisante pour ne pas la citer. On peut se servir des parties qui n'ont pas été falsifiées mais il faut éviter de l'utiliser sans discrimination. Cette attitude est diamétralement différente de celle du christianisme qui, en principe, accepte la Bible telle qu'elle est, mais l'interprète parfois différemment.

Assassins des prophètes

Une des accusations récurrentes les plus graves dirigées contre les juifs est le meurtre des prophètes qui leur ont été envoyés : « La colère de Dieu les éprouva parce qu'ils n'avaient pas cru aux Signes de Dieu, parce qu'ils tuaient injustement les prophètes » (2 : 61) ; « Nous avons conclu l'alliance avec les fils d'Israël et nous leur avons envoyé des prophètes. Mais chaque fois qu'un prophète s'est présenté à eux en contrariant leurs désirs, ils ont accusé de mensonges plusieurs prophètes et ils ont tué les autres » (5 : 70).

Ces paroles du Coran et toutes les autres mentions de cette accusation qui en sont inspirées ne se réfèrent à aucune circonstance attestée par la Bible où des juifs auraient mis à mort tel ou tel prophète. Abraham Geiger pense qu'il s'agit ici de la crucifixion de Jésus (bien que, selon le Coran, Jésus n'aurait pas véritablement été crucifié). Une autre possibilité serait qu'il s'agit d'une référence à l'assassinat du prophète Zacharie ou encore du père de Jean-Baptiste, lui aussi nommé Zacharie[21].

D'autres chercheurs, comme Josef Horovitz, ont mis en relation ce verset avec un passage du Nouveau Testament dont il se fait l'écho : « Jérusalem, Jérusalem, toi qui tues les prophètes et lapides ceux qui te sont envoyés ! » (Matthieu 23 : 37 ; Luc, 13 : 34 ; Romains 11 : 3 ; I Thessaloniciens 2 : 14-15[22]). On ne saurait exclure que ces passages soient eux-mêmes inspirés par les paroles du prophète Élie, qui auraient donc été connues des premiers musulmans : « Je suis dévoré de zèle pour le Seigneur, le Dieu des armées, car les Israélites ont abandonné ton alliance, ils ont renversé tes autels et passé tes prophètes au fil de l'épée » (I Rois 19 : 10) ; « Votre épée a dévoré vos prophètes, comme un lion destructeur » (Jérémie 2 : 30).

La position que le Coran adopte concernant la culpabilité des juifs dans la crucifixion de Jésus est ambiguë. D'un côté, il place dans leur bouche un aveu : « Oui, nous avons tué le Messie, Jésus fils de Marie, l'Envoyé de Dieu » (4 : 157), ce qui est cohérent avec la réputation qui leur est faite de « tueurs de prophètes et d'envoyés » ; d'un autre côté, le Coran maintient que Jésus n'a en réalité pas été crucifié : « Mais ils ne l'ont pas tué ; ils ne l'ont pas crucifié ; plutôt, cela leur est apparu ainsi. (4 : 157) » Cette question du regard coranique sur la crucifixion a suscité de nombreuses recherches, et l'opinion dominante est que le Coran reprend ici la conception des docétistes. Pour ces derniers, qui se rattachaient aux gnostiques, Jésus n'était pas réellement un humain mais seulement une manifestation divine dont le corps n'était qu'une apparence ; il ne pouvait pas mourir et sa crucifixion n'avait été qu'une illusion[23].

Ainsi donc, dans les paroles d'Élie, connu dans le Nouveau Testament et dans le Coran, l'abandon de l'Alliance, dont il a été question plus haut, s'exprime par le meurtre des prophètes. Autrement dit l'abandon de l'Alliance rabaisse le peuple au point qu'il en vient à tuer les envoyés de Dieu. On ne sait si la source de cette accusation était connue des premiers musulmans mais il ne fait pas de doute qu'elle repose tant sur le Coran lui-même, où elle est mentionnée neuf fois (bien que parfois les juifs ne soient pas explicitement désignés), que sur l'exégèse inspirée par la polémique antijuive.

Aux principales caractérisations négatives des juifs que nous venons d'examiner, on pourrait en ajouter d'autres. Une des plus répandues dans le Coran est qu'ils pratiquent l'usure (voir par exemple 4 : 161 ; 5 : 62). Mais ce qui compte, ce n'est pas l'énumération des griefs contre eux, c'est surtout le fait que cette vision négative globale des juifs sert de fondement à leur délégitimation et à leur rabaissement. Ainsi les juifs sont-ils condamnés à la misère et à un statut inférieur en raison de leurs péchés : « Ils furent frappés par l'humiliation et la pauvreté » (2 : 61). Leur infériorité doit être marquée par l'imposition de la capitation (*jizya*), comme nous le verrons au chapitre v. En outre, selon le Coran, le nombre élevé de commandements bibliques (613 selon la tradition juive), en regard du nombre restreint des prescriptions coraniques, est une punition divine infligée aux juifs[24].

Toutes ces accusations dirigées contre les juifs doivent être replacées dans une tradition de polémique antijuive qui a précédé l'islam. Plusieurs éléments, comme la rupture de l'Alliance et le meurtre des prophètes, se trouvent déjà dans la polémique chrétienne ; l'idée que les juifs avaient falsifié l'Écriture était déjà répandue par les Samaritains ; l'usure fait partie des stéréotypes anciens. Le lien de cause à effet qu'établit le Coran entre les caractéristiques des juifs et le fait que Dieu se détourne d'eux, d'où leur délégitimation, provient aussi de traditions religieuses antérieures à l'islam. Selon le célèbre paradigme de l'« esprit » contre la « chair » et de l'« amour » vs. la « Loi », initié par Paul, le christianisme considérait déjà que le joug des commandements était un châtiment imposé aux juifs et non une marque d'élection. De même, la soumission des juifs au pouvoir chrétien exprimait la volonté de Dieu qui s'était détourné d'eux car ils avaient refusé de croire en Jésus. On voit par là que le Coran est l'héritier de stéréotypes anciens.

« *Transformés en singes et en porcs* »

L'idée coranique (7 : 163-166 et 2 : 65-66) selon laquelle des juifs auraient été transformés ou réincarnés (*musîkhu*) en singes parce qu'ils auraient transgressé le shabbat connaît une large postérité dans la littérature postcoranique. Un autre verset parle plus généralement des « gens du Livre » (*ahl al-kitâb*), y compris donc les chrétiens, « transformés en singes et porcs » (5 : 59-60). La tradition sunnite classique y voit un épisode ponctuel et s'interroge surtout sur le sens réel ou imagé de cette métamorphose, ce qu'elle induit en termes de porosité entre les règnes animal et humain, et le destin de ces singes : tous les singes actuels descendent-ils de ces hommes transformés en singes[25] ?

Dans d'autres écrits musulmans, en particulier chez les sectes shî'ites dites « hétérodoxes » ou « exagératrices » (*ghulât*), ces épisodes sont lus dans le contexte de la doctrine de la transmigration de l'âme humaine. L'âme humaine, en fonction de la gravité des péchés, peut transmigrer de diverses manières, y compris dans des animaux, ces divers degrés du changement de l'âme étant décrits par des mots à rimes : *naskh*, *maskh*, *waskh*, etc.[26]

Ces versets coraniques ont inspiré l'expression *awlâd al-qirada wa-l-khanâzîr*, « descendants des singes et des porcs », une des insultes les plus communes visant les juifs et des chrétiens, comme une recherche rapide sur Internet suffit pour l'attester. Plus précisément, les juifs sont devenus des « fils de singes » et les chrétiens les « fils de porcs ». La tradition musulmane s'interroge en interne pour savoir s'il faut prendre ces épithètes au sens littéral et si elles s'appliquent aux juifs et aux chrétiens de toutes époques. Dans une lecture maximaliste de ces versets, si « les juifs » ont été transformés « en singes », faut-il en déduire que les juifs d'aujourd'hui sont en réalité des singes dont la forme humaine n'est qu'apparente ? Cette lecture est très clairement repoussée, au motif que la justice divine ne saurait souffrir que les descendants soient punis pour les fautes de leurs ancêtres. Ce qui n'empêche pas l'insulte de perdurer.

Le hadîth des pierres et des arbres

Ce processus de délégitimation des juifs, qui atteint son paroxysme du vivant de Muhammad avec l'expulsion des juifs de Médine et de ses environs voire, comme on l'a vu, avec le massacre des hommes de la tribu des Banû Qurayza et l'asservissement de ses femmes, s'est prolongé tout au long de l'histoire islamique. Les juifs sont régulièrement accusés de fomenter des complots contre Muhammad et de chercher à subvertir l'islam. La littérature du Hadîth, c'est-à-dire des traditions orales remontant au Prophète, est remplie de considérations péjoratives envers les juifs, dans l'esprit de ce qui ressort du Coran et de la *Sîra* ou biographie du Prophète. On trouvera une synthèse de l'image donnée des juifs dans la littérature du Hadîth dans l'article de Haggai Ben-Shammai, « Jew-Hatred in the Islamic Tradition and the Koranic Exegesis[27] » (« La haine du Juif dans la tradition islamique et l'exégèse coranique »).

L'un de ces hadîths les plus connus est en

même temps tout à fait singulier en ce qu'il présente la lutte entre l'islam et le judaïsme comme une lutte éternelle, qui se prolonge dans tout le temps historique, et qui ne trouvera son terme qu'à l'ère eschatologique : « Le Jour du Jugement dernier ne viendra pas avant que les musulmans ne combattent les juifs, quand les juifs se cacheront derrière les rochers et les arbres. Les rochers et les arbres diront : "Ô Musulman, ô serviteur de Dieu ('Abdallâh), il y a un juif derrière moi, viens le tuer !" Seul l'arbre du *gharqad* ne le dira pas, parce que c'est en effet un arbre appartenant aux juifs[28]. »

Ce hadîth, bien attesté par de nombreuses sources islamiques anciennes et modernes, a connu une seconde vie à notre époque dans le contexte du conflit israélo-arabe qui a revêtu l'aspect religieux d'un conflit entre judaïsme et islam. C'est ainsi qu'il se trouve cité sans précautions oratoires ou contextuelles dans la Charte du Hamas ainsi que dans de nombreuses autres sources contemporaines, comme une rapide recherche du mot *gharqad* sur Google suffit pour s'en convaincre. Il faut cependant relever que la nouvelle Charte du Hamas, proclamée en 2017, omet la mention de ce hadîth. Ce fait nouveau ne se prête pas à une interprétation univoque : il est possible qu'il révèle un souci nouveau du Hamas de se prémunir contre les accusations d'antisémitisme portées envers le mouvement, mais on ne peut pas exclure qu'il soit aussi le symptôme de luttes internes au mouvement[29].

Il est révélateur que des prédicateurs musulmans contemporains interprètent le travail du KKL (Keren Kayemet Le-Israël ou Fonds national juif)[30], qui vise à planter des forêts en Israël, comme une entreprise de culture intensive de cet arbre appelé *gharqad :* les juifs seraient donc persuadés que cet arbre les protégera à l'heure du conflit eschatologique entre l'islam et le judaïsme. Le présupposé d'une telle croyance est assez surprenant : il suppose que non seulement les juifs connaissent ce hadîth, mais encore qu'ils y croient et qu'ils modèlent leurs actions en conséquence. Une telle opinion est notamment explorée par un idéologue du Hamas, le Palestinien As'ad Buyud al-Tamîmî, dans son livre *Zawâl Isrâ'îl haqîqa hatmiyya* (« La disparition d'Israël est une vérité absolue[31] »).

L'« âne chargé de livres »

Cette parabole, qui sera souvent reprise par la littérature juive (on la trouve déjà chez les auteurs andalous comme Bahya ibn Paquda et Yehuda al-Harizi), résume l'attitude complexe du Coran envers les juifs : « Ceux qui étaient chargés de la Torah et qui, par la suite, ne l'ont plus assumée [littéralement "ne s'en sont pas chargés"] ressemblent à l'âne chargé de livres » (62 : 5). Notons en passant que la parabole est introduite par le terme *mathal*, « exemple, parabole », qui revient près de cent fois dans le Coran et qui a son exact correspondant dans la littérature midrashique, *mashal*, où il s'agit d'un procédé fréquent.

Les juifs ont donc été chargés de la Torah, d'un héritage important et vénérable que le Coran ne minimise pas, mais eux, qui en sont les porteurs, le négligent. Ils ne font que le porter concrètement comme un âne qui ne sait pas ce qu'il a sur le dos. Si les juifs avaient su reconnaître la valeur de l'héritage qui leur a été confié, ils auraient réglé leur comportement sur lui au lieu de le déformer, de le falsifier et de le rejeter. S'ils avaient respecté dans leur conduite l'héritage divin, ils n'auraient pas été abandonnés par Dieu et condamnés à l'abaissement et à la misère auxquels les réduit le Coran. Ce genre de remontrances n'est pas étranger à la Bible, où il est courant que les prophètes réprimandent le peuple, par exemple chez Isaïe : « La révélation de tous ces événements demeure pour vous comme le texte d'un livre scellé. L'offre-t-on à un illettré en le priant de lire, il répond : "Je ne sais pas lire" » (Isaïe 29 : 12). Il faut cependant noter que la comparaison du peuple juif à un âne chargé de livres constitue aussi une mise en garde à l'intention des musulmans : beaucoup d'hommes se comportent comme ces juifs à l'égard de la Parole révélée, les musulmans sont donc invités à en tirer la leçon pour ne pas trébucher comme l'ont fait les juifs.

Plus généralement, il convient de se poser la question : à qui s'adresse le Coran ? Les versets critiquant l'infidélité des juifs jouent semble-t-il toujours un double rôle : d'une part instaurer la communauté musulmane en nouveau « peuple élu », mais dans le même temps la mettre en garde : si les musulmans ne restent pas fidèles à la Parole divine, alors ils ne valent pas mieux que ces juifs.

III

LES RÉCITS BIBLIQUES ET LEURS PROLONGEMENTS POSTBIBLIQUES DANS LE CORAN

Le Coran est riche de principes de foi, d'idées et de récits connus par la Bible et la littérature postbiblique. Cela est évident pour tout lecteur familier de la Bible et de la littérature juive ou chrétienne postérieure, même dans une lecture superficielle du Coran. Parfois, il lui faut plus d'efforts pour les reconnaître car ils ont subi un remaniement sensible afin de s'intégrer dans le narratif coranique et ses traits spécifiques. Ce lien entre le Coran et la Bible, ainsi que les sources postbibliques, a été étudié par de nombreux savants depuis les débuts de l'islamologie il y a plus de deux siècles, parmi les plus éminents desquels se trouvent Abraham Geiger, Ignaz Goldziher, Helmut Speyer, David Sidersky, Joseph Horovitz, Shlomo Dov Goitein, Hava Lazarus-Yafeh, Uri Rubin et bien d'autres, et plus récemment Sydney Griffith dans son livre *The Bible in Arabic : The Scriptures of the « People of the Book » in the Language of Islam* et Gabriel S. Reynolds dans son œuvre *The Qur'an and the Bible : Text and Commentary*.

Le vocabulaire hébraïque du Coran

Rappelons tout d'abord combien le Coran est empreint d'une terminologie religieuse étrangère à la langue arabe préislamique en raison des contacts des musulmans avec différentes cultures. La recherche moderne s'est beaucoup consacrée à cette question en étudiant soit un terme particulier, soit un groupe de mots, ou encore en élaborant des travaux monographiques sur le sujet comme l'enquête pionnière d'Arthur Jeffery, *The Foreign Vocabulary of the Qur'ān*. Dans ce livre, on trouve une discussion très précise de nombreux termes importants du Coran dont l'origine biblique ou postbiblique est évidente. Ils n'auraient certainement pas pu entrer dans le Coran si les rédacteurs de celui-ci n'avaient pas été en contact avec des sages juifs. Nous pouvons citer entre autres des expressions eschatologiques telles que *yawm al-dîn*, « le jour du jugement [dernier] », qui pourrait venir de l'hébreu *yom ha-din* ; *jahannam*, la géhenne, issue du mot *gehinnom* ou *gehinnam* ; *jannât 'adn*, « le jardin d'Éden », issu de *gân 'éden* ; ou encore *Ya'jûj wa-Ma'jûj*, « Gog et Magog », deux étranges peuplades de la Bible que le Coran évoque en relation avec les exploits d'Alexandre, appelé dans le Coran l'homme à deux cornes, *Dhû l-qarnayn* (18 : 82-98). On trouve encore d'autres exemples tel le mot *ahbâr* désignant un sage juif ou un rabbin, dérivé de *haber*, terme hébraïque qui désigne un « confrère », un membre des milieux rabbiniques ; *asbât*, « tribus » (sing. *sibt*, mais uniquement attesté au pluriel dans le Coran) qui vient de l'hébreu *shebet* (pl. *shebatim*), désignant les douze tribus d'Israël issues des douze fils de Jacob – d'ailleurs le mot apparaît toujours soit dans l'expression *Ya'qûb wa-l-asbât*, « Jacob et les tribus », soit dans la phrase *wa-qatta'nâhumu thnatâ 'ashrata asbâta*, « nous les avons divisés en douze tribus » (7: 160) ; *Sakîna* qui vient très probablement du mot hébraïque *shekhina*, expression typiquement rabbinique pour désigner la « Présence divine »[1] ; *'elyon*, l'adjectif hébraïque qui rappelle *'illiyyûn* signifiant « suprême », « en haut », dans l'évocation du monde d'en haut, ou encore *shaytan* pour son homologue biblique *Satan*, le Diable. On terminera cette énumération partielle avec les mots bien connus de *salât* (« prière ») et *zakât* (« aumône ») désignant deux des futurs cinq piliers de l'islam. Ils tirent certainement leur origine des mots *sêlôta* et *zekhûta* en araméen / syriaque dont l'usage est partagé par les juifs et les chrétiens de l'Orient de cette époque.

Le Coran et la Genèse

Si le Coran se fait l'écho de la Bible, c'est avec un goût prononcé pour le Pentateuque, cependant que d'autres livres bibliques brillent par leur absence. Les héros de la Genèse sont bien représentés avec Adam, Noé, Loth, Abraham et ses fils, Jacob, Joseph et ses frères. Le prophète Moïse, l'une des figures centrales du Coran, fait l'objet de longues narrations où sont décrits les épisodes de sa vie, en particulier son affrontement avec Pharaon et son rôle de guide des Hébreux, de la sortie d'Égypte à l'entrée en Terre sainte. D'autres figures bibliques reçoivent une attention très mesurée comme Saül (Tâlût), David et Goliath (Jâlût), Salomon et Jonas avec de brèves allusions éparses ici ou là ; en revanche, les grands prophètes auxquels la Bible consacre des livres entiers comme Isaïe, Jérémie et Ézéchiel sont complètement passés sous silence. L'absence flagrante de grandes figures bibliques comme les trois grands prophètes sus-cités a certes été comblée dans la littérature postcoranique, avec le genre littéraire appelé « les récits des prophètes », *qisas al-anbiyâ'*. Les récits de ce genre comprennent des chapitres sur des figures absentes du Coran aussi bien que des figures mentionnées fugitivement, parfois simplement par leur nom sans qu'il soit rien ajouté de plus, comme Élie (Ilyâs), Élisée (Alyasa‘) et Job (Ayyûb).

Une autre caractéristique de ces récits bibliques, ou plutôt semi-bibliques, du Coran tient à ce que dans son évocation des figures bibliques, celui-ci semble souvent plus tributaire de la littérature juive postbiblique (Talmud et Midrash) que de la Bible hébraïque elle-même. Avant de les examiner, quelques remarques s'imposent cependant sur la forme des récits coraniques. Leur première caractéristique, et la plus frappante, est qu'ils sont brefs, tronqués et elliptiques. Il est en effet très rare d'y trouver de longs récits continus et complets. Le même personnage – Noé, Abraham, Loth ou Moïse – est susceptible de se retrouver en plusieurs passages du Coran, mais chaque fois dans le cadre d'un récit partiel, de sorte que si l'on veut savoir ce qui caractérise tel ou tel personnage dans le Coran, il faudra recueillir ici et là des informations qui se répètent ou parfois se complètent. Par exemple, pour Noé, on trouve un récit détaillé dans la sourate 11 (verset 25-48), la sourate 7 (versets 59-64) et dans la sourate 26 (versets 105-121) qui incluent les remontrances de Noé à son peuple qui refuse de l'écouter et le Déluge qui s'abat en punition. Par ailleurs, dans de nombreuses autres sourates, Noé est mentionné brièvement en relation avec quelques détails de sa vie ou celle de sa famille, par exemple en 66 : 10, où sa femme et la femme de Lot sont qualifiées de traîtresses, ou en 23 : 25, où il est dit que Noé est accusé par les siens d'être possédé par les djinns – autant d'éléments qui n'apparaissent pas dans la Bible. Dans la Genèse, le dialogue entre Noé et le peuple est également absent, car c'est de Dieu que vient la décision d'envoyer le Déluge ; le Coran suit pour sa part un schéma qui met en relief la mission du prophète (ici Noé) qui fustige son peuple à cause de ses péchés et devant son durcissement annonce le châtiment.

L'une des explications quant à la nature elliptique des récits coraniques est que le Coran n'envisage pas de raconter toute l'histoire de telle ou telle figure biblique mais se contente de l'évoquer devant un public qui la connaît déjà ; c'est pourquoi des allusions suffisent. La racine *dh-k-r*, équivalant à l'hébreu *z-k-r*, « rappeler, se rappeler », revient ainsi près de trois cents fois, comme un leitmotiv : « Rappelez-vous ce qui a été dit… » Cette tendance se rencontre même dans les introductions à ces cycles de récits, par exemple *udhkur fî-l-kitâb*, « Rappelle dans le Livre… ! », en 19 : 16 pour ouvrir l'histoire de Marie / Myriam ; au verset 41 pour l'histoire d'Abraham ; au verset 51 pour celle de Moïse ; au verset 54 pour celle d'Ismaël ; et au verset 56 pour celle d'Idrîs, qui est identifié à Hénoch. La mention du nom du prophète amène le récit de son histoire. Seule celle de Joseph fait exception, la sourate le concernant étant particulièrement longue et détaillée – ce qui n'est d'ailleurs pas sans parallèle avec la Torah, où le récit de Joseph, particulièrement long (quatorze chapitres sur les cinquante que compte la Genèse), fait figure de véritable roman.

Un autre trait caractéristique du Coran est qu'il omet souvent de mentionner le nom des héros du récit. Lorsqu'il évoque Caïn et Abel par exemple, il les désigne simplement comme « les deux fils d'Adam ». De même à propos de Joseph et ses frères, le Coran ne nomme aucun des frères de Joseph, mais seulement son père Jacob, Joseph lui-même ainsi que celle que la Genèse connaît seulement comme la « femme de Putiphar », le ministre égyptien auquel Joseph avait été vendu comme esclave et que le Coran surnomme *imra'at al-'azîz* (« la femme du Puissant »).

Autre trait caractéristique des récits coraniques, le fait qu'y soient incluses des injonctions morales et des réprimandes à l'intention des auditeurs et lecteurs. Cette préoccupation explique sans doute qu'ils négligent les faits concernant les personnages : ce ne sont pas les récits en eux-mêmes qui ont de l'importance, mais la leçon qu'on peut et doit en tirer. Les prophètes du Coran, dont la majorité sinon tous sont aussi considérés comme prophètes dans la tradition juive, sont appelés « annonciateurs » (*mubashirûn*) et « avertisseurs » (*mundhirûn*). Tel est donc l'essentiel de leur mission et, par conséquent, celle de Muhammad, qui est leur ultime continuateur : annoncer la parole de Dieu et mettre en garde contre toute infraction. Ainsi Noé, qui est vu comme un prophète dans le Coran (à la différence de la Bible où il ne réussit pas à se faire entendre et semble presque muet), est un prédicateur qui ne cesse de parler, de réprimander et de mettre en garde. Contrairement à la Bible, le Coran ne dit rien des fils de Noé et ignore leurs noms ; seul l'un d'eux est l'interlocuteur de son père, qui le tance vertement.

Examinons maintenant quelques récits bibliques et de quelle manière ils sont repris dans le Coran. Il est clair que tout choix ne peut donner qu'une image incomplète. Les exemples que nous avons retenus permettront de mieux évaluer le lien entre les récits coraniques et leurs parallèles dans les sources juives.

Caïn et Abel

Le Coran, on l'a vu, ne mentionne pas leurs noms mais les évoque de façon vague : « les deux fils d'Adam » (5 : 27). C'est la tradition musulmane postcoranique qui les désignera au moyen d'une paire de noms unis par la rime : Hâbîl et

Qâbîl, tantôt dans cet ordre, tantôt dans l'ordre inverse.

Pour l'essentiel, l'histoire des deux frères telle qu'on la trouve dans le Coran (5 : 27-32) est analogue au récit biblique (Genèse 4 : 1-16), mais elle est caractérisée par une plus grande concision. D'après la version coranique, les deux fils apportèrent un sacrifice à Dieu qui agréa uniquement l'offrande de l'un d'entre eux. Contrairement à la Bible, le Coran ne précise ni l'identité de celui qui offrit son sacrifice, ni la nature de celui-ci. De la phrase coranique selon laquelle « Dieu n'agrée que les offrandes de ceux qui le craignent », on peut déduire que l'un des deux frères, à savoir Caïn (comme l'affirment la Bible ainsi que la tradition musulmane), vit son offrande refusée parce qu'il n'était pas mû par la crainte de Dieu. En outre, à l'instar du récit de la Genèse, la tradition post-coranique, comme d'habitude plus prolixe, nous fournit davantage de détails sur les causes de la colère de Caïn, qui semblent clairement reprises des traditions midrashiques juives : celui-ci, qui s'adonnait à l'agriculture, choisit comme offrande les moins beaux parmi les fruits qu'il avait fait pousser, tandis qu'Abel, berger, apporta les animaux les plus remarquables de son troupeau. Que Dieu ait agréé le sacrifice d'Abel alors qu'il avait refusé celui de Caïn excita la colère de ce dernier et l'incita à tuer son frère.

Le texte coranique et les sources postbibliques juives font état de deux ajouts au récit biblique de manière analogique. Le premier concerne le jugement moral porté sur le meurtre, et le second la question de la sépulture de la victime. Le Coran dénonce la gravité du meurtre en disant :

> Voilà pourquoi Nous avons prescrit aux fils d'Israël : « Celui qui a tué un homme (*nafs*) qui lui-même n'a pas tué, ou qui n'a pas commis de violence sur la terre, est considéré comme s'il avait tué tous les hommes » (5 : 32).

Cette équivalence entre le meurtre d'un seul homme et l'anéantissement de l'humanité tout entière apparaît déjà dans l'exégèse rabbinique ancienne des reproches que Dieu adresse à Caïn en Genèse 4, 10, comme le commente la Mishna[2] :

> … C'est pour enseigner que tout homme qui détruit une seule personne[3], l'Écriture lui impute (le crime) comme s'il avait anéanti un univers entier ; par contre, tout homme qui maintient en vie une seule personne est comme s'il avait maintenu en vie un univers entier (Mishna, traité *Sanhedrin* 4 : 5).

Le Coran précise encore la manière dont le premier meurtrier de l'humanité a été amené à donner une sépulture à sa victime :

> Dieu envoya surgir un corbeau qui se mit à gratter la terre pour lui montrer comment cacher le cadavre de son frère. Il dit : « Malheur à moi ! Suis-je incapable d'être comme ce corbeau et de cacher le cadavre de mon frère ? » (5 : 31).

Ces détails ne figurent pas dans la Bible, mais présente des analogies certaines avec le Midrash Tanhuma (sur Genèse 10) qui dit :

> Lorsque Caïn tua Abel, ce dernier était resté couché par terre et Caïn ne savait comment faire. Dieu y fit passer deux corbeaux se bataillant ; l'un tua l'autre, puis creusa avec ses pattes un trou dans le sol et y enterra le mort. S'inspirant de cet exemple, Caïn creusa dans la terre et y ensevelit Abel[4].

La structure générale de ce récit coranique, qui adjoint à un noyau biblique des éléments qui ont leur source dans la littérature rabbinique, n'est pas rare dans le Coran.

Abraham

Parmi les prophètes bibliques, Abraham occupe une place centrale dans le Coran. La sourate 14 porte même son nom, bien que seuls quelques versets (35-40) y parlent de lui. Les informations le concernant sont, comme c'est souvent le cas pour d'autres personnages, dispersées à travers le texte. Parmi les éléments connus par la Bible, on trouve : la visite des trois anges venus lui annoncer la naissance d'un fils (11 : 69-76, avec un peu moins de détails que dans la Genèse) ; la dispute d'Abraham avec Dieu à propos de Sodome, bien que le nom de la ville ne soit pas cité et qu'il y soit simplement fait mention du « peuple de Lot » (*qawm Lût*, 11 : 74-76 et 29 : 32) ; le sacrifice des oiseaux (2 : 260) qui renvoie à « l'alliance entre les morceaux (*berit bein ha-betarim*) » (Genèse 15 : 1-21), et surtout le sacrifice du fils d'Abraham (37 : 102-112).

C'est en effet cet épisode biblique qui a pris une place importante dans le Coran, où il est présenté d'une manière différente du récit de la Genèse. Tout d'abord, il y est résumé à l'extrême. Abraham n'y reçoit pas d'ordre divin pour sacrifier son fils. Il dit à celui-ci : « Ô mon fils ! Je me suis vu moi-même en songe et je t'immolais ; qu'en penses-tu ? » Et son fils lui répond : « Ô mon père ! Fais ce qui t'est ordonné. Tu me trouveras patient » (37 : 102). Le fils accepte son sort sans hésiter, il ne demande même pas, comme Isaac dans la Bible : « Voici le feu et le bois ; mais où est la brebis pour l'holocauste ?! » (Genèse 22 : 6). Dans les deux récits, Dieu arrête la main d'Abraham qui s'apprêtait à sacrifier son fils et c'est un bélier qui est sacrifié à la place de celui-ci. La plus grande différence entre les deux récits réside dans l'identité du fils. La Genèse précise : « Prends ton fils, ton unique, celui que tu aimes, Isaac ; et rends-toi au pays de Moria, où tu l'offriras en holocauste sur l'une des hauteurs que je t'indiquerai » (Genèse 22 : 2). Plusieurs *midrashim* soulignent la gradation dramatique dans la désignation de la victime :

> Dieu lui dit : « Je t'en prie, prends ton fils… » Il lui répond : « Mais j'ai deux fils ! – Ton unique… – Mais chacun est unique pour sa mère ! – Celui que tu aimes… – Y aurait-il des frontières dans mes entrailles ? –… Isaac. » Pourquoi Dieu ne lui a-t-il pas révélé le nom dès le départ ? Pour accroître l'affection d'Abraham envers Isaac et accroître ainsi son mérite (Genèse Rabba 55 : 7).

Le Coran, pour sa part, et contrairement à ce qu'on croit souvent, ne précise pas l'identité du fils, évoquant juste « l'annonce d'un garçon doux et patient » (37 : 101) ; il est révélateur que la traduction « officielle » saoudienne de Muhammad Hamidullah se sente obligée de préciser, entre parenthèses, « Ismaïl ». Ce sont les exégètes qui, par la suite, ont cherché à répondre à cette question. Le grand compilateur Tabarî rapporte de nombreux avis dont beaucoup – et lui-même – penchent pour Isaac, dans la mesure où c'est Isaac, et non Ismaël, qui a fait l'objet d'une annonce divine. À l'inverse, plusieurs autres exégètes penchent pour Ismaël ; c'est désormais l'opinion la plus répandue dans l'islam, mais elle n'a jamais fait l'objet d'un consensus, et n'a pas toujours été majoritaire.

À côté des éléments bibliques qui, de toute évidence, concourent à l'édification de la figure coranique d'Abraham, le Coran emprunte aussi beaucoup à la littérature juive postbiblique. L'exemple le plus célèbre en est le débat d'Abraham avec les idolâtres de son temps dont il brise les statues (21 : 52-70 ; 29 : 24 ; 37 : 88-98), absent de la Genèse mais bien attesté dans le Midrash et très présent dans la culture juive comme geste fondateur du monothéisme d'Abraham (voir par exemple *Genèse Rabba* 38 : 13). Abraham commence par affirmer que la prosternation devant les idoles est chose vaine et de là il parvient à la croyance en un Dieu unique et au rejet d'autres pouvoirs, que ce soient les astres ou les idoles :

> Lorsque la nuit l'enveloppa, il (Abraham) vit une étoile et il dit : « Voici mon Seigneur ! » Mais il dit, lorsqu'elle eut disparu : « Je n'aime pas ceux qui disparaissent. » Lorsqu'il vit la lune qui se levait, il dit : « Voici mon Seigneur ! » Mais il dit, lorsqu'elle

> eut disparu : « Si mon Seigneur ne me dirige pas, je serai au nombre des égarés. » Lorsqu'il vit le soleil qui se levait, il dit : « Voici mon Seigneur ! C'est le plus grand ! » Mais il dit, lorsqu'il eut disparu : « Ô mon peuple ! Je désavoue ce que vous associez à Dieu. Je tourne mon visage, comme un vrai croyant, vers celui qui crée les cieux et la terre. Je ne suis pas au nombre des polythéistes » (6 : 76-79).

La découverte de la vérité monothéiste par le biais de la méditation sur les phénomènes cosmiques est un thème abondamment attesté dans la littérature juive pré-coranique. Le récit coranique rapporté ici rappelle fortement le Livre des Jubilés (XII, 16-18), antérieur à l'ère chrétienne, ainsi que divers midrashim, comme le passage de Genèse Rabba (39 : 1), qui compare apparemment le monde à une tour illuminée, ce dont Abraham déduit qu'il doit y avoir quelqu'un qui gouverne cette tour, et c'est alors que Dieu se révèle à lui en lui disant : « C'est moi qui gouverne cette tour », c'est-à-dire le monde. Il faut encore noter qu'en retour, la formulation coranique, plus explicitement cosmologique, a été par la suite largement reprise et acculturée chez les auteurs juifs, notamment par Maïmonide.

Selon divers chercheurs, cette vision d'Abraham en tant que fondateur du monothéisme doit beaucoup au tournant opéré par Muhammad après l'hégire. Dans la plupart des sourates de La Mecque, Abraham est présenté comme un prophète comme les autres, sans statut particulier. En revanche, pendant la période de Médine, après la rupture entre Muhammad et les juifs, Abraham devient une figure centrale et un exemple aux yeux de Muhammad. Le Coran proclame :

> « Abraham n'était ni juif ni chrétien mais il était un vrai croyant soumis à Dieu (*hanîf muslim*) ; il n'était pas au nombre des polythéistes » (3 : 67).

Soulignons au passage que le terme *muslim* appliqué à Abraham ne signifie pas encore ici qu'il appartient à l'islam, mais qu'il est un vrai croyant soumis à Dieu[5]. Tel est aussi le sens de *hanîf* qui lui est associé, un terme d'origine syriaque qui, dans le Coran, signifie « monothéiste pur, non affilié à une religion particulière[6] ». L'idée sous-jacente est la volonté de présenter Abraham comme le père du monothéisme et d'ôter ainsi aux juifs et aux chrétiens leur hégémonie sur Abraham et leur prétention à voir en lui le père de leur religion respective. À partir du Coran se joue tout un glissement de sens et d'identifications successives, où la *hanîfiyya*, le « monothéisme non confessionnel », est identifiée à l'*islâm*, la « soumission à Dieu », lequel devient l'islam comme religion. Ce dernier ne se pense donc pas seulement comme une nouvelle phase de l'histoire de la révélation divine dans le monde, mais aussi et peut-être surtout comme un retour à un monothéisme originel en amont des divisions religieuses dont les conflits entre juifs et chrétiens sont la triste illustration. Muhammad se présente donc autant comme un nouvel Abraham qu'un nouveau Moïse. Le verset coranique *Inna l-dîn 'inda Llâhi l-islâm*, « la religion aux yeux de Dieu est l'*islâm* (3 : 19), est lu par 'Abd Allâh b. Mas'ûd, un célèbre compagnon de Muhammad, comme *Inna l-dîn 'inda Llâhi l-hanîfiyya*, « la religion aux yeux de Dieu est la religion des *hanîfs*[7] », que la suite du verset oppose clairement aux disputes théologiques qui divisent juifs et chrétiens.

Si Abraham est une figure unificatrice, le père commun du judaïsme, du christianisme et de l'islam comme l'indiquent nombre d'éléments bibliques et midrashiques intégrés dans sa biographie telle qu'elle ressort du Coran, il est aussi une figure propre à l'islam dans la mesure où Muhammad se voit en prophète *arabe* dont Abraham serait l'archétype. Ainsi, certains épisodes de la vie d'Abraham sont censés se passer dans la péninsule Arabique. Lui-même le proclame : « Notre Seigneur ! J'ai établi une partie de mes descendants dans une vallée stérile, auprès de ta Maison sacrée » (14 : 37). La « vallée stérile » est celle de La Mecque où se trouve la Ka'ba, appelée dans ce verset la « Maison sacrée ». Dieu en indique l'emplacement à Abraham et lui enjoint d'appeler au pèlerinage : « Appelle les hommes au Pèlerinage : ils viendront à toi, à pied ou sur toute monture élancée. Ils viendront par des chemins encaissés pour témoigner des bienfaits qui leur ont été accordés pour invoquer le nom de Dieu aux jours fixés... » (22 : 27). Abraham et son fils Ismaël sont présentés comme ceux qui ont restauré la Ka'ba (2 : 127).

L'islamisation de la Ka'ba et du pèlerinage à La Mecque et ses environs est donc rattachée par le Coran à Abraham. La tradition postcoranique l'accentue encore : la course (*sa'y*) imposée aux pèlerins entre les deux collines al-Safâ et al-Marwa rappelle celle de Hagar après qu'elle eut été chassée par Sarah avec Ismaël quand elle cherchait de l'eau pour abreuver son fils, comme le rapporte la Genèse ; le puits qu'elle aurait alors trouvé sur l'indication d'un ange, toujours selon la Bible, serait celui de Zamzam, proche de la Ka'ba. On voit donc comment des éléments importants de l'histoire biblique d'Abraham, conjugués avec d'autres typiquement musulmans, concourent à créer l'image d'un prophète arabe vivant et agissant dans la péninsule Arabique. C'est ainsi que La Mecque, jadis lieu de culte païen, se transforme en sanctuaire du monothéisme, et par là prépare la voie à Muhammad, dont la mission est de ramener les Arabes – voire toute l'humanité – à l'*islâm* déjà annoncé par Abraham mais entre-temps oublié par les idolâtres.

Joseph

Le récit biblique concernant Joseph constitue, lui aussi, un bel exemple du traitement des sources bibliques et postbibliques juives dans le Coran et l'exégèse musulmane. En effet, l'histoire de Joseph telle qu'elle est rapportée dans les textes musulmans entre très souvent en résonance avec des *midrashim* connus, qui s'intéressent notamment à différents moments du récit de la Genèse : Joseph réprimandé par son père au sujet de ses rêves ; le désaccord entre les frères sur son sort ; sa vente en Égypte ; son erreur en prison de s'en remettre au grand échanson plutôt qu'à Dieu seul. Si l'on menait une lecture très attentive de tous les textes exégétiques musulmans, nul doute que l'on découvrirait encore beaucoup d'autres vestiges du Midrash.

Il faut noter la différence entre le début des deux narrations biblique et coranique. La Genèse commence par évoquer la préférence de Jacob pour son fils Joseph, ce qui suscite la jalousie compréhensible de ses frères, et poursuit avec les songes de Joseph (celui des épis et celui du soleil, de la lune et des étoiles qui se prosternent devant lui), dont l'interprétation ne peut qu'accroître la haine de ses frères. Le deuxième songe provoque une réprimande de la part de Jacob : « "Que signifie, lui dit-il, ce songe que tu as eu ? Va-t-il falloir que nous venions, moi, ta mère et tes frères, nous prosterner à terre devant toi ?" Ses frères furent alors jaloux de lui, mais son père garda le souvenir de cet événement » (Genèse 37 : 10-11). Le récit biblique donne une base à la haine des frères qui va se manifester plus tard lorsqu'ils vont se concerter, en se demandant s'il faut le tuer, le jeter dans une citerne ou le vendre comme esclave.

Le récit coranique ignore pour sa part la préférence de Jacob, et c'est à son père seul que Joseph raconte son rêve sur le soleil, la lune et les étoiles qui se prosternent à ses pieds. C'est alors que Jacob met en garde son fils et lui déconseille de raconter ce songe à ses frères, de peur qu'ils ne s'en prennent à lui ; il n'exclut pas quelque machination de Satan. Les frères concluent que leur père préfère Joseph et son frère (à savoir Benjamin, dont le nom n'est d'ailleurs pas cité) sans que la raison en soit explicitement donnée : « Joseph et son frère sont plus chers à notre père, bien que nous soyons plus nombreux. Notre père se trouve dans un égarement manifeste » (12 : 7).

Le Coran omet aussi de dire que c'est Jacob qui a envoyé Joseph trouver ses frères, le faisant ainsi tomber dans un piège qui entraînera son esclavage (Genèse 37 : 13-14). Ce sont ses frères qui insistent pour que Jacob leur envoie Joseph : « Ô notre père, pourquoi n'as-tu pas confiance en nous au sujet de Joseph... Envoie-le demain avec nous ; il s'ébattra, il jouera tandis que nous veillerons sur lui » (12 : 12-13). Ainsi, malgré de fortes similitudes dans la trame principale, les deux récits divergent sensiblement sur certains points. La divergence la plus évidente concerne la tentative de séduction de Joseph par la femme de Putiphar, qui, dans le Coran, est appelée *imra'at al-'azîz* (« la femme du puissant ») et qui deviendra dans la littérature arabe l'héroïne de leur amour impossible, dans le roman classique *Yûsuf et Zulaykha*.

Le Coran dit : « Elle pensait certainement à lui et il [Joseph] aurait pensé à elle s'il n'avait pas vu la claire preuve de son Seigneur » (12 : 24). Alors que selon le récit biblique, Joseph résiste vaillamment à la tentation – céder serait un péché contre Dieu et contre son maître –, selon le Coran, Joseph était sur le point de céder. Abraham Geiger et à sa suite d'autres chercheurs ont attiré l'attention sur des similitudes entre ce passage du Coran et différents *midrashim* rapportés dans le Talmud tel celui-ci :

> « Elle le saisit par son vêtement en disant : Couche avec moi » (Genèse 39 : 12). À ce moment, Joseph entrevit par la fenêtre l'image de son père, qui lui dit : « Joseph ! Les noms de tes frères sont appelés à être inscrits sur les pierres du pectoral du grand prêtre et toi parmi eux. Veux-tu que ton nom soit effacé ? » (Talmud de Babylone, traité *Sota* 36b[8]).

La divergence entre le récit biblique et le récit coranique peut donc s'expliquer par une source postbiblique, en l'occurrence le Midrash. Dans le Coran comme dans le Midrash, c'est l'apparition miraculeuse de son père qui, à la dernière minute, empêche Joseph de céder à la tentation. « La claire preuve de son seigneur » (*burhâna rabbihi)* qu'évoque le Coran ne renverrait donc pas nécessairement à une manifestation divine mais plutôt à une vision de l'image de Jacob.

L'apparition de Jacob à son fils Joseph se retrouve chez plusieurs commentateurs du Coran. Ainsi, on peut lire : « Lorsque Joseph vit face à lui l'image de son père en train de se mordre les doigts, il sursauta, et de l'eau sortit [euphémisme pour une émission de sperme] de son orteil[9]. » Cette description énigmatique (à savoir du sperme émanant de l'orteil) entre elle aussi en résonance avec un *midrash* peu connu (quoique la littérature kabbalistique en fasse grand cas). En explication de la formule de bénédiction de Jacob à

Joseph : « les bras de ses mains se sont tendus (*wa-yafozzu zero'ei yadaw*) » (Genèse 49 : 24), le Talmud raconte que Joseph, pour maîtriser son désir, « a enfoncé ses mains dans le sol et une émission de sperme (*zera'*) est sortie des ongles de ses doigts ». Cette lecture rabbinique est provoquée par le pléonasme « les bras de ses mains » (*zero'ei yadaw*), qui est alors lu *zera' yadaw*, « la semence de ses mains ». Ce midrash est passé dans la tradition exégétique musulmane en perdant ce qui la justifiait dans le verset biblique pour devenir un élément « légendaire ».

Une autre anecdote mérite de retenir l'attention. Selon le récit coranique, après avoir confessé sa faute, la femme de Putiphar se justifie devant les femmes de la ville et fait comprendre la tentation qu'elle a subie en les mettant à leur tour à l'épreuve :

> Les femmes disaient en ville : « La femme du Grand Intendant s'est éprise de son serviteur : il l'a rendue éperdument amoureuse de lui ; nous la voyons complétement égarée ! » Après avoir entendu leurs propos, celle-ci leur adressa des invitations, puis elle leur fit préparer un repas et elle donna à chacune d'elles un couteau. Elle dit alors à Joseph : « Parais devant elles ! » Quand elles le virent, elles le trouvèrent si beau qu'elles se firent des coupures aux mains. Elles dirent : « À Dieu ne plaise ! Celui-ci

n'est pas un mortel ; ce ne peut être qu'un ange plein de noblesse » (12 : 30-31).

Si on ne trouve aucune mention de cet épisode dans la Bible, on le retrouve bien dans le Midrash Tanhuma et d'autres sources midrashiques :

> Les femmes égyptiennes se réunirent chez la femme de Putiphar afin de voir la beauté de Joseph. La maîtresse de maison donna à chacune d'elles des cédrats et un couteau, puis elle appela Joseph et le plaça devant ses invitées. À la vue de la beauté de Joseph, elles se coupèrent les doigts. La femme de Putiphar leur dit alors : Voilà ce qui vous arrive en une heure, et moi qui le vois tout le temps, combien plus suis-je tentée ! (Midrash Tanhuma, *parashat Wayeshev* 5[10]).

Dans son article « Joseph among the Ishmaelites : Q 12 in light of Syriac sources[11] », consacré à une analyse approfondie de l'histoire de Joseph dans le Coran, Joseph Witztum remarque que, outre les sources juives, certaines sources chrétiennes, notamment les Pères de l'Église syriaques, doivent aussi être prises en compte pour expliquer le Coran. Cet article examine avec précision d'autres aspects de l'histoire de Joseph en les comparant à des sources syriaques datant pour la plupart du IVe et du Ve siècle, l'une écrite en prose et les autres en poésie rythmée. Ce sont des homélies d'Ephrem (mort en 373), de Balaï (actif au début du Ve siècle) et de Jacob de Séroug (mort en 503). Aux comparaisons que l'on peut faire entre le récit coranique sur Joseph et ses frères et les sources juives postbibliques, Witztum ajoute des comparaisons convaincantes du Coran avec les sources syriaques qui impliquent une plus grande proximité car elles diffèrent toutes du récit biblique sur des points précis : mêmes omissions, mêmes élaborations, mêmes modifications, sans que cela coïncide avec les sources juives.

Un exemple d'omission est donné dans le début du récit mentionné plus haut. Ni le récit coranique ni les sources syriaques ne commencent avec la préférence marquée par Jacob à Joseph et par la haine provoquée chez les frères par le comportement de Joseph et de son père. Tout ce qui pourrait être reproché à Joseph y est gommé et l'histoire commence avec les rêves de Joseph mais présentés différemment. Alors que dans la Bible le héros raconte son premier rêve à ses frères, puis son deuxième rêve à son père qui le réprimande, dans les sources syriaques et le Coran, Joseph veut d'abord comprendre le sens des rêves qu'il rapporte seulement à son père, et celui-ci lui interdit de les raconter à ses frères, ce qui prouve qu'il y croit.

Quant à la tentative de séduction par la femme de Putiphar, selon la Genèse, elle aurait calomnié et fait jeter en prison Joseph, mais elle ne réapparaît pas par la suite ; tandis que dans le Coran (12 : 50-54), comme nous l'avons vu plus haut, ainsi que dans les sources syriaques, cette femme confesse sa faute et exprime son repentir. Malgré ces parallèles, on trouve aussi quelques différences. Ainsi les sources syriaques mettent-elles l'accent sur le pardon de Joseph et sa générosité, tandis que le Coran souligne l'innocence de Joseph tout en montrant le repentir de la femme de Putiphar.

Witztum relève aussi le rôle typologique de ce récit. À la suite d'autres chercheurs, il souligne le double but du récit coranique sur Joseph : encourager Muhammad dans sa lutte contre ses rivaux qui sont ainsi mis en garde contre le sort qui attend les non-croyants, et en outre présenter le prophète comme l'héritier de la tradition biblique. La lecture de l'histoire de Joseph prend également dans la littérature syriaque un tour typologique : Joseph joue le rôle de Jésus et les frères (les loups du récit) celui des juifs, ainsi que dans l'exégèse coranique où les ennemis sont non pas les juifs mais les gens de La Mecque.

David

David est une figure importante du Coran bien qu'il comporte peu de détails à son sujet. Il y est présenté comme un prophète et un roi, mais tout ce qui est rapporté dans les livres de Samuel, des Chroniques et des Psaumes n'est que très peu répercuté dans le Coran. On n'y trouve que de brèves allusions à ses luttes internes et ses combats contre les ennemis d'Israël, notamment les Philistins (2 : 248-251). Le seul combat mentionné est celui qui le met aux prises avec Goliath (Jâlût). De ses nombreux fils et des rivalités qui les opposent entre eux ou à lui, seul le nom de Salomon (Sulaymân) est retenu. Il est dit dans le Coran qu'après le combat contre Goliath, « Dieu accorda à David la royauté et la sagesse ; il lui enseigna ce qu'il voulut » (2 : 251). Dans ce verset, la sagesse se repère au don de la prophétie. Que Dieu ait donné la science à David et à son fils Salomon (27 : 15) signifie selon les exégètes du Coran qu'ils ont reçu la faculté de comprendre le langage des oiseaux et des animaux, comme cela ressort de certains *midrashim*. Dieu aurait fait de David son lieutenant (*khalîfa*) sur terre (38 : 26), ce qu'il n'avait accordé qu'à Adam (2 : 30). Il lui aurait aussi conféré le privilège de distinguer entre la vérité et le mensonge. C'est pourquoi David est représenté comme un juge siégeant auprès de son fils Salomon :

> Et David, et Salomon, quand tous deux arbitraient au sujet d'un champ cultivé où des moutons erraient la nuit. Nous avons été témoin de leur jugement. Nous avons fait comprendre cette affaire à Salomon. Nous avons donné à tous deux la Sagesse et la Science (21 : 78).

David occupe enfin une place à part, aux côtés de Moïse, de Jésus et de Muhammad, en ce qu'il a reçu du Dieu un Livre révélé, *al-Zabûr*, que l'on identifie généralement aux Psaumes (4 : 163 et 17 : 55).

La plus longue référence à David dans le Coran se trouve dans la sourate 38. Elle s'ouvre sur les railleries des Arabes à l'encontre de Muhammad : ils lui reprochent de vouloir fabriquer une seule divinité à partir des nombreuses autres auxquelles ils sont attachés. En réaction à la prédication de Muhammad qui leur annonce l'approche du Jugement dernier, ils s'écrient : « Notre Seigneur ! Envoie-nous rapidement notre part avant le jour du Jugement » (38 : 16). Aussitôt après, Muhammad leur rappelle « Notre serviteur David, doué de force et plein de repentir » (38 : 17) et fait allusion à l'épisode de la relation entre David et Bethsabée en reprenant l'image du berger riche qui veut s'accaparer l'unique brebis du berger pauvre.

Le prophète Nathan, qui dans la Bible est l'auteur de cette parabole et qui réprimande David pour le grave péché commis, n'est pas mentionné dans le Coran et la parabole se transforme en conversation entre deux hommes qui passent en jugement devant David :

> L'histoire des plaideurs t'est-elle parvenue ? Ils montèrent au sanctuaire. Ils pénétrèrent auprès de David qui en fut effrayé et ils dirent : « N'aie pas peur ! Nous sommes deux plaideurs, injustes l'un envers l'autre. Juge-nous en toute justice ; ne sois pas partial, conduis-nous sur la voie droite. Celui-ci est mon frère : il possède quatre-vingt-dix-neuf brebis, et moi, je n'ai qu'une seule brebis. Il m'a dit : "Confie-la-moi" ; puis il a eu le dessus dans la discussion ! » David dit : « Il t'a lésé en te demandant ta brebis en plus de ses brebis. » Beaucoup d'associés se causent des torts réciproques à l'exception du petit nombre de ceux qui croient et qui font des œuvres bonnes. David comprit que Nous avions seulement voulu l'éprouver. Il demanda pardon à son Seigneur ; il tomba prosterné et se repentit. Nous lui avons pardonné. Il a près de Nous une place et un beau lieu en retour. Ô David ! Nous avons fait de toi un lieutenant sur la terre ; juge les hommes selon la justice ; ne suis pas ta passion, elle t'égarerait loin du chemin de Dieu (38 : 21-26).

Quiconque ne connaîtrait pas l'histoire du péché de David qui a pris l'épouse d'Urie le Hittite (II Samuel 11 : 1-27) et la parabole de la brebis du pauvre qui lui est appliquée pour cela (*ibid.* 12 : 1-25) ne peut rien comprendre à ce passage du Coran. La seule allusion qui y est faite est la demande de pardon de David sans que l'on sache de quoi il est coupable, ainsi que l'exhortation à ne pas suivre sa passion, dont on ne peut savoir d'ailleurs s'il s'agit d'un conseil moral d'ordre général ou si elle répond à une infraction particulière. Il ne fait pas de doute que, dans ce cas aussi, la clef de ce passage se trouve dans le récit biblique.

Il faut aussi noter encore une importante différence d'avec le récit biblique. Alors que la Bible ne cherche pas à taire certains détails gênants de la vie des héros et présente aussi bien leurs faiblesses que leurs qualités, le Coran les évite autant que possible. Cette tendance s'est même développée par la suite et est devenue une doctrine établie connue sous le nom de *'ismat al-anbiyâ'* (« l'infaillibilité des prophètes ») ; elle implique que les prophètes ne sont exposés ni au péché ni à l'erreur. Les sages de l'islam ont fait un effort considérable pour purifier les prophètes et d'autres héros – en particulier les Imâms dans le shî'isme – de tout ce qui pourrait entacher leur image dans le Coran ou dans les traditions extérieures parvenues dans la littérature musulmane[12].

Cette tendance à donner une image impeccable des héros de l'histoire sainte, tandis que les antagonistes voient leur portrait noirci, est cependant déjà bien présente dans la littérature juive post-biblique.

La volonté de laver David du péché d'adultère avec Bethsabée se rencontre aussi dans la littérature rabbinique en contradiction évidente avec la lettre du texte qui abonde en détails et nous dit même qu'après les remontrances du prophète Nathan, David a reconnu sa faute (II Samuel 12 : 13 et Psaume 51). Le Talmud fait des contorsions exégétiques pour innocenter David, dans une formule célèbre : « Celui qui dit que David a péché se trompe purement et simplement[13]. » Le Talmud explique ainsi que, sur le plan légal sinon moral, David n'a commis aucune transgression, en particulier parce qu'Urie, avant de partir à la guerre, avait divorcé de Bethsabée afin qu'elle puisse se remarier s'il disparaissait au combat sans qu'on puisse témoigner de sa mort. David n'a donc pas couché avec une femme mariée ; tout au plus lui reproche-t-on d'avoir voulu aller trop vite pour s'unir avec celle qui lui était destinée « depuis les six jours de la Création ». Ce dédouanement de David, qui commence à poindre dans le Coran, est largement développé dans la littérature postcoranique. Pierre Lory résume ainsi l'attitude musulmane quant à la faute de David :

> La faute si grave de David ne résulte plus d'un penchant charnel incontrôlé : c'est une épreuve induite par Dieu, dont le but est le progrès spirituel et moral du prophète. David en ressort grandi, malgré la gravité de son acte. Par ailleurs, et de façon plus secondaire, la possibilité qu'un prophète de plus haut niveau spirituel puisse en même temps disposer d'un harem important a permis aux musulmans de réfuter les critiques de certains juifs médinois concernant le nombre des épouses de Mahomet[14].

A. H. Johns souligne le lien entre la figure de David et Muhammad. Selon lui, la mention de David n'est pas fortuite ; elle a pour but de marquer une analogie entre eux et de faire de David une source d'inspiration pour Muhammad. Tous deux sont prophètes et subissent les railleries de leur peuple, mais de même que David a réussi dans toutes ses entreprises à l'intérieur comme à l'extérieur, de même Muhammad connaîtra le succès[15].

Saül / Tâlût

Saül, premier roi d'Israël, est mentionné dans le Coran (2 : 247 et 249) sous le nom de Tâlût, sur le modèle de Jâlût, le nom arabe de Goliath qui apparaît tout de suite après – on trouve d'autres noms formés selon la même structure, comme les deux couples Ya'jûj wa-Ma'jûj (Gog et Magog) ou bien les anges Hârût et Mârût (2 : 102), déchus après s'être compromis avec les filles des humains, dans la reprise coranique de Genèse 6 : 4 et de ses amplifications midrashiques. Tous les commentateurs partagent l'avis selon lequel le nom Tâlût vient de la racine arabe *t-w-l*, qui signifie « être grand ». Il semble que le nom arabe conserve le souvenir de la haute taille de Saül que la Bible décrit ainsi : « Pas un fils d'Israël plus beau que lui ; et il dépassait de la tête tout le peuple » (I Samuel 9 : 2). Seule la tradition postcoranique, comme par exemple l'ouvrage d'al-Tha'labî, *Qisas al-anbiyâ'* (« Récits des prophètes »), conserve son nom hébreu, accolé à celui de son père, tel qu'il apparaît dans la Bible : Sha'ûl ben. Qîsh[16].

L'histoire de Saül, comme celle d'autres figures bibliques apparaissant dans le Coran, est racontée avec une grande concision. Dans un passage formé de seulement quatre versets (2 : 246-250), on trouve plusieurs éléments sur lesquels la Bible s'étend fort longuement : la demande que fit le peuple d'Israël à son prophète (le nom de ce dernier n'est pas précisé non plus, mais la tradition exégétique l'identifie généralement à Samuel, conformément à la Bible) de lui donner un roi ; l'élection par Saül d'un groupe d'hommes issu de son peuple pour partir au combat contre leurs ennemis ; et enfin le choix qui se porta sur David pour affronter Goliath et la victoire de David sur ce dernier[17].

La demande du peuple d'Israël à son prophète pour avoir un roi qui le dirigera lors de son combat contre l'ennemi concorde parfaitement avec le récit biblique se trouvant dans I Samuel 8 : 4-22. Cependant, le récit coranique diffère de ce dernier quant à la réaction du peuple à la nomination du souverain. La Bible ne fait allusion qu'à la réaction d'une minorité : « Toutefois il y eut des misérables pour dire : "À quoi cet homme pourrait-il nous servir ?" Aussi, par mépris, ne lui apportèrent-ils aucun présent » (I Samuel 10 : 27). Le Coran, en revanche, rapporte que la nomination de Saül / Tâlût suscita une opposition au sein de tout le peuple : « Comment aurait-il de l'autorité sur nous ? Nous avons plus de droit que lui à la royauté, et il n'a même pas l'avantage de la richesse » (2 : 247). Les commentateurs du Coran, tel Tabarî, expliquent que le peuple d'Israël fonda son opposition sur le fait que Tâlût appartenait à la tribu peu prestigieuse de Benjamin, puisque ne se distinguant ni par la prophétie (comme la tribu de Lévi), ni par la royauté (comme celle de Juda[18]).

Il est probable que la tradition expliquant l'opposition à Saül en raison de son ascendance soit l'écho des paroles que la Bible met dans la bouche de Saül lui-même. Lorsque Samuel lui annonce son élection comme roi d'Israël en lui disant : « À qui d'ailleurs doit revenir tout ce qu'Israël a de précieux ? N'est-ce pas à toi et à toute ta famille ? » (I Samuel 9 : 20), Saül réagit avec étonnement et humilité : « Je ne suis qu'un Benjaminite, de la plus petite tribu d'Israël ; et ma famille est la moindre de toutes les familles de Benjamin. Pourquoi me tenir pareil langage ? » (9 : 21).

En réaction à l'opposition du peuple d'Israël, nous rapporte le Coran, leur prophète leur rétorque fermement que « Dieu l'a choisi de préférence sur vous tous, et il lui a octroyé une supériorité sur vous grâce à la science et à la stature dont il est doué » (2 : 247). En outre, continue le verset, « Dieu donne sa royauté à qui Il veut », c'est-à-dire à Saül / Tâlût. Pour persuader les fils d'Israël de se soumettre à la royauté de Saül, Dieu place devant leurs yeux le signe de sa royauté : « Voici ce que sera le signe de sa royauté : l'arche viendra vers vous, portée par les anges. Elle contient une présence divine (*sakîna*) venue de votre Seigneur et une relique laissée par la famille de Moïse et par la famille d'Aaron » (2 : 248). R. Blachère remarque au sujet de ce passage : « Il est à peine besoin de souligner le parallèle établi ici entre le conseil des Israélites rejetant la royauté de Saül et le conseil des Mecquois et des juifs médinois refusant de reconnaître Mahomet[19]. »

Un autre épisode auquel fait allusion le Coran est l'élection des guerriers destinés à combattre les ennemis d'Israël. Le texte coranique ne nomme pas ces ennemis, mais la tradition postérieure précise qu'il s'agissait là des Cananéens ou des Amalécites, toujours en conformité donc avec le texte biblique. Tâlût choisit ses combattants en les soumettant à l'épreuve de boire de l'eau d'un fleuve : « "Dieu va sûrement vous éprouver à une rivière, dit Saül à ses hommes, et celui qui y boira ne fera partie des miens, et celui qui n'y boira pas sera des miens – à l'exception de celui qui puisera un peu d'eau avec la main". Ils burent ensuite, sauf un petit nombre d'entre eux » (2 : 249). Ceux qui burent l'eau, à savoir la majorité du peuple, prouvèrent immédiatement qu'il n'était pas en leur pouvoir de combattre Goliath, mais la minorité qui comptait, d'après la tradition, 310 hommes ou un peu plus, était prête à combattre une armée bien plus nombreuse, et même à la vaincre. Il est à noter que cet épisode est rapporté dans la Bible non au sujet de Saül mais à celui de Gédéon, qui fit subir une épreuve semblable à ses guerriers avant de partir combattre les Madianites (Juges 7 : 4-7).

La victoire du peuple sous la conduite de David sur ses ennemis conduits par Goliath est racontée très brièvement ; de plus, la dimension dramatique du combat tel que le décrit la Bible (I Samuel 17-18) est complètement occultée. Le Coran rapporte en quelques mots que « David tua Goliath. Dieu accorda à David la royauté et la sagesse ; il lui enseigna ce qu'il voulut » (2 : 251). Cependant cette lacune, ressentie fortement par la tradition musulmane, est largement comblée dans la littérature postcoranique. De nombreux éléments concernant les relations de Saül et David racontés dans la Bible et dans le Midrash sont rapportés dans la littérature exégétique et historiographique musulmane, par exemple dans la monumentale *Histoire universelle* de Tabarî. Ces ouvrages regorgent de récits colorés sur la jalousie de Saül à l'égard de David après la victoire éclatante de celui-ci sur Goliath ou encore sur la poursuite de David par Saül ; ils se distinguent même par des nuances absentes du Midrash. Remarquable entre toutes est la tradition racontant que Saül reconnut avoir commis une faute en ressentant de la jalousie envers David, et que pour se faire pardonner il fut prêt à sacrifier à

Dieu sa vie et celle de ses enfants dans le combat contre les ennemis de son peuple.

La vache rousse (al-baqara)

Al-Baqara, « La Vache », est le titre de la deuxième sourate du Coran, ainsi intitulée car elle fait mention du commandement de la vache rousse (2 : 67-73). Il n'est pas inutile de rappeler ici cette disposition si particulière que la tradition juive en a fait le symbole de l'insondabilité des prescriptions divines. Le livre des Nombres (chap. 19) décrit le rituel nécessaire pour se purifier de l'impureté contractée au contact d'un cadavre. Les prêtres doivent prendre une vache entièrement rousse n'ayant jamais connu le joug, la brûler intégralement et mélanger ses cendres dans de l'eau vive. Les « eaux lustrales » ainsi obtenues servent à l'aspersion de l'individu impur le troisième puis le septième jour après son contact avec un cadavre.

La description que donne le Coran de ce commandement, sous la forme d'un dialogue entre Moïse et le peuple d'Israël, ressemble à de nombreux égards à celle de la Bible. Moïse transmet au peuple d'Israël le commandement divin : « En vérité, Dieu vous ordonne d'immoler une vache » (2 : 67). Les Israélites montrent un grand étonnement, et pensent que Moïse se moque d'eux. Lorsqu'il réitère ses paroles et les assure de sa sincérité, ils lui demandent de se renseigner pour eux auprès de Dieu sur la nature de cette vache. Moïse leur donne des éclaircissements : « Ce sera une vache, ni vieille ni jeune, mais d'âge moyen » (2 : 68). Mais cette réponse ne les satisfait pas encore : « Ils dirent : "Demande pour nous à ton Seigneur de nous indiquer clairement ce qu'elle doit être ; toutes les vaches sont semblables à nos yeux..." » (2 : 70). Moïse leur délivre alors des précisions supplémentaires : « Dieu dit : oui, ce sera une vache qui n'aura pas été avilie par le labour de la terre, ou par l'arrosage des champs, une vache sans marque et sans défaut » (2 : 71). La description coranique est beaucoup plus concise que celle qu'on trouve dans la Bible et qui contient différents aspects du rite du sacrifice de la vache, mais elle lui ressemble en ce qui concerne les caractéristiques de la vache elle-même.

Par contre, lorsque le Coran explique le sens du commandement, il diverge complètement de la prescription biblique puisqu'il dit : « Rappelez-vous qu'après avoir tué un homme, vous vous êtes rejeté ce crime les uns sur les autres ; mais Dieu a mis au grand jour ce que vous cachiez. Nous avons dit : "Frappez le cadavre par un membre de la vache. Voici comment Dieu rend la vie aux morts..." » (2 : 72-73). Le Coran reprend en fait ici un autre commandement biblique, qui met en œuvre lui aussi une génisse n'ayant pas connu le jour, ce qu'on appelle « la génisse dont on aura brisé la nuque » (en hébreu *'egla 'arufa*). Voici le texte biblique :

> « Lorsque [...] on trouvera gisant dans la campagne le corps d'un homme assassiné sans qu'on sache qui l'a frappé, alors tes anciens et tes juges viendront mesurer les distances qui séparent le cadavre des villes d'alentour. Les anciens de la ville estimée la plus proche prendront alors une génisse avec laquelle on n'a pas encore travaillé et qui n'aura pas porté le joug. Ils la feront descendre dans un ravin arrosé par un ruisseau, et où il n'y ait ni culture ni semailles, et là, dans le ruisseau, ils lui briseront la nuque... Alors tous les anciens de cette ville la plus proche du cadavre se laveront les mains au-dessus de la génisse... Ils diront ces paroles : "Nos mains n'ont point versé ce sang, et nos yeux ne l'ont point vu" » (Deutéronome 21 : 1-7).

Comme l'ont montré les chercheurs, dont A. I. Katsh dans son ouvrage *Judaism in Islam*, le Coran synthétise donc deux thèmes bibliques distincts : l'épisode de la vache rousse et celui de la génisse dont on aura brisé la nuque. Katsh a également prêté attention au fait que la littérature rabbinique ancienne fait le lien entre ces deux prescriptions bibliques et les discute conjointement (par exemple dans le *Sifrei*, c'est-à-dire le midrash halakhique sur les Livres des Nombres et du Deutéronome). Katsh en conclut qu'« il est probable que les fréquentes comparaisons talmudiques entre la vache rousse et la génisse dont on aura brisé la nuque aient entraîné la synthèse de deux épisodes par Muhammad[20] ».

Les midrashim et les ***isrâ'îliyyât***

Les récits coraniques évoquant les personnages bibliques ont de nombreux parallèles non seulement dans la Bible mais encore dans la littérature postbiblique juive. Autrement dit, beaucoup de thèmes de l'exégèse rabbinique sont insérés dans les épisodes bibliques rapportés dans le Coran comme s'ils faisaient partie intégrante de la Bible ; a contrario, de nombreux détails bibliques y sont complètement occultés. Quelques générations après l'achèvement du Coran, les lettrés musulmans, ayant amélioré sensiblement leur connaissance de la Bible et des sources rabbiniques, produisirent une littérature exégétique extrêmement riche. Ainsi, les recueils de hadîths et particulièrement le genre littéraire déjà évoqué appelé « les récits des prophètes » regorgent de détails bibliques et postbibliques.

Tous ces midrashim auxquels recourt la tradition musulmane postcoranique se regroupent sous l'appellation d'*isrâ'îliyyât*. Ignaz Goldziher, l'un des pionniers des études sur les *isrâ'îliyyât*, les répartit en trois catégories : a) les propos et les récits complétant les données du Coran sur des thèmes bibliques. Ce genre d'*isrâ'îliyyât* se retrouve dans toute la littérature musulmane ; b) Des récits connus sous le nom de *'ahd banî isrâ'îl*, « l'époque des fils d'Israël ». En dépit de cette appellation, ces textes peuvent être exempts de la moindre allusion à des figures hébraïques ; c) des récits folkloriques et miraculeux dont l'origine juive n'est que partielle.

Particulièrement importantes, les *isrâ'îliyyât* de la première catégorie permettent de combler les nombreuses lacunes qui caractérisent les récits coraniques. Toutefois, les sources musulmanes qui les utilisent ne précisent pas leur provenance. À l'instar des épisodes bibliques relatés dans le Coran de manière paraphrastique mais non en traduction littérale, les *isrâ'îliyyât* ont été soigneusement réécrites et réadaptées. Il est donc particulièrement difficile de retracer leur origine. En effet, elles sont citées après une vague introduction comme : « J'ai trouvé dans la Torah », « Il est écrit dans la Torah », « il est écrit dans les livres » (*maktûb fî-l-kutub*). Ces expressions ne signifient pas nécessairement qu'il s'agisse du Pentateuque voire de la Bible mais plutôt de la littérature postbiblique. Identifier avec précision ces *isrâ'îliyyât* nécessite donc une connaissance exhaustive des littératures juive et chrétienne.

Il est évident que les juifs convertis à l'islam ainsi que les lettrés musulmans en relation avec leurs homologues juifs et chrétiens ont été les maillons essentiels de la transmission des sources. D'après les textes historiques musulmans, ces traditions furent mises par écrit entre la fin du VIIe et tout le VIIIe siècle. On attribue à Wahb b. Munabbih, un célèbre savant musulman d'origine juive, l'ouvrage intitulé *Kitâb al-isrâ'îliyyât*. C'est apparemment le premier écrit du genre[21].

Quelques exemples parmi les abondants enseignements des midrashim juifs ayant pris la forme de hadîths dans les recueils aussi bien sunnites que shî'ites : c'est le cas de l'histoire de Joseph. Les traditions musulmanes traitent de plusieurs épisodes de cette histoire, comme le désaccord des frères sur le sort réservé à Joseph, sa vente comme esclave aux Égyptiens, sa punition pour avoir manqué de respect à son père ou encore l'erreur commise en prison consistant à se fier au ministre de Pharaon plutôt que de s'en remettre à Dieu[22]. Par ailleurs, dans de nombreuses traditions, la description du Trône divin et des quatre anges qui l'entourent rappelle l'évocation du « Char divin » dans la prophétie d'Ézéchiel[23].

L'usage massif de ces données midrashiques

dans la littérature religieuse musulmane n'a pas encore suscité l'attention que le sujet mérite et malgré les travaux d'islamologues éminents déjà mentionnés, il reste encore de nombreux textes à étudier.

IV

LOI CORANIQUE ET LOI JUIVE

La ressemblance entre les lois religieuses du judaïsme et de l'islam est considérable, tout au long de leur histoire. Ici, nous nous focaliserons essentiellement sur la strate coranique de l'islam. On sait que les parties juridiques du Coran se sont surtout constituées après l'hégire de 622 : alors que les sourates de la période mecquoise ont une orientation apocalyptique et eschatologique, celles de Médine sont plus juridiques. À La Mecque, Muhammad était persuadé que la fin du monde était proche et cela se reflète dans les sourates mecquoises, du moins dans les plus anciennes d'entre elles qui évoquent la résurrection des morts et le Jugement dernier. Dans ces mêmes sourates, la dimension juridique est pratiquement absente et seules deux obligations cultuelles sont mentionnées : la prière (*salât*) et l'aumône (*zakât*), sans plus de règles d'application.

Déjà à la fin de cette période mecquoise, et a

fortiori après l'hégire, l'idée de l'approche de la fin des temps commençait à s'estomper. Les visions apocalyptiques laissèrent place au combat contre les Arabes de La Mecque, à la diffusion de l'islam et au dialogue avec les juifs de Médine. Dans un premier temps, l'espoir de convertir ceux-ci prévalut, mais par la suite se développa une hostilité grandissante à leur égard, comme nous le verrons plus loin. C'est alors que la dimension juridique est devenue dominante. La législation très détaillée de cette époque concerne l'armée et la guerre, le partage du butin, la prière, le jeûne, le pèlerinage, la pureté et l'impureté des femmes après leurs menstruations ou un accouchement, les règles alimentaires et les animaux permis ou non, l'interdiction du mois intercalaire dans le calendrier et du prêt à intérêt, etc.

Compte tenu de l'importance de ces aspects légaux, les chercheurs sont unanimes à attribuer cette prépondérance des aspects légaux dans le Coran médinois à l'influence de la communauté juive locale. Pour un grand nombre de spécialistes, la similitude entre la jurisprudence musulmane et celle des juifs est si troublante qu'il semble que de nombreuses lois du Coran ne peuvent avoir été formulées que dans une relation dialectique constante avec la *halakha* (loi juive) biblique et postbiblique. Il est clair que les adeptes des deux religions vivaient dans un voisinage étroit. On observe en outre que certains thèmes juridiques du Coran évoluent en fonction de l'attitude changeante que l'islam naissant adopte vis-à-vis du judaïsme.

La recherche comparée sur les liens entre islam et judaïsme sur le plan juridique a commencé à prendre une place importante dans le domaine de l'islamologie à partir de la deuxième moitié du XIXe siècle. Arent Jan Wensinck, dans son livre *Muhammad and the Jews of Medina*, dont l'édition originale en néerlandais date de 1908, analyse longuement le développement du culte musulman sous l'effet des influences juives. Il montre que les commandements fondamentaux de l'islam, comme la prière et le jeûne, ressemblent dans leurs moindres détails aux injonctions analogues dans la religion juive. Ces dernières en seraient même les inspiratrices. Les heures fixes de la prière, le rituel préalable de purification, l'orientation géographique constituent des principes liturgiques et normatifs fondamentaux communs aux deux religions. Il semble que ces réglementations de l'islam n'auraient pu se cristalliser si le judaïsme avait été complètement ignoré. Ces sujets, dont débat l'islamologie depuis ses débuts, agitent toujours la recherche sur l'islam de nos jours, comme nous le montrent les autres contributions sur ce thème, telles les études de Robert Brunschvig, « Herméneutique normative dans le judaïsme et dans l'islam[1] » et son « Vœu ou serment : Droit comparé du judaïsme et de l'islam[2] ». Il y a quelques années, le livre de Haggai Mazuz, *The Religious and Spiritual Life of the Jews of Medina* (Leyde, 2014), est venu compléter les études anciennes comme celles de Wensinck, Brunschvig et bien d'autres après eux. L'auteur y examine une série de points religieux caractéristiques du judaïsme médinois qui a laissé son empreinte dans l'islam naissant. Mazuz consacre son deuxième chapitre à la *halakha* et aux coutumes. Il passe au crible des sujets comme le shabbat, le jeûne, la prière, le mariage, l'adultère et son châtiment, les lois de pureté conjugale ou encore celles de la guerre. Cela permet de constater également à quel point le judaïsme médinois ressemble au judaïsme rabbinique ou au contraire en diverge[3].

De même que le Coran fait écho à des récits bibliques sans citer la Torah mot à mot, de même, pour les règles juridiques, le lien entre le Coran et la Bible ou écrits postbibliques n'est pas textuel, autrement dit il ne s'agit pas de citations directes mais de ressemblances thématiques générales. On est cependant parfois très proche du mot à mot, par exemple avec la « loi du talion ». Le Coran s'exprime ainsi :

> Nous leur avons prescrit, dans la Torah : vie pour vie, œil pour œil, nez pour nez, oreille pour oreille,

dent pour dent. Les blessures tombent sous la loi du talion (5 : 45).

On est très proche de la formulation du Lévitique :

> Et si quelqu'un fait une blessure à son prochain, comme il a agi lui-même on agira à son égard : fracture pour fracture, œil pour œil, dent pour dent ; selon la lésion qu'il aura faite à autrui, ainsi lui sera-t-il fait (Lévitique 24 : 19-20).

La ressemblance ne saurait être accidentelle. Plus encore, la façon dont le Talmud interprète ces versets, non pas selon leur sens apparent, mais dans le sens d'une compensation financière proportionnelle au dommage causé – puisque aussi bien le préjudice d'une blessure à la jambe n'est-il pas le même selon que l'on est sportif ou écrivain –, semble-t-elle aussi avoir un écho dans le Coran :

> La loi du talion vous est prescrite en cas de meurtre : l'homme libre pour l'homme libre ; l'esclave pour l'esclave ; la femme pour la femme. On doit user de procédés convenables envers celui auquel son frère a remis une partie de la dette, et lui-même dédommagera celui-ci de la meilleure façon. Cela constitue un allégement et une miséricorde accordés par votre Seigneur. Un châtiment douloureux

est réservé à quiconque, après cela, aura transgressé la loi (2 : 178).

Les commentateurs du Coran et les juristes musulmans débattent depuis les premiers siècles pour savoir comment concilier ces deux versets coraniques : disent-ils en réalité la même chose (et quoi précisément) ou la contradiction est-elle insoluble, auquel cas l'un des deux versets vient « abroger » l'autre – et lequel est l'abrogé (*mansûkh*), lequel l'abrogeant (*nâsikh*) ? Les différentes écoles juridiques de l'islam divergent sur cette question, comme sur beaucoup d'autres. Ce qui nous importe ici, c'est que le Coran reprend les deux positions connues des sources juives : l'interprétation strictement littérale de la loi du talion et l'interprétation douce (« une miséricorde accordée par votre Seigneur »).

On ne saurait traiter, dans ce petit livre, tous les parallèles entre loi juive et musulmane. Nous nous intéresserons à quatre sujets essentiels : la prière (*salât*) et plus spécifiquement la question de la direction que le croyant musulman adopte en priant (*qibla*) ; le jeûne (*sawm*) ; les lois alimentaires ; et la fixation du calendrier. Ces quatre thèmes sont révélateurs, non seulement de la proximité du judaïsme et de l'islam, mais surtout, pour nous dans ce livre, de la manière dont l'islam s'est construit à la fois avec et contre sa référence juive.

Les lois de la prière et la qibla

Chez les Arabes d'avant l'islam, il n'existait pas de prières quotidiennes qui aient pu servir de modèle à la prière musulmane. Il existait cependant des formules rituelles que les Arabes païens récitaient lors de leurs pèlerinages aux divers sanctuaires, lesquels étaient dispersés à travers la péninsule Arabique. Il s'agissait surtout de professions de foi, d'expression de fidélité au service des divinités, de consultations de celles-ci et de demandes de bénédictions avant d'entreprendre quoi que ce soit. Du fait qu'on ne possède aucune attestation de prière préislamique, il y a lieu de souligner que même le mot pour dire « prière » n'existait pas en arabe avant l'islam et que le terme coranique *salât* n'est pas d'origine arabe mais est emprunté à l'araméen *selôta*, en usage aussi bien chez les juifs que chez les chrétiens d'Orient. Ainsi ce mot n'apparaît pas dans la poésie préislamique et l'on peut supposer qu'il n'est entré dans la langue arabe qu'après l'avènement de l'islam. Les Arabes l'ont vraisemblablement pris chez les juifs et les chrétiens locuteurs de l'araméen ou du syriaque avec lesquels ils étaient en contact.

Ni la structure de la prière musulmane ni son contenu ne ressemblent à ceux de la prière juive. La prière musulmane se distingue en effet par sa simplicité et sa grande brièveté, alors que la prière juive est connue pour être longue. Il existe néanmoins d'importantes ressemblances dans leur déroulement.

Un élément central dans l'une comme dans l'autre est l'intention (en arabe *niyya*) et aussi l'importance de la direction (*qibla*). Selon la tradition musulmane, avant que soit fixée la formule de l'appel à la prière (*adhân*) que récite le muezzin, il était coutume d'appeler à la prière au son du *shofar* des juifs (*bûq al-yahûd*), c'est-à-dire de la corne de bélier, et par la suite en sonnant la cloche (*nâqûs*) comme chez les chrétiens. L'adoption d'un autre usage – l'appel du muezzin – reflète la volonté de se distinguer des juifs et des chrétiens.

Le choix du vendredi comme jour de la grande prière résulte lui aussi probablement d'une dialectique entre la prière juive et la polémique contre les juifs de Médine à ce sujet. Il y a lieu de supposer que la prière de la mi-journée du vendredi (*salât al-jum'a*) n'a pas été instituée à La Mecque avant l'hégire car la minorité musulmane n'y jouissait pas encore d'un statut suffisant entre le début de la prédication de Muhammad en 610 et la prise de contrôle de la ville en 630. Selon la tradition musulmane, les musulmans de Médine avaient observé que les juifs et les chrétiens avaient les uns et les autres un grand rassemblement hebdomadaire et ils avaient voulu les imiter.

La recherche islamologique s'interroge sur le choix du vendredi pour la grande prière musulmane. Shlomo Dov Goitein, qui a développé les études de Carl Heinrich Becker et de Wensick, explique ce choix du fait que le vendredi était jour de marché à Médine et que, ce jour-là, les juifs faisaient leurs préparatifs pour le shabbat. Comme cela est de coutume les jours de marché, il y avait affluence non seulement des habitants du lieu, mais aussi des villages avoisinants. Le vendredi convenait donc parfaitement au culte musulman puisqu'il attirait des foules – parmi lesquelles de nombreux juifs de Médine. Cela entretenait l'espoir de faire parvenir le message de l'islam aux oreilles de plus de monde que les jours ordinaires. Le lien entre l'activité commerciale et la prière du vendredi apparaît clairement dans les versets où elle est mentionnée :

> Ô vous les croyants ! Quand on vous appelle à la prière du vendredi, accourez à l'invocation de Dieu ! Interrompez tout négoce : c'est un bien pour vous, si vous saviez ! Lorsque la prière est achevée, dispersez-vous dans le pays ; recherchez la grâce de Dieu ; invoquez souvent le Nom de Dieu. – Peut-être serez-vous heureux ! – Quand ils entrevoient

la possibilité d'un négoce ou d'un plaisir, ils s'y précipitent et ils te laissent debout ! Dis : « Ce qui se trouve auprès de Dieu est meilleur que le plaisir et que le négoce ! » – Dieu est le meilleur dispensateur de tous les biens ! (62 : 9-11).

Ces versets attestent que le vendredi de l'islam diffère du shabbat en ce qu'il n'est pas un jour de repos. L'interruption du commerce ou de toute autre activité ne concerne que l'heure de la prière. À la fin de celle-ci, les fidèles sont appelés à retourner à leurs affaires : « dispersez-vous dans le pays ; recherchez la grâce de Dieu ».

Il apparaît clairement que la fixation de la prière au vendredi reflète la conscience de l'existence d'une communauté juive dont on s'efforce de se différencier en substituant le vendredi au shabbat sans qu'il soit un jour de repos, tout en voulant l'attirer en fixant un moment commode pour elle.

Passons maintenant à la polémique concernant l'orientation de la prière. Celle-ci est mentionnée dans le Coran dans deux passages différents aux échos polémiques. Toutefois, à la simple lecture des versets, il est malaisé de savoir contre qui sont dirigées ces invectives et seule une lecture des commentaires du Coran permet de conclure qu'il s'agirait d'une polémique antijuive. Dans le premier passage, il est dit : « L'Orient et l'Occident appartiennent à Dieu. Quel que soit le côté vers lequel vous vous tourniez, la face de Dieu est là » (2 : 115). Même si la signification originelle du verset n'est pas très claire, les commentateurs le comprennent comme voulant dire que la direction de la prière est secondaire, contrairement à ce que prétendent les juifs. Cependant, plus loin dans la même sourate, on trouve des versets dont l'aspect polémique est évident :

> Les insensés d'entre les hommes disent : « Qui donc les a détournés de la *qibla* vers laquelle ils s'orientaient ? » Dis : « L'Orient et l'Occident appartiennent à Dieu ; il guide qui Il veut dans un chemin droit. » […]. Nous n'avions établi la *qibla* vers laquelle vous vous tourniez que pour distinguer ceux qui suivent le Messager [Muhammad] de ceux qui retournent sur leurs pas […]. Nous te voyons souvent tourner la face vers le ciel ; nous t'orientons vers une *qibla* qui te plaira. Tourne donc ta face dans la direction de la Mosquée sacrée ! Où que vous soyez, tournez votre face dans sa direction […] » (2 : 142-144).

Ces versets obscurs ne livrent que des bribes d'indices. Néanmoins, la tradition les a interprétés comme témoins d'une polémique vivace entre Muhammad et les juifs de Médine au sujet de la direction vers laquelle devait se tourner le croyant en prière. À l'époque où Muhammad s'était rapproché des juifs de la ville, pendant près d'une année et demie depuis son arrivée, le Prophète ordonnait à ses fidèles de prier en direction de Jérusalem (c'est pourquoi on appela la ville *ûlâ l-qiblatayn*, « la première des deux directions de prière [en islam] »). Même si l'identité des groupes de gens désignés dans les mots « pour distinguer ceux qui suivent le Messager de ceux qui s'en retournent sur leurs pas » nous est inconnue, il est clair que la mention qui en est faite va de pair avec une condamnation polémique. Les commentateurs y voient une allusion à la période qui suit la rupture avec les juifs. De fait, le temps du rapprochement avec eux s'était caractérisé par l'adoption d'idées, de rituels, de lois et de coutumes d'origine juive. L'époque qui suivit la séparation vit se dessiner la volonté de créer une religion bien distincte de celle des juifs comme l'indique le hadîth bien connu : « ne ressemblez pas aux juifs et aux chrétiens » (*lâ tashabbahû bi-l-yahûd wa-l-nasârâ*) ou cet autre hadîth : « Manifestez votre divergence avec les juifs » (*khâlifû l-yahûd*[4]). Autrement dit, les changements dans les préceptes musulmans ont été introduits afin, d'une part, de dissiper le lien évident avec le judaïsme et le christianisme, d'autre part d'affirmer l'originalité de la position musulmane. En effet, l'islam naissant voyait dans les deux religions qui l'avaient précédé une source d'inspiration et en même temps une menace pour son identité. Alors que les juifs et les premiers musulmans priaient ensemble dans la direction de Jérusalem, les musulmans ultérieurs se mirent à se tourner vers « la maison du Seigneur » (*bayt Allâh*) située à La Mecque. Cette décision illustre à elle seule la volonté de se détacher du judaïsme.

Pour compléter le tableau complexe de la recherche sur ces versets polémiques, il faut se référer à un important article d'Uri Rubin, « Les directions de prière (*qibla*) dans l'espace sacré[5] », où il exprime un avis différent de l'opinion régnante. Sur la base d'une nouvelle analyse des hadîths concernant ce sujet, il renverse l'ordre généralement admis : ce ne serait pas la séparation d'avec les juifs qui aurait entraîné le changement de la direction de la prière – de Jérusalem vers La Mecque – mais c'est ce changement qui aurait causé la rupture entre Muhammad et les juifs. Rubin affirme aussi que le changement de la *qibla* fait partie de toute une évolution interne de l'islam, qui a conduit à accorder à la Ka'ba un rôle cultuel prépondérant. Selon lui, cela symbolise l'arrachement aux précédentes religions du judaïsme et du christianisme ; or le fait de se tourner vers la Syrie et la terre d'Israël en faisait partie. La Mecque et Jérusalem étaient des foyers de sainteté avant l'avènement de l'islam, c'est pourquoi le maintien de la prière en direction de Jérusalem pendant un an et demi après l'hégire ne doit pas être seulement considéré comme un moyen d'attirer les juifs vers l'islam. Selon Rubin, la sainteté de Jérusalem pour l'islam est essentielle et ne correspond pas uniquement à une stratégie du prophète après l'hégire. En d'autres termes, le statut de Jérusalem n'est pas un enjeu politique tardif de l'islam devenu empire, mais un enjeu religieux clair dès l'époque de Muhammad. La terre d'Israël en général et Jérusalem en particulier tiennent une place absolument centrale dans le judaïsme et le christianisme, or ce sont ces deux religions qui constituent l'arrière-plan culturel de l'islam naissant. Il n'est donc pas étonnant que ce dernier ait hérité de ces conceptions, lui qui se revendique de cet héritage.

Les lois du jeûne

Le jeûne était pratiqué par les païens de la péninsule Arabique avant l'islam. Ils jeûnaient au mois de Rajab, que l'on a fait correspondre au septième mois du calendrier musulman. De nombreuses traditions attestent que le jeûne était très répandu à cette période-là, sans que l'on puisse en déterminer la cause ou le but. Au début de l'islam, il fallut combattre pour supprimer cet usage et conférer au Ramadan son statut unique de mois du jeûne. Quoi qu'il en soit, la centralité du jeûne dans l'islam – un des cinq piliers de la foi – s'est établie lors du séjour de Muhammad à Médine.

Une tradition veut qu'à son arrivée à Médine, Muhammad ait observé les juifs jeûner « le dixième jour du premier mois » et leur ait demandé :

> Quel est ce jour que vous jeûnez ? Ils [les juifs] répondirent : « C'est un grand jour durant lequel Dieu sauva Moïse et son peuple, et noya Pharaon et son peuple. Moïse le jeûna alors pour remercier Dieu, donc, nous le jeûnons également. » Le Prophète Muhammad répondit : « Nous sommes plus dignes de nous réclamer de Moïse que vous ! » Ainsi, il jeûna ce jour et ordonna de le jeûner[6].

Ce jeûne observé par les juifs de Médine s'appelait selon la tradition musulmane le jeûne de ʿÂshûrâ, c'est-à-dire le jeûne du dixième jour du mois de Muharram, qui est le premier mois du calendrier musulman. ʿÂshûrâ est probablement un mot araméen de la racine *ʿ-s-r*, « dix », qui, de l'avis général des chercheurs, se référait au jeûne de Kippour fixé, comme on le sait, au dixième jour du mois de Tishri, septième mois de l'année selon le décompte biblique (Lévitique 23 : 27), mais premier mois selon la tradition juive postbiblique.

La raison donnée par l'islam à la fixation de ce jeûne – présenté comme le jour le plus important du calendrier juif – est la volonté de souligner le lien entre Muhammad et Moïse – alors même que, dans la Torah, le jeûne de Kippour n'a pas de lien direct avec la sortie d'Égypte, mais se rattache plutôt au pardon de Dieu après le Veau d'or.

La justification des commandements de l'islam par l'existence de commandements semblables dans la tradition juive (ou chrétienne) est, comme on le voit, un phénomène répandu dans la tradition musulmane. Nous verrons plus loin que le pèlerinage (*hajj*), qui est lui aussi l'un des cinq piliers de l'islam, est rattaché à Abraham. Dans ces deux cas, le sentiment d'un lien étroit entre Muhammad et les prophètes bibliques (Moïse ou Abraham) conduit à faire adopter par l'islam un usage ancien. Le postulat de base est le même dans les deux cas : le prophète Muhammad se voit comme le continuateur des prophètes bibliques, c'est pourquoi les commandements et les pratiques qu'ils prônaient sont adoptés dans l'islam ancien.

Ce lien avec Moïse n'est toutefois pas la seule explication de l'instauration donnée du jeûne de 'Âshûrâ. Selon d'autres traditions, cela marquerait le jour où Noé serait sorti de l'Arche ; ou encore, on raconte qu'avant l'islam la tribu de Muhammad, les Quraysh, avait coutume de jeûner ce jour-là. On a sans doute ici un processus semblable à celui que nous avons pu observer pour la direction de la prière : on a d'abord fixé un jour de jeûne sur le modèle de Yom Kippour, en soulignant le lien avec Moïse, puis on s'est efforcé de rattacher cet usage à une autre figure plus universelle, comme Noé, pour finalement y voir une pratique purement arabe sans aucun lien avec le judaïsme. La différenciation d'avec le judaïsme trouve son expression dans l'annulation du jeûne de 'Âshûrâ et sa transformation en jeûne facultatif cependant qu'était institué un autre jeûne, celui du Ramadan. Ce jour de 'Âshûrâ sera cependant récupéré dans la piété shî'ite où il marque jusqu'à aujourd'hui le souvenir du martyre du troisième Imâm, Husayn, petit-fils du Prophète, tué à Karbala par les armées omeyyades. Dans la conscience shî'ite, l'instauration précoce du jeûne de 'Âshûrâ par Muhammad à Médine prend donc encore un autre sens, celui d'une anticipation de l'histoire sainte des Imâms.

Le ramadan, pour sa part, confère au jeûne un caractère strictement musulman qui le différencie des religions antérieures à l'islam. Ce processus s'accorde avec la chronologie généralement admise de l'ordre des révélations des chapitres du Coran : Selon celle-ci, en effet, le verset ordonnant le jeûne du ramadan (2 : 185) aurait été révélé à Muhammad la deuxième année de l'hégire, soit en l'an 624, date qui marque la fin des efforts de Muhammad pour se rapprocher des juifs de Médine. Elle signale l'approfondissement du fossé entre juifs et musulmans.

Bien que l'instauration du ramadan marque apparemment une séparation complète d'avec le judaïsme, on peut y reconnaître quelques éléments qui maintiennent un lien avec lui. Goitein a attiré l'attention sur la ressemblance entre islam et judaïsme qui tous deux établissent un lien entre le commandement du jeûne et la révélation de l'Écriture sainte. Selon l'islam : « Le Coran a été révélé durant le mois de ramadan. C'est une Direction pour les hommes ; une manifestation claire de la Direction et de la Loi… » (2 : 185).

Cette association entre la révélation de la parole divine et le mois du jeûne ne peut, selon Goitein, être sortie du néant. Selon le Midrash, le jeûne de Kippour tombe précisément à la date où Moïse est redescendu du Sinaï avec les secondes Tables de la Loi, après la faute du Veau d'or et le pardon (soit trois fois quarante jours après la fête de Shavu'ot où Moïse reçoit les premières Tables de la Loi[7]).

Même dans divers détails relatifs au déroulement du jeûne prescrit dans le Coran, on trouve des échos de la Loi juive telle qu'elle s'exprime dans le premier recueil de lois postbiblique, la Mishna. Que l'on considère les deux exemples suivants :

D'une part, le Coran autorise à manger les nuits de Ramadan jusqu'à l'aube, laquelle est définie comme le moment où on distingue les couleurs : « Mangez et buvez jusqu'à ce que l'on puisse distinguer à l'aube un fil blanc d'un fil noir » (2 : 187). De nombreux chercheurs soulignent la ressemblance avec la définition de la Mishna, célèbre puisqu'elle se trouve presque au tout début du premier traité : « On peut réciter la prière matinale du Shema' à partir du moment où l'on peut distinguer un fil bleu d'un fil blanc » (Mishna, traité *Berakhot* I, 2). Ces ressemblances ne doivent pas faire oublier les différences : certes dans les deux cas, la distinction des couleurs permet de déterminer l'aube, mais dans la Mishna, c'est à propos de la prière, et dans le Coran, à propos du jeûne. Dans la Mishna, les couleurs sont le bleu et le blanc (comme dans la taleth), dans le Coran, le blanc et le noir sans que l'on puisse savoir si la ressemblance est purement fortuite ou si elle résulte d'un emprunt[8].

D'autre part, le Coran autorise le fidèle empêché d'observer entièrement le commandement du jeûne de le compléter à un autre moment : « Celui d'entre vous qui est malade ou qui voyage jeûnera ensuite un nombre égal de jours » (2 : 184). Ce point est développé dans la littérature postcoranique et s'applique à d'autres cas tels que celui de l'accouchée ou de la femme en période de menstruation qui, en raison de leur impureté, ne peuvent jeûner toute la durée du ramadan. Cette disposition se rencontre également dans la Bible et dans la littérature talmudique. Le précédent biblique est celui de la « deuxième Pâque » (*Pessah Sheni*), Pâque de remplacement : « Si l'un de vous ou de vos descendants se trouve souillé par un cadavre ou en voyage au loin, il ne devra pas omettre de célébrer la Pâque » (Nombres 9 : 9). La solution proposée est alors de célébrer la fête un mois jour pour jour (le 15 Iyyar) après la date originelle (le 15 Nissan). Dans la Mishna, une solution analogue est conseillée pour la prière : quiconque a manqué l'une des trois prières journalières peut la rattraper à l'occasion de la prière suivante, dans des conditions bien définies.

Bien que les domaines où cette réglementation s'applique ne soient pas identiques – dans un cas le jeûne, dans l'autre Pâque et la prière –, on ne peut que noter la ressemblance sur ce point, à savoir la solution proposée au fidèle qui a manqué d'accomplir son devoir religieux en son temps. On peut certes toujours prétendre que cette ressemblance est fortuite et qu'elle ne suppose pas de lien direct, mais l'hypothèse inverse paraît fort plausible : dans l'environnement juif où est apparu l'islam, il est possible que de telles réglementations soient passées du judaïsme à l'islam encore en formation.

Les lois alimentaires

L'islam et le judaïsme ont en commun d'avoir des interdits alimentaires concernant certains animaux, mais en dehors de ce fait la ressemblance sur ce point est minime. Les lois alimentaires de l'islam – et bien entendu de la strate qui se reflète dans le Coran – sont simples et limitées, la liste des animaux interdits à la consommation est très restreinte : « Ô vous qui croyez ! Mangez de ces bonnes choses que nous vous avons accordées ; remerciez Dieu, si c'est lui que vous adorez. Dieu vous a seulement interdit la bête morte, le sang, la viande de porc et tout animal sur lequel on aura invoqué un autre nom que celui de Dieu… » (2 : 172-173 ; voir aussi 5 : 3-5 qui contient quelques autres interdictions ; 6 : 145-146). Rien de comparable avec les listes bibliques où sont énumérées nombre d'espèces animales interdites à la consommation (Lévitique 11 : 1-47 ; Deutéronome 14 : 3-21). Le dénominateur commun est l'interdiction de la viande de porc, du sang ainsi que des charognes.

L'abondance des interdits propre au judaïsme dans ce domaine est interprétée dans le Coran

– comme c'était le cas de la polémique chrétienne contre le judaïsme[9] – comme un châtiment imposé aux juifs : « Nous avons interdit toute bête à ongles à ceux qui pratiquent le judaïsme. Nous leur avons interdit la graisse des bovins et des ovins [...] Nous les avons ainsi punis pour leur rébellion. Nous sommes véridiques » (6 : 146), et de manière semblable : « Nous avons interdit aux juifs d'excellentes nourritures qui leur étaient permises auparavant : c'est à cause de leur prévarication ; parce qu'ils se sont souvent écartés du chemin de Dieu » (4 : 160).

L'idée que la plupart des interdits alimentaires imposés aux juifs n'existaient pas à l'origine mais qu'ils sont apparus par le suite pour les punir de leurs péchés s'ancre dans un autre verset qui évoque Jacob – sous l'appellation d'Israël – en affirmant que du temps de ce patriarche, toutes les nourritures étaient permises. « Tout élément était licite pour les fils d'Israël, à part ce qu'Israël [Jacob] s'était interdit à lui-même avant que la Torah n'ait été révélée » (3 : 93).

Contrairement aux versets cités plus haut, ce verset ne présente pas les interdits alimentaires comme une punition imposée aux juifs, il fait seulement allusion au fait que ces interdits n'ont pas toujours existé. La restriction exprimée par les mots « à part ce qu'Israël s'était interdit à lui-même » se réfère de toute évidence à l'interdiction du nerf sciatique consécutive à la lutte avec l'ange. Au terme de la lutte qui dure jusqu'au lever de l'aurore, la cuisse de Jacob se démet : « C'est pour cela que les Israélites, aujourd'hui encore, ne mangent point du nerf sciatique qui est l'articulation de la hanche, car il avait touché Jacob à ce nerf, sur l'articulation de la hanche... » (Genèse 32 : 33). Le Coran n'évoque pas cet épisode biblique dont la seule réminiscence est l'interdiction du nerf sciatique. Il est intéressant de noter que Jacob n'apparaît pas dans ce verset coranique sous le nom de Jacob mais sous celui d'Israël, qui lui a est donné par l'ange avec lequel il se bat (Genèse 32 : 29). L'appellation Israël pour Jacob ne se retrouve qu'une autre fois dans le Coran (19 : 58) ; dans les seize autres occurrences, il est appelé de son nom plus courant Ya'qûb (Jacob).

Un autre point commun entre islam et judaïsme est la sévérité avec laquelle tous deux condamnent la consommation de bêtes offertes en sacrifice aux idoles. Ainsi : « Voici ce qui vous a été interdit : la bête morte, le sang, la viande du porc ; et ce qui a été immolé à un autre Dieu [...] » (5 : 3). Cet interdit est très présent dans le Talmud. On le trouve déjà aussi dans le christianisme primitif qui, au concile de Jérusalem, interdit « les viandes sacrifiées aux idoles » ainsi que le sang et les animaux étouffés (Actes des apôtres 15 : 29).

Dans son livre *The Jewish Foundation of Islam*, Charles Torrey écrit que l'intention de Muhammad était à l'origine d'imiter les lois alimentaires juives, mais que les conditions et les « coutumes de l'Arabie nécessitaient toutefois quelques différences. Les lois d'Israël sont désormais supplantées par l'application qu'en fait l'islam[10] ». Quoi qu'il en soit, les interdits alimentaires et les lois qui en découlent, par exemple les règles de l'abattage rituel ou celles qui concernent les usages non alimentaires des animaux interdits à la consommation, ont continué à se développer parallèlement dans le judaïsme et l'islam, comme on le verra dans le dernier chapitre[11].

Le calendrier et l'année embolismique

Rappelons brièvement les raisons qui font du calendrier un problème et un enjeu. Tout calendrier consiste en une tentative d'harmoniser le cycle solaire – qui définit une année de 365 jours ¼, et dont dépendent les saisons climatiques – et le cycle lunaire – qui définit des mois de 29 ou 30 jours, ce qui veut dire qu'une « année » de douze mois lunaires compte 354 jours. Les Romains, et à leur suite l'Occident chrétien, ont opté pour un calendrier essentiellement solaire dont les mois de 30 ou 31 jours ne sont pas du tout fonction du cycle lunaire. Les juifs, pour leur part, doivent prendre en compte des injonctions bibliques divergentes : d'une part les mois, et donc les fêtes qui tombent un certain jour du mois, doivent être fixées en fonction de la nouvelle lune, d'autre part ces mêmes fêtes doivent tomber à des saisons agricoles précises : la fête de Pessah doit en particulier tomber au printemps. Il en est résulté une science complexe par laquelle on rajoute, sept fois au cours de cycles de dix-neuf années, soit tous les deux ou trois ans, un treizième mois, afin que les saisons ne « glissent » pas de dix jours à chaque année qui passe.

Du côté musulman, on sait que le calendrier est strictement lunaire : le mois du ramadan, comme tous les autres mois, se décale d'année en année, passant de l'été à l'hiver en une dizaine d'années. On sait en outre que l'an 1 du calendrier musulman est celle de l'hégire, c'est-à-dire de l'« émigration » (*hijra*) du Prophète à Médine, fuyant La Mecque. Fixer un calendrier, c'est donc à la fois donner un sens global au temps long de l'histoire universelle et maîtriser politiquement le temps court du quotidien.

La question de la fixation du calendrier islamique a fait l'objet d'une polémique contre différents groupes, d'abord contre les Arabes païens au sein desquels l'islam est né, puis contre d'autres religions, en particulier le judaïsme. En se détachant d'une coutume fortement enracinée, les premiers musulmans ont ainsi exprimé leur volonté de se distinguer des autres communautés. Ce nouveau calendrier dit « hégirien » a été établi, selon la tradition, par le deuxième calife 'Umar b. al-Khattâb (calife de 634 à 644).

Dans le Coran, c'est essentiellement la pratique de l'ajout d'un treizième mois intercalaire qui fait polémique :

> Le nombre des mois, pour Dieu, est de douze mois inscrits dans le Livre de Dieu, le jour où Il créa les cieux et la terre [...]. Le mois intercalaire (*al-nasî'*) n'est qu'un surcroît d'infidélité (*ziyâda fi-l-kufr*) ; les incrédules s'égarent ainsi : ils le déclarent non sacré une année, puis l'année suivante ils le déclarent sacré, afin de se mettre d'accord sur le nombre de mois que Dieu a déclarés sacrés. Ils déclarent ainsi non-sacré ce que Dieu a déclaré sacré ! (9 : 36-37).

Sans en préconiser encore formellement l'interdiction, le Coran fait de cette intercalation d'un mois supplémentaire la marque d'une infidélité à la Loi divine fixée à l'aube de la création. La question se pose alors : contre qui cette polémique est-elle dirigée ? Les commentateurs classiques d'hier et d'aujourd'hui expliquent généralement cette polémique dans le contexte arabe païen : les

Arabes de l'époque s'accordaient sur le fait que certains mois de l'année étaient des mois sacrés, consacrés aux pèlerinages ; mais certaines tribus manipulaient le calendrier, en rajoutant des mois, pour des raisons de confort. Pour autant, il serait très étonnant que les juifs ne soient pas visés par cette polémique, alors qu'ils sont le seul groupe dont on sait qu'ils pratiquaient, et pratiquent encore, cet ajout d'un mois intercalaire. En outre, cette sourate 9 (*al-Tawba*) appartient à la fin de l'époque médinoise. D'après de nombreux chercheurs, elle serait même la dernière dans l'ordre de la révélation coranique. Elle appartient donc aux jours où la rupture entre Muhammad et les juifs médinois semble définitivement consommée. Dans toute cette sourate, et encore plus particulièrement dans les versets qui jouxtent ceux concernant l'intercalation du mois, la critique contre les juifs et les chrétiens se manifeste de la manière la plus virulente – ce n'est pas pour rien que les jihadistes contemporains puisent dans cette sourate beaucoup de leurs références. Quelques exemples : le fameux verset 29 de la *jizya* (impôt de capitation, tribut) marque la position coranique sur le statut inférieur des gens du Livre (c'est-à-dire les juifs et les chrétiens) sous le pouvoir islamique. Dans la suite du verset, on trouve l'obligation de s'opposer à eux les armes à la main s'ils ne s'acquittent pas de leur tribut :

« Combattez-les jusqu'à ce qu'ils payent directement le tribut (*jizya*) après s'être humiliés[12]. » Dans le verset qui suit (30), les juifs et les chrétiens sont blâmés pour leur croyance déficiente dans le monothéisme puisqu'ils attribuent un fils à Dieu : « Les juifs ont dit : "'Uzayr est le fils de Dieu" ; les chrétiens ont dit : "Le Messie est le Fils de Dieu !" Telle est la parole qui sort de leurs bouches ; ils répètent ce que les incrédules disaient avant eux. Que Dieu les anéantisse ! Ils sont tellement stupides ! » (9 : 30[13]). Il existe d'autres affirmations accusatrices contre les juifs et les chrétiens dans les versets qui suivent, comme le 32 : « Ils voudraient, avec leurs bouches, éteindre la lumière de Dieu, alors que Dieu ne veut que parachever sa lumière, en dépit des incrédules » ou bien le 34 : « … Beaucoup de docteurs [juifs] et de moines (*al-ahbâr wa-l-ruhbân*) mangent en pure perte les biens des gens, et ils écartent ceux-ci du chemin de Dieu. »

C'est précisément au cœur de ces violentes polémiques que l'on trouve le verset sur l'intercalation du mois. Le contexte semble être antijuif et antichrétien. Pourtant, il est remarquable que, à ma connaissance, aucune source musulmane n'ait justifié l'interdiction de l'intercalation du mois au nom de l'opposition au judaïsme. Ce seront les astronomes musulmans qui mentionneront l'influence du judaïsme sur les habitudes arabes préislamiques dans l'intercalation d'un mois. Ainsi, comme le dit le célèbre savant Abû Rayhân al-Bîrûnî (mort en 1048) : « Ils [les Arabes] ont appris l'intercalation du mois des juifs qui vivaient dans leur voisinage et ce, plus de deux siècles avant l'hégire et ils se sont mis à adopter cette pratique juive en ajoutant un mois entre l'année [lunaire] et l'année solaire[14]. » À la lecture de ce témoignage, on constate que l'influence des sources juives sur les Arabes résulte bien d'échanges entre les deux communautés vivant l'une à côté de l'autre, avant et après l'islam.

Cependant, il nous semble que la précision donnée dans le verset (« … Le nombre des mois, pour Dieu, est de douze mois inscrits dans le Livre de Dieu, *le jour où Il créa les cieux et la terre* ») n'est pas sans faire écho avec une vision diamétralement opposée que l'on trouve dans la littérature talmudique. En effet, dans certains passages du Talmud traitant de l'année embolismique, le calendrier n'est plus l'apanage de Dieu mais appartient aux sages juifs qui en décident. Dans le Pentateuque, on trouve le verset : « Voici les fêtes du Seigneur, les convocations saintes, vous *les* (*otam*) proclamerez en leur temps » (Lévitique 23 : 4). Dans les midrashim du Talmud, le complément d'objet direct *otam* est lu *attem*, « vous », le verset étant alors lu : « c'est vous et vous seuls qui les proclamerez ». Dieu délègue au tribunal rabbinique la maîtrise du calendrier, et par là du temps et de la Création. (Talmud de Babylone, traité *Rosh ha-shana* 24a). Le point de vue des Sages juifs s'avère donc en totale opposition avec celui du Coran qui interdit l'année embolismique au nom du principe que le calendrier est fixé dès la Création du monde. Nul homme n'y peut ajouter ou retrancher quoi que ce soit. Il s'agit là d'une divergence de fond entre les théologies juive et musulmane.

En guise de conclusion

Ces exemples sur des sujets halakhiques confirment bien que les relations entre le judaïsme et le message coranique étaient aussi étroites que complexes à l'époque dite médinoise qu'elles le seront à l'époque classique. Proches et éloignées à la fois, ces relations témoignent que si les savants musulmans faisaient allusion à des textes bibliques et postbibliques et adoptaient des idées juives, ils s'efforçaient en même temps de se démarquer du judaïsme. Dans le verset 2 : 143 inséré dans la suite des versets au sujet de la *qibla*, se trouve une expression résumant parfaitement cette dialectique : « Ainsi Nous avons fait de vous une communauté éloignée des extrêmes (*ummatan wasatan*) » ou « une communauté médiane ». Pour tous les commentateurs, ce verset clé désigne l'islam comme la voie royale, la « voie du milieu », la religion qui ne penche jamais vers les extrêmes, à la différence du judaïsme et du christianisme. Ainsi, le judaïsme que les premiers musulmans connurent à Médine fut aussitôt considéré comme une religion contraignante. Beaucoup des commandements que doivent pratiquer les juifs – comme par exemple les interdits alimentaires beaucoup plus stricts que ceux des musulmans et bien sûr des chrétiens – sont d'après le Coran une punition imposée à eux par Dieu à cause de leurs péchés.

V

LES SOURCES CORANIQUES DE LA *DHIMMA*

Le statut juridique des juifs ainsi que des adeptes d'autres religions sous le règne de l'islam ne se dégage pas explicitement du Coran. Cette question n'est apparue que dans la période postcoranique, lorsqu'a émergé un Empire musulman réunissant sous les ailes de l'islam de nombreuses minorités religieuses pour lesquelles il a fallu définir des règles et des conditions leur permettant de vivre à l'ombre de l'islam. Bien que ce sujet n'ait pas donné lieu à un traitement explicite dans le Coran, celui-ci contient pour autant un nombre non négligeable de versets où se reflète la condition inférieure attribuée aux juifs et qui ont servi de point d'ancrage à leur statut juridique. Le premier de ces versets s'énonce ainsi :

> L'humiliation (*al-dhilla*) les a frappés, là où ils se trouvaient, à l'exception de ceux qui étaient protégés par un lien avec Dieu ou un lien avec les

> hommes. Ils ont encouru la colère de Dieu ; la pauvreté (*al-maskana*) les a frappés. Il en fut ainsi, parce qu'ils ne croyaient pas aux Signes de Dieu et qu'ils tuaient injustement les prophètes (3 : 112).

La condition des « peuples du Livre » dont parle ce verset, ainsi que l'explicite le contexte, est l'humiliation (*al-dhilla*) continue. À cela s'ajoute la pauvreté (*maskana*) justifiée par le Coran par les deux grands péchés des « peuples du Livre » évoqués plus haut (chap. 2) : la non-reconnaissance des signes divins et l'assassinat des prophètes qui leur avaient été envoyés. Ce verset mentionne aussi des exceptions auxquelles l'humiliation ne s'applique pas : « ceux qui étaient protégés par un lien avec Dieu ou avec les hommes ». Il s'agit de juifs et de chrétiens qui, au début de l'islam, étaient protégés par des alliances conclues avec les tribus arabes. Cependant, le Coran n'interdit pas de les humilier ; il commande seulement de les protéger, comme le montre le commentaire de notre verset par le célèbre exégète Ismâ'îl b. 'Umar Ibn Kathîr (mort en 1373). Il expose que les principes de base des lois de protection qui se sont développées par la suite dans l'islam sont ancrés dans le verset : ainsi « Dieu a établi qu'ils – les juifs – seraient toujours dans l'abaissement et la sujétion (*al-dhilla wa-l-saghâr*) en tout lieu où ils se trouveront et qu'ils n'auront de protection que par l'entremise du “lien avec Dieu” ; c'est-à-dire la protection (*al-dhimma*) de Dieu et le paiement de la capitation (*jizya*) ainsi que par le “lien avec les hommes” qui est d'assurer leur sécurité (*amân*[1]) ».

Un autre verset, peut-être encore plus connu que le précédent, est le célèbre « verset de la *jizya* » :

> Combattez ceux qui ne croient pas en Dieu et au jour dernier ; ceux qui ne déclarent pas illicite ce que Dieu et son Messager ont déclaré illicite ; ceux qui, parmi les gens du Livre, ne pratiquent pas la vraie religion. Combattez-lez jusqu'à qu'ils payent directement (*'an yadin*) le tribut (*al-jizya*) après s'être humiliés (9 : 29[2]).

Ce verset a occupé de nombreux chercheurs et suscité un nombre important d'études destinées à éclaircir le contexte général et les expressions spécifiques qui s'y trouvent. Par exemple, que signifie l'expression vague *'an yadin* que Denise Masson, Régis Blachère et d'autres traduisent par « directement » ? Cette expression qui littéralement signifie « au moyen » ou « par [le truchement de] la main » a reçu diverses autres interprétations. La plus stricte d'entre elles veut que, lors du paiement de la *jizya*, le non-musulman qui jouit de la protection doive mettre solennellement sa main près de celle du collecteur d'impôts en signe de reconnaissance de sa propre infériorité et de sa sujétion à l'islam. Une autre interprétation – qui décrit une réalité idéale, voire utopique, celle de la proximité entre le protégé et le musulman – donne à l'expression *'an yadin* le sens de « dans la mesure de ses moyens* ». De fait, on a connu des époques et des lieux sous gouvernement islamique où la *jizya* a été considérée comme un impôt progressif à prélever proportionnellement aux moyens du protégé[3].

Quoi qu'il en soit, l'examen de ce verset et du précédent – ainsi que de l'ensemble des autres versets critiques envers les juifs, que nous avons vus au chapitre II – montre qu'ils ont joué un rôle important dans la discrimination envers les juifs sur le plan juridique et sur d'autres. L'infériorité et l'abaissement des juifs et autres peuples du Livre n'est cependant qu'une face de la monnaie, l'autre face étant la supériorité affirmée de l'islam en tant que religion et culture. On trouve le fondement de ce principe dans de nombreux versets du Coran, comme par exemple : « C'est Lui qui a envoyé Son Messager avec la Direction et la Religion Vraie pour la faire prévaloir sur

---

* Ce sens du mot *yad* (« capacité ») est proche de l'expression hébraïque *hissiga yado*, (« il trouve les moyens », littéralement : « sa main a trouvé [les moyens] ») ; voir, par exemple, en Lévitique 25 : 49.

toute autre religion, en dépit des polythéistes » (9 : 33 ; cf. aussi 48 : 28 et 61 : 9), ainsi que : « Le culte de celui qui recherche une autre religion en dehors de l'*islâm* n'est pas accepté. Cet homme sera, dans le futur, au nombre de ceux qui ont tout perdu » (3 : 85). Cette idée a été largement développée dans la littérature du Hadîth et de nombreuses traditions attribuées au prophète Muhammad la confirment, par exemple la très célèbre « L'islam est suprême et rien ne lui est supérieur (*al-islâm ya'lû wa-lâ yu'lâ 'alayhi*) ». On trouve d'autres enseignements traditionnels qui explicitent plus particulièrement la supériorité de l'islam sur les religions révélées qui l'ont précédé, à savoir le judaïsme et le christianisme, comme « Faites attention à ne glorifier ni le judaïsme ni le christianisme (*lâ turfa'anna fîkum lâ yahûdiyya wa-lâ nasrâniyya*[4]) ».

Toutefois, cette prise de position idéologique, soulignée par les versets coraniques et les enseignements prophétiques cités ici (et bien d'autres encore), ne s'est cristallisée que quelques générations après l'apparition de l'islam, pour prendre alors une forme juridique définitive généralement désignée sous le nom de pacte de 'Umar.

Le pacte de ‘Umar

On considère, en général, le recueil de mesures légales connu sous le nom de pacte de ‘Umar comme le fondement idéologique et juridique qui définit les rapports de l’islam aux peuples du Livre. Ce pacte est traditionnellement attribué au calife ‘Umar Ibn al-Khattâb (calife de 634 à 644), mais a été probablement élaboré pendant le règne du calife omeyyade ‘Umar b. ‘Abd al-‘Azîz (calife de 717 à 720), connu pour son hostilité à l’égard des juifs et des chrétiens. Il s’agit d’un recueil de lois discriminatoires définissant le statut juridique des « gens du Livre », c’est-à-dire les juifs, les chrétiens et d’autres peuples vivant en terre d’Islam, comme les *majûs* (« mages »), à savoir les zoroastriens, qui ont réussi à faire admettre l’Avesta comme livre sacré alors même qu’il ne relève pas du monothéisme abrahamique. Ces « gens du Livre » se voient accordé le statut de *dhimmîs*, de minorités soumises mais « protégées » par le pouvoir islamique, contrairement aux païens qui n’ont le choix qu’entre la conversion et la mort, au mieux l’esclavage.

Plus précisément, toutes les versions du pacte de ‘Umar et toutes ses versions mentionnent uniquement les chrétiens, et les limitations religieuses qu’elles énoncent, par exemple l’interdiction d'élever des églises et des monastères, de sonner les cloches pour appeler à la prière, de célébrer des cérémonies bruyantes, ne concernent que le christianisme. Cela résulte sans aucun doute du fait que les chrétiens étaient majoritaires dans les territoires conquis par l'islam. Pour autant, ces limitations ont été étendues aussi aux juifs et aux zoroastriens – de sorte que tout ce qui est dit des chrétiens dans ce document les concerne eux aussi.

Le pacte de 'Umar, auquel à travers les siècles ont été adjoints de nouveaux décrets, comme ceux attribués au calife abbasside al-Mutawwakil (qui a régné entre 847 et 861), reflète fidèlement la position de tous les légistes musulmans, quelle que soit leur école, vis-à-vis des religions du Livre. Toutefois, l'étude rigoureuse de la littérature juridique musulmane en ce qui concerne ceux qui sont considérés comme des protégés (*dhimmîs*) peut nous permettre de saisir dans toute leur complexité les relations entre la théorie juridique proprement dite et sa réalisation dans la pratique, au point qu'on est en droit de s'interroger : ces lois de la *dhimma* ont-elles reflété des situations réelles ou bien ne sont-elles que la description d'un idéal que l'on s'efforcerait de réaliser sans jamais pouvoir parfaitement l'atteindre ? En réalité, il n'existe pas de réponse simple à cette question. Claude Cahen écrivait notamment : « En fait, il ne semble pas que ces prescriptions, dont les modalités varient fréquemment, aient jamais été respectées de façon durable (d'où leur répétition par les souverains piétistes), et il est même douteux qu'on se soit réellement soucié de les faire appliquer hors de Baghdâd et des grands centres musulmans[5]. »

Voici le texte du Pacte, dans la traduction d'Antoine Fattal[6] :

> « On tient de 'Abd al-Rahmân ibn Ghamm ce qui suit : lorsque 'Umar ibn al-Khattâb eut accordé la paix aux chrétiens de Syrie, nous lui écrivîmes une lettre ainsi conçue :
> Au nom d'Allah, le Bienfaiteur miséricordieux ! Ceci est une lettre adressée par les chrétiens de telle ville, au serviteur d'Allah, 'Umar ibn al-Khattâb, commandeur des Croyants :
> Quand vous êtes venu dans ce pays, nous vous avons demandé la sauvegarde pour nous, notre progéniture, nos biens et nos coreligionnaires. Et nous avons pris par-devers vous l'engagement suivant :
>
> • Nous ne construirons plus dans nos villes et dans leurs environs ni couvents, ni églises, ni cellules de moines, ni ermitages. Nous ne réparerons point, ni de jour ni de nuit, ceux de ces édifices qui tomberaient en ruine, ou qui seraient situés dans les quartiers musulmans.
> • Nous tiendrons nos portes ouvertes aux passants et aux voyageurs.

• Nous donnerons l'hospitalité à tous les musulmans qui passeront chez nous et les hébergerons durant trois jours.
• Nous ne donnerons asile, ni dans nos églises ni dans nos demeures, à aucun espion. Nous ne cacherons rien aux musulmans qui soit de nature à leur nuire.
• Nous n'enseignerons pas le Coran à nos enfants.
• Nous ne manifesterons pas publiquement notre culte et ne le prêcherons pas.
• Nous n'empêcherons aucun de nos parents d'embrasser l'islam, si telle est sa volonté.
• Nous serons pleins de respect envers les musulmans. Nous nous lèverons de nos sièges lorsqu'ils voudront s'asseoir.
• Nous ne chercherons point à leur ressembler, sous le rapport des vêtements, par la *qalansawa* (coiffe en forme de cône), le turban ou les chaussures, ou par la manière de peigner nos cheveux.
• Nous ne ferons point usage de leur parler ; nous ne prendrons pas leurs *kunya*s (titres honorifiques).
• Nous ne monterons point sur des selles.
• Nous ne ceindrons pas l'épée. Nous ne détiendrons aucune espèce d'arme et n'en porterons point sur nous.
• Nous ne ferons point graver nos cachets en caractères arabes.
• Nous ne vendrons point de boissons fermentées.
• Nous nous tondrons le devant de la tête.
• Nous nous habillerons toujours de la même manière, en quelque endroit que nous soyons ;

nous nous serrerons la taille avec le *zunnâr* (ceinture portée par les *dhimmîs*).
• Nous ne ferons point paraître nos croix et nos livres sur les chemins fréquentés par les musulmans et dans leurs marchés.
• Nous ne battrons le *nâqûs* (la cloche) dans nos églises que très doucement.
• Nous n'y éléverons pas la voix en présence des musulmans.
• Nous ne ferons pas les processions publiques du dimanche des Rameaux et de Pâques. Nous n'éléverons pas la voix en accompagnant nos morts.
• Nous ne prierons pas à voix haute sur les chemins fréquentés par les musulmans et dans leurs marchés.
• Nous n'enterrerons point nos morts dans le voisinage des musulmans.
• Nous n'emploierons pas les esclaves qui sont échus en partage aux musulmans.
• Nous n'aurons point de vue sur les maisons des musulmans.

(Lorsque j'apportai cette lettre à 'Umar, il ajouta : "Nous ne battrons aucun musulman.")

Telles sont les conditions auxquelles nous avons souscrit, nous et nos coreligionnaires, et en échange desquelles nous recevons la sauvegarde. S'il nous arrivait de contrevenir à quelques-uns de ces engagements dont nos personnes demeurent garantes, nous n'aurons plus droit à la *dhimma* et nous serions passibles des peines réservées aux rebelles et aux séditieux.

'Umar ibn al-Khattâb répondit à 'Abd al-Rahmân ibn Ghamm : « Sanctionne leur requête, mais non sans avoir ajouté à ce qu'ils ont souscrit les deux conditions suivantes que je leur impose : "Ils ne pourront pas acheter d'individus faits prisonniers par des musulmans. Celui qui aura frappé un musulman de propos délibéré ne bénéficiera plus de la garantie de ce pacte." »

Comme on peut le voir, ces lois reflètent des aspects différents des relations de l'islam et des populations qui lui sont assujetties : l'interdiction de bâtir des lieux de culte ou de restaurer ceux qui ont été détruits ; l'obligation d'héberger des musulmans et l'interdiction d'offrir un refuge aux espions et ennemis de l'islam ; l'interdiction de manifester ostensiblement une autre religion ; l'interdiction de chevaucher une monture sellée – ce qui équivaut à exclure l'usage de toute monture noble comme le cheval ; l'interdiction du port d'armes et l'obligation de porter des vêtements spécifiques permettant de distinguer les protégés de leurs patrons musulmans. Tout ce que les protégés reçoivent en échange de ces limitations et du paiement de la *jizya* est la liberté de culte et la vie sauve.

Les chercheurs s'accordent sur le fait que les

restrictions imposées par le pacte de ʿUmar ont été influencées par le droit byzantin et le droit sassanide, car la première vague de conquêtes musulmanes en dehors de la péninsule Arabique a déferlé sur des régions appartenant à ces deux empires. Dans chacun des deux empires rivaux, la religion majoritaire était religion d'État (christianisme chez les uns, zoroastrisme chez les autres) et reconnaissaient des minorités religieuses tolérées, en particulier les juifs, mais soumises à de fortes restrictions (Code Théodosien, en 404) et à des persécutions épisodiques, comme sous les règnes de Justinien côté byzantin, en 553, ou de Yazdegerd II côté perse, en 456.

Une longue codification

La législation de l'islam sur le statut des juifs en tant que *dhimmîs* n'a débuté que deux siècles après l'apparition de l'islam. Elle se reflète bien dans la littérature des quatre écoles juridiques de l'islam sunnite ainsi que dans les écrits juridiques shîʿites. Toutefois, les règles juridiques concernant les *dhimmîs* ne font pas à l'origine l'objet d'une section spécifique dans les codes, mais sont dispersées sous d'autres rubriques. Si l'on prend par exemple *Kitâb al-mabsût*, un code juridique de l'école hanafite, l'une des quatre écoles de l'islam sunnite, dû à Shams al-Dîn al-Sarakhsî (m. 1090), on voit que la question du mariage avec les *dhimmîs* est incluse dans un sous-chapitre du traité du mariage (*kitâb al-nikâh*) et que les règles commerciales du traité des ventes (*kitâb al-bay'*) comprennent un sous-chapitre traitant du commerce avec les *dhimmîs*. Il en va de même dans les codes des autres écoles sunnites et le grand codificateur shî'ite Abû Ja'far al-Tûsî (m. 1067) suit une voie semblable dans ses deux écrits juridiques *Tahdhîb al-ahkâm* (« Rectification des principes ») et *al-Istibsâr fî-mâ ukhtulifa min al-akhbâr* (« Éclaircissements du problème des traditions sujettes à divergences »).

Ce n'est que vers la fin du Moyen Âge qu'a commencé la systématisation de la législation concernant les protégés, illustrée notamment par la vaste monographie d'Ibn Qayyim al-Jawziyya (m. 1350), *Ahkâm ahl al-dhimma* (« Les lois concernant les *dhimmîs* »). Les règles discriminatoires concernant les *dhimmîs* qui étaient formulées de manière concise et sèche dans le pacte de 'Umar s'y trouvent plus élaborées et détaillées[7]. Cette littérature juridique débat de la question de savoir s'il y a lieu de renouveler le pacte de 'Umar et dans quelles conditions, mais la position dominante de la littérature musulmane classique est qu'il est valide à travers les générations et qu'il faut s'y tenir.

Entre la théorie et la réalité

Il ne fait aucun doute que le pacte de ʿUmar sert de base à l'attitude généralement adoptée envers les juifs et les autres minorités au cours de l'histoire musulmane mais, pour avoir une image de la situation réelle des juifs à l'ombre de l'islam, il faut examiner avec précision l'application de ces lois suivant le lieu et le temps. En outre, il ne faut pas négliger la part de la subjectivité de chaque chercheur qui peut l'amener à privilégier certains traits par rapport à d'autres ou à exprimer sa vision globale de la situation juridique des juifs sous l'islam.

Juifs en terre d'Islam, l'important ouvrage de Bernard Lewis, l'un des plus grands islamologues du XXe siècle et du début du XXIe siècle, s'ouvre sur cette belle réflexion :

> Deux clichés dominent à peu près tout ce que l'on a pu écrire sur la tolérance ou l'intolérance dans le monde islamique. Le premier nous présente un cavalier arabe fanatique surgissant du désert, une épée dans une main, le Coran dans l'autre, et offrant à ses victimes le choix entre les deux. Cette vision, rendue célèbre par Edward Gibbon dans son *Histoire du déclin et de la chute de l'Empire romain*, est non seulement fausse mais impossible

> […]. L'autre cliché, presque aussi absurde, se complaît dans la description d'une utopie interconfessionnelle et multiraciale dans laquelle hommes et femmes de races et de religions différentes auraient coexisté dans la plus parfaite harmonie, bénéficié des mêmes droits et des mêmes chances, et œuvré ensemble pour le progrès de la civilisation. Transposées en termes juifs, ces deux visions stéréotypées reviendraient à dire que l'islam de l'époque classique ressemblait à l'Amérique contemporaine, ou, inversement à l'Allemagne hitlérienne, mais en pire – si cela est concevable. Bien entendu ces deux représentations donnent une image très déformée de la réalité ; comme bien des stéréotypes, elles renfermement cependant des éléments de vérité[8].

Bernard Lewis, ainsi que Marc Cohen dans son livre cité plus haut et Michel Abitbol dans son livre *Le Passé d'une discorde : Juifs et Arabes du VIIᵉ siècle à nos jours*[9] voient dans l'histoire des juifs sous la domination de l'islam un mouvement perpétuel entre ces deux extrêmes présentés. Autrement dit, l'histoire des juifs sous l'islam n'est pas monolithique. L'historien qui recherche la vérité n'a pas droit aux généralisations ; chaque lieu et chaque époque nécessitent une recherche particulière. Il ne fait pas de doute que l'histoire des juifs sous l'islam comporte des situations où les juifs ont souffert de discrimination et ont connu une vie plus amère encore que celle imposée par le pacte de ‘Umar. Dans son livre *Les Dhimmis*, Bat Ye’or[10] en donne quantité d’exemples et l’on pourrait encore en ajouter[11]. Néanmoins, sans vouloir minimiser les malheurs et les persécutions qui se sont abattus sur les juifs en terre d’Islam au cours de leur histoire, il est difficile d’adopter l’une ou l’autre des positions extrêmes. Il y a beaucoup de vrai dans les évocations de Bat Ye’or, ou encore dans le livre de Paul Fenton *Le Pogrome de Fès ou le tritel 17-19 avril 1912*[12] ; cependant, on ne saurait en étendre la description à d’autres lieux et d’autres temps sans commettre une entorse à la réalité. Quand des autorités musulmanes ont estimé que telle ou telle restriction imposée aux *dhimmîs* n’était pas observée assez strictement, elles avaient l’habitude de publier le pacte de ‘Umar dans son intégralité et de rappeler le devoir de s’y tenir scrupuleusement. Rares furent cependant les cas où une communauté juive entière eut à souffrir en conséquence de la non-observance du pacte par un ou plusieurs de ses membres.

De la modernité au fondamentalisme

Il faut enfin noter que la *dhimma* a officiellement été abolie dans la quasi-totalité des États musulmans : d’abord dans l’Égypte de Mehmet

Ali et dans tout l'Empire ottoman entre 1839 et 1856 dans le cadre des réformes modernisatrices appelées *Tanzîmât* – ce qui inclut la Turquie, l'Irak, le Yémen, la Tunisie, la Syrie, etc. ; plus tard au Maroc, en 1912, dans le cadre du protectorat français. Aucun de ces pays n'a réinstitué la *dhimma* au moment des indépendances, puisque aussi bien leur Constitution n'est pas islamique. Parmi les pays islamiques où résident des communautés non musulmanes, seul l'Iran applique encore la *dhimma*, et encore, sous une forme assez différente de l'islam classique. Nous en reparlerons au chapitre suivant.

C'est surtout sur le plan de l'idéologie politique que la *dhimma* s'exprime aujourd'hui. Dans les discours antijuifs que tiennent de nos jours certaines autorités islamiques, revient souvent l'affirmation que les juifs n'ont pas le droit de dominer des musulmans quel que soit le lieu ou le temps. À leurs yeux, la souveraineté de l'État d'Israël où des musulmans sont, pour la première fois dans l'histoire de l'islam, sous domination juive, constitue donc une anomalie intolérable. En effet, non seulement les juifs n'ont pas le droit de dominer des musulmans, mais c'est le contraire qui doit se produire comme cela a été le cas tout au long de l'histoire, car l'islam doit dominer toutes les autres religions. Ainsi que l'enseigne un hadîth cité plus haut : « L'islam est supérieur à tout et rien ne lui est supérieur. » Du côté des islamistes comme du côté de ceux qui agitent la peur d'un islam conquérant, la *dhimma* existe dans le discours, soit comme idéal, soit comme repoussoir, bien plus que dans les faits.

VI

LA PLACE DU JUDAISME ET DES JUIFS DANS LE SHÎ'ISME DUODÉCIMAIN

Étant donné que le sunnisme et le shî'isme se fondent en grande partie sur les mêmes sources religieuses, en premier lieu le Coran, on peut s'attendre à ce que leur attitude théologique et juridique vis-à-vis des juifs et leur religion soit similaire. De fait, les deux grandes branches de l'islam partagent beaucoup de points communs dans leur attitude vis-à-vis du judaïsme, notamment concernant les aspects positifs et négatifs des juifs et de leur religion, et ce aussi bien à l'époque ancienne que récente.

Malgré cette similitude de positions vis-à-vis des juifs et d'autres peuples du Livre*, il est pos-

* Une grande partie de ce qui est dit dans le shî'isme au sujet des juifs et de leur religion est aussi valable vis-à-vis des chrétiens et des zoroastriens (en arabe : *majûs*). Notons que malgré l'équivalence quasi constante des positions juridiques à l'égard des fidèles de ces trois religions, il existe des différences dans l'attitude du shî'isme vis-à-vis de chaque

sible de dégager quelques conceptions spécifiques du shî'isme par rapport aux juifs et au judaïsme dans deux secteurs de la vie religieuse. Le premier est celui du droit, qui se fonde sur des considérations théologiques, domaine auquel seuls quelques rares spécialistes ont jusqu'à présent accordé une attention particulière[1]. La question principale qui s'y pose est la suivante : doit-on considérer les peuples du Livre comme rituellement impurs (*najis*) ? Cette question a, dans la littérature juridique shî'ite, certaines implications, notamment quant à la consommation de la nourriture et notamment des bêtes abattues rituellement par les peuples du Livre et quant à la possibilité ou non d'épouser les femmes issues de ces derniers.

Le deuxième domaine dans lequel le shî'isme présente des conceptions spécifiques vis-à-vis des juifs et de leur religion est le domaine doctrinal. L'attitude shî'ite est ici presque aux antipodes de celle existant sur le plan juridique : dans de multiples traditions, on trouve les shî'ites identifiés au peuple d'Israël ou encore – de façon plus modérée – les descendants d'Israël sont présentés comme étant le prototype de la Shî'a. On est souvent surpris de retrouver dans le discours

---

communauté. Dans ce chapitre, seule l'attitude à l'égard des juifs et de leur religion est étudiée.

shî'ite cette approche, qui rappelle fortement l'attitude traditionnelle du christianisme s'identifiant au « Vrai Israël » (*Verus Israël*) ; elle est pourtant bien attestée[2].

L'impureté des ahl al-kitâb

La controverse entre sunnites et shî'ites sur cette question se fonde sur les mêmes versets coraniques, la référence principale étant : « Ô vous qui croyez, les *mushrikûn* ne sont qu'impureté (*najas*) ; qu'ils n'approchent plus la Mosquée sacrée (*al-masjid al-hâram*) » (9 : 28).

Deux tendances majeures se font jour dans l'exégèse de ces versets. La première, qui se fonde sur le contexte des versets précédents, tient que le terme *mushrikûn*, de la racine *sh-r-k* qui revient 168 fois dans le Coran et qui signifie « associer », presque toujours avec le sens précis d'« associer d'autres divinités à Allâh », se réfère aux seuls polythéistes mecquois auxquels il s'agissait désormais d'interdire l'accès à l'enceinte sacrée (le *harâm*) de La Mecque. La deuxième lecture, en revanche, soutient que le verset concerne tous les polythéistes sans exception, ainsi que toutes les mosquées.

Plus encore, la tendance générale est d'inclure dans ce terme de *mushrikûn* également les juifs et les chrétiens, soit parce qu'il est pris dans un sens vague, soit sur la base du verset disant que les juifs ont divinisé ʿUzayr de même que les chrétiens ont divinisé Jésus (voir plus haut pp. 88-92). Si la plupart des savants sunnites limitent cette interdiction à La Mecque, une tendance plus « dure », dont l'origine remonterait au calife omeyyade ʿUmar b. ʿAbd al-ʿAzîz déjà mentionné au chapitre précédent, l'étend « à toutes les mosquées sous n'importe quel prétexte[3] ». En revanche, les codificateurs sunnites ne prennent pas la mention d'« impureté » (*najâsa*) dans son sens littéral et n'en déduisent pas que les juifs ou les chrétiens seraient rituellement impurs. L'impureté dont il est question concerne au premier chef les règles de la prière et la nécessité d'être en état de pureté rituelle (*tahâra* en arabe comme en hébreu) pour l'accomplir, mais on se doute bien qu'elle induit des représentations plus larges.

Dans le shîʿisme duodécimain, la tendance majoritaire qui ressort des exégèses coraniques, de la littérature du Hadîth et des écrits juridiques est clairement sur la ligne « dure » que l'on vient d'évoquer.* L'étude des grandes sommes ency-

---

* Le shîʿisme zaydite maintient une position semblable à celle des duodécimains concernant les *ahl al-kitâb*, tandis que l'ismaélisme est sur la même ligne que l'opinion majoritaire sunnite. En ce qui concerne les zaydites voir Toby, *Les Juifs du Yémen, à l'ombre de l'Islam, des origines à nos jours*, p. 80.

clopédiques shî'ites comme *Bihâr al-anwâr* de Muhammad Bâqir al-Majlisî (mort en 1699[4]) et, beaucoup plus récemment, l'ouvrage encyclopédique du juriste contemporain Ayatu'llâh Muhammad al-Husaynī Shîrâzî[5] montrent une tendance très nette à inclure les juifs dans la catégorie des *mushrikûn* et à prendre l'impureté que leur impute ce verset au sens littéral. D'après ces sources, ces derniers doivent être considérés comme des infidèles et donc comme impurs. Le shî'isme, tout comme le sunnisme d'ailleurs, justifie cette prise de position en élargissant la signification du terme *shirk* (associationnisme, polythéisme, idolâtrie). Néanmoins, la position shî'ite sur cette question semble beaucoup plus tranchée. Dans l'élaboration de leur argumentation, les savants shî'ites se fondent sur des versets coraniques qui remettent en question le monothéisme des juifs. Une synthèse de la question détaillant les opinions exprimées sur ce sujet tout au long de l'histoire du shî'isme est offerte dans l'ouvrage.

Selon al-Majlisî, l'impureté des peuples du Livre doit se comprendre selon deux aspects : leur « impureté spirituelle » (*najâsa ma'nawiyya*[6]) causée par « leur méchanceté foncière et la corruption de leurs croyances » (*khubth bâtinihim wa-sû'i i'tiqâdihim*[7]) ; et leur impureté concrète, physique, souvent appelée impureté juridique (*najâsa shar'iyya*[8]), c'est-à-dire définie par des prescriptions légales, et qui découle de cette impureté spirituelle. Elle se divise dans la jurisprudence shî'ite en plusieurs sous-chapitres : Est-il permis de toucher un membre des gens du Livre ou un objet touché par lui ? Est-il licite de mettre un vêtement qu'il a mis auparavant ? Est-il permis de dormir dans son lit ?, etc[9].

Les savants, des plus « souples » aux plus « rigoureux », exposent leurs opinions en s'appuyant sur des traditions attribuées au Prophète et aux Imâms. En voici quelques exemples : On demanda aux Imâms Muhammad al-Bâqir (mort v. 731-2) et Ja'far al-Sâdiq (m. 765) : « Est-il licite de serrer la main d'un juif ou d'un chrétien » ? Ils répondent que l'acte est permis s'il est accompli « à travers un vêtement, mais si [le juif ou le chrétien] te sert la main [directement], tu dois te la laver[10] ». De même, « s'il est permis de prier en mettant un vêtement acheté à un musulman [sans le laver auparavant] ; cependant, s'il a été acheté à un chrétien, il n'est licite de prier en le portant qu'après l'avoir lavé[11] ».

Il existe pourtant bien d'autres traditions remontant aux Imâms qui véhiculent des positions différentes plus souples[12], autorisant d'effectuer les ablutions rituelles avant la prière avec un objet touché par un juif ou en utilisant l'eau contenue dans un tel objet[13] ou encore permettant de porter des vêtements préalablement revêtus par un zoroastrien (*majûsî*[14]). Les textes se font d'ailleurs parfois l'écho de la perplexité des disciples face à cette tolérance des Imâms : « Comment pouvez-vous être aussi indulgents [par rapport à l'impureté des gens du Livre] étant donné qu'ils boivent du vin et mangent du porc ? » Les Imâms insistent alors sur la nécessité d'être souple[15]. D'autres traditions présentent les Imâms comme étant plus exigeants avec eux-mêmes qu'envers leurs disciples, ainsi l'Imâm al-Sâdiq : « Comment les musulmans doivent-ils se comporter lorsqu'ils sont à table et qu'arrive, de manière inattendue, un zoroastrien ? Doivent-ils l'inviter à partager leur repas ? » L'Imâm leur répond : « Personnellement, je ne me mets pas à table avec un zoroastrien, mais il me déplaît de vous interdire une chose que vous avez coutume de faire dans vos pays[16]. »

Les relations sociales

Les deux implications principales de la question de l'impureté des juifs sont la consommation de la chair des bêtes rituellement abattues par eux et le mariage avec des femmes issues de leurs communautés, deux thèmes déjà associés dans le Coran :

> Aujourd'hui, les bonnes choses vous sont permises. La nourriture de ceux auxquels le Livre a été donné vous est permise, et votre nourriture leur est permise. L'union avec les femmes croyantes et de bonne condition, et avec les femmes de bonne condition faisant partie du peuple auquel le Livre a été donné avant vous, vous est permise, si vous leur avez remis le douaire, en hommes contractant une union régulière et non comme des débauchés ou des amateurs de courtisanes… (5 : 5).

À première vue, ces propos, renforcés par d'autres versets, permettent explicitement aussi bien la consommation de la nourriture que le mariage avec les femmes issues des gens du Livre. Pourtant ces versets ont fait l'objet d'interminables controverses chez les savants sunnites et shî'ites. Si l'on retrouve chez les uns comme chez les autres des positions aussi bien souples que rigides, la tendance dominante est différente dans les deux branches de l'islam. L'opinion majoritaire parmi les juristes sunnites penche du côté de l'indulgence sur ces deux questions : la consommation des bêtes abattues selon le rituel des peuples du Livre est licite et il n'y a pas de mal à épouser des femmes parmi eux, bien qu'il soit évidemment préférable de se marier avec les femmes musulmanes[17]. Ils en veulent pour preuve l'histoire des premiers temps de l'islam, qui relate les mariages du prophète Muhammad et ses Compagnons avec des femmes juives ou chrétiennes.

Dans le droit shî'ite, c'est la tendance rigoriste qui est dominante. Même les savants indulgents préconisent des mesures préventives concernant le contact avec les juifs et les chrétiens et interprètent ces versets explicites du Coran dans un sens compatible avec leur position. Ainsi, la seule nourriture des gens du Livre qui soit permise sont les aliments crus ou « secs » tels que les graines et les légumes, mais pas leur viande ni les plats cuits par eux, car « la viande et les aliments humides touchés par eux sont impurs et leur consommation est interdite[18] ». Ils justifient (rejoints en cela par certains sunnites) l'interdiction de consommer la nourriture ou la bête rituellement abattue par les juifs et les chrétiens par le fait qu'ils ne prononcent pas la formule qu'on appelle *tasmiya,* c'est-a-dire le verset *Bismi Llâhi l-rahmâni l-rahîm* (« Au nom de Dieu, celui qui fait miséricorde, le Miséricordieux ») avant d'abattre la bête*, et que, quand bien même ils le feraient, le soupçon d'associationnisme qui pèse sur leur foi invalide leur intention[19].

Le même genre d'attitude négative prédomine en ce qui concerne le mariage avec les femmes

---

* Voir les versets coraniques comme 2 : 173 ; 6 : 118 et 121.

appartenant aux gens du Livre, les shî'ites considérant qu'il n'est pas permis de se marier avec elles sauf dans le cadre d'une union spécifique appelée *nikâh al-mut'a*[20], littéralement « mariage de plaisir », mariage à durée déterminée qui se dissout de lui-même à la fin d'une période spécifiée au départ, sans acte de divorce. Ce type de mariage, on s'en doute, est bien moins respectable que le mariage traditionnel. Ces prises de position ne sont pas uniquement théoriques et ont souvent été strictement appliquées, comme le montre l'étude significative de Sorour Soroudi[21] à travers des exemples concrets de rapports entre juifs et shî'ites en Iran au cours des derniers siècles[22].

Les origines du rigorisme shî'ite

S'il y a toujours eu des juristes shî'ites soutenant des opinions beaucoup plus modérées, que citent aussi bien al-Majlisî que l'ayatollâh Shîrâzî, ces derniers sont cependant tous unanimes à soutenir que la position permissive demeure marginale : « Tous nos savants juristes s'accordent à considérer comme impurs au moins les infidèles qui ne sont ni juifs ni chrétiens et la majorité d'entre eux soutiennent en outre que même ces deux derniers groupes sont également impurs[23]. » Laquelle, de la position permissive et de la position stricte, peut être dite correspondre à l'attitude du shî'isme ancien, c'est-à-dire avant l'« occultation » du douzième et dernier Imâm en 874, concernant les juifs et les chrétiens ? (La Perse, rappelons-le, n'est devenue majoritairement shî'ite qu'avec l'avènement de la dynastie safavide au XVIe siècle.) S'agit-il en outre de développements doctrinaux internes au shî'isme ou bien faut-il les imputer à des influences extérieures ou encore à une conjugaison des deux ?

Sur le premier point, le point de vue interne au shî'isme est que la tendance la plus authentique est bien celle qui prône la séparation d'avec l'« autre » et le devoir de le considérer comme impur. Abû Ja'far al-Tûsî, un des plus grands docteurs shî'ites duodécimains de tous les temps (m. 1067), explique que les opinions permissives sont purement circonstancielles. Elles se justifient d'une part par l'hostilité de la majorité sunnite aux opinions légales shî'ites divergentes, danger qui justifie la fameuse *taqiyya*, « précaution » ou dissimulation des divergences doctrinales. Elles constituent d'autre part un recours en cas de nécessité absolue et de danger pour la vie du fidèle, circonstances exceptionnelles dans lesquelles il devient licite de consommer des animaux rituellement abattus par des juifs et des chrétiens ou de se marier avec une femme issue de ces groupes[24].

Quant à l'origine interne ou externe de la notion

d'impureté des juifs et des chrétiens, il est difficile, en l'état actuel de la recherche, de s'en faire une opinion définitive. Il est cependant possible d'émettre quelques hypothèses. Commençons par celles déjà proposées par des islamologues reconnus. I. Goldziher, dans son article « Islamisme et Parsisme », souligne les remarquables ressemblances entre les lois régissant la pureté et l'impureté chez les zoroastriens et chez les shî'ites[25]. Rappelons que le zoroastrisme, religion d'État sous les Sassanides, n'était pas seulement pratiqué en Perse mais également dans toute la Mésopotamie, qui faisait partie de l'Empire, et que cette région de l'Irak actuel est le berceau du shî'isme. L'étude déjà mentionnée de S. Soroudi enrichit les découvertes de Goldziher par de nouvelles données et montre que de nombreuses restrictions posées par le droit zoroastrien afin de protéger la pureté des fidèles en contact avec un non-zoroastrien ou un zoroastrien pécheur ou apostat ressemblent de façon remarquable aux règles de pureté shî'ites. Par exemple, la religion zoroastrienne interdit à ses fidèles de s'attabler en compagnie d'un hérétique (*druvand*) ou d'un musulman. De plus, il est interdit de consommer la viande d'une bête rituellement abattue par ces derniers. Il n'est pas permis non plus de consommer de la graisse qui a été préparée par un hérétique, d'utiliser de l'eau ou des ustensiles touchés par un hérétique ou un musulman, d'accéder à un lieu de culte autre que le zoroastrisme ou de toucher les objets de culte qui s'y trouvent[26].

A. J. Wensinck suggère pour sa part que l'islam, toutes tendances confondues, a été, dès ses débuts, massivement influencé par des sources juives. D'après lui, cette influence peut expliquer les positions rigoristes du shî'isme concernant l'impureté des non-musulmans et la question de la consommation de leur nourriture[27]. De fait, les règles de pureté rituelle jouent un rôle majeur dans le judaïsme biblique et postbiblique jusqu'à la destruction du Temple qui en rend la plupart des règles caduques, et la littérature rabbinique ancienne fait largement état de dispositions supplémentaires décrétant l'impureté des non-juifs ou visant à limiter l'interaction avec eux. Cette opinion est partagée par Michael Cook, qui détecte des influences juives dans les écoles juridiques musulmanes développées en Irak, berceau du Talmud dit « de Babylone », et tout particulièrement dans le shî'isme duodécimain[28]. Par ailleurs, les recherches récentes de Y. Elman[29] ou encore S. Secunda[30] ont montré l'influence décisive des croyances, des rituels et du droit zoroastriens sur le Talmud de Babylone. Il est donc fort difficile de démêler, au sein des religions pratiquées dans l'ère irakienne des tout débuts de l'islam, ce qui relève des normes propres de chacune et ce qui relève d'influences réciproques.

Sans nier la vraisemblance de ces deux hypothèses, dont la première, l'influence zoroastrienne, nous paraît plus plausible, on peut en proposer une troisième, qui expliquerait le développement de la doctrine de l'impureté à partir de concepts internes au shî'isme. On peut en effet penser que l'attitude vis-à-vis de l'autre et le besoin de séparation se sont développés dans le shî'isme à partir de la prise de conscience de sa singularité et de son élection. Peut-être le statut minoritaire du shî'isme au sein de l'islam l'a-t-il amené à développer une doctrine d'élection et de supériorité par rapport aux musulmans sunnites et aux non-musulmans, de manière parallèle au judaïsme rabbinique dans la diaspora, sans être pour autant influencé par lui. Les shî'ites se considèrent comme appartenant à une communauté d'élus que Dieu a choisie avant même la création du monde sensible. Cette notion se manifeste de plusieurs façons. D'après la doctrine shî'ite, les Imâms et leurs fidèles ont été créés d'une argile particulière (*tîna*) extraite du Trône divin. Cette « matière première » n'est pas mélangée avec celle avec laquelle tout le reste de l'humanité a été créée[31]. De plus, la lumière divine traverse les Imâms qui sont considérés comme des êtres choisis par Dieu. À l'opposé, les infidèles, c'est-à-dire les adversaires des shî'ites, même « musulmans », ont été créés d'une matière inférieure et impure tirée de l'enfer[32]. Cette perception de soi en tant que communauté d'élus peut expliquer l'existence de règles juridiques ayant pour objectif de consolider les barrières entre les élus et la masse, les purs et les impurs. Le même genre d'attitude existe, sous une forme ou une autre, aussi bien dans le zoroastrisme que le judaïsme.

Ce sentiment d'élection et le fait d'être une minorité persécutée tout au long de son histoire peuvent expliquer le besoin d'isolement et de séparation. Mary Boyce, éminente spécialiste des religions iraniennes anciennes, soutient que dans la religion zoroastrienne un rapport similaire existe toujours entre une théologie de l'élection et ses implications cultuelles et juridiques à travers un système rigoureux de lois de pureté et d'impureté. « Les lois de pureté [dans le zoroastrisme], écrit Boyce, puisent leur force de leur base doctrinale fondée dans le dualisme de Zoroastre qui conçoit le monde comme le champ d'un conflit éternel entre le Bien, dont la pureté fait évidemment partie, et le Mal qui met constamment en danger le Bien et la pureté[33]. »

Une dialectique similaire est perceptible dans les écrits des sectes juives de la mer Morte entre une théologie de l'élection et de la supériorité d'une communauté d'une part, et un système rigoureux de lois de pureté d'autre part[34]. Par ailleurs, la possibilité d'une influence des religions iraniennes sur ces écrits du tournant de l'ère chrétienne est un thème important qu'on ne peut évidemment pas aborder ici. La recherche en histoire comparée des religions peut mettre en lumière d'autres croyances comportant ce genre de dialectique. Notre hypothèse, selon laquelle les règles de pureté du shî'isme sont les conséquences d'une tension intrinsèque de cette religion, n'exclut donc pas l'hypothèse des influences extérieures mais peut la compléter.

Fils d'Israël, prototypes et témoins de la préexistence des shî'ites

Au vu de tout cela, le fait que le shî'isme revendique une filiation exclusive avec le peuple d'Israël paraît surprenante. La conception d'Israël comme prototype de la Shî'a est exprimée dans des traditions exégétiques attribuées aux Imâms Muhammad al-Bâqir et Ja'far al-Sâdiq. Dans leurs commentaires du verset « Ô fils d'Israël ! Souvenez-vous des bienfaits dont je vous ai comblés ! Je vous ai préférés à tous les mondes » (2 : 47), les premiers commentaires coraniques imâmites attribuent à l'Imâm al-Sâdiq l'idée selon laquelle, au niveau de la signification ésotérique du verset, le véritable peuple élu dont il y est question n'est autre que la famille du prophète Muhammad (*ahl al-bayt*), c'est-à-dire les Imâms shî'ites[35].

On trouve dans la même littérature une autre illustration de cette identification de la famille de Muhammad, c'est-à-dire des Imâms, avec le peuple d'Israël. Le Prophète aurait dit : « Je suis 'Abd Allâh et mon nom est Ahmad* et je suis aussi le fils de 'Abd Allâh et mon nom est Israël**. Tout ce que Dieu a ordonné à Israël, Il l'a ordonné à moi aussi et partout où Il s'est référé à lui, Il s'est référé à moi aussi[36]. » Cette tradition repose sur un jeu de mots sur les deux significations du nom 'Abd Allâh : son sens littéral « serviteur de Dieu » et l'allusion au nom du père du Prophète. L'implication de cette identification de Muhammad avec Israël / Jacob est que le Prophète et ses descendants sont considérés comme la continuation des Israélites de la Bible. Une interprétation de cette tradition est offerte par al-Majlisî :

> « La parole divine "Ô fils d'Israël ! Souvenez-vous des bienfaits dont je vous ai comblés. Je vous ai

---

* Le nom Ahmad est dit être l'appellation allusive de Muhammad dans le Coran 61 : 5.

** La tradition fait référence à la figure biblique de Jacob qui fut par la suite appelé Israël : « On ne t'appellera plus Jacob, mais Israël, car tu as été fort contre Dieu et contre tous les hommes et tu l'as emporté. » (Genèse 32 : 29).

préférés à tous les mondes" peut s'entendre dans le sens ésotérique comme faisant référence à la famille de Muhammad, car [le nom] Israël signifie *'abd Allâh* [serviteur de Dieu*]. [Selon le hadîth du Prophète :] "je suis le fils de 'Abd Allâh et je suis [aussi] 'Abd Allâh", comme le dit Dieu : "Gloire à celui qui a fait voyager de nuit son serviteur** de la Mosquée sacrée à la Mosquée très éloignée..." (17 : 1). Par conséquent, toutes les mentions positives des fils d'Israël les concernent au niveau exotérique (*zâhir*), alors qu'au niveau ésotérique (*bâtin*), elles me concernent, moi, et ma maisonnée[37]. »

Parallèlement à cette première tendance d'identification de la Shî'a aux fils d'Israël bibliques, les sources shî'ites duodécimaines font état d'une seconde où les descendants d'Israël sont présentés comme des prototypes ou des préfigurations de la Shî'a. Ainsi les Hébreux de la Bible, mais aussi du Coran, victimes de l'oppression de Pharaon en Égypte, sont considérés comme les modèles des shî'ites et leurs souffrances symbolisent celles que les shî'ites subissent de la part de leurs ennemis. De la même façon, la délivrance des

---

* Ce n'est que partiellement vrai. Le nom hébreu « Israël » contient l'élément théophore *el* qui signifie Dieu (Allâh). Mais on comprend mal comment l'élément *'abd* (serviteur) est associé au mot.

** Selon les exégètes, ce « serviteur » désigne Muhammad.

Hébreux du joug des Égyptiens et leur victoire finale sur ces derniers sont présentées comme un message d'espoir présageant la victoire des shî'ites sur leurs ennemis. L'un des fondements coraniques sur lequel s'appuie cette conception sont les versets 28 : 3-6 :

> « Nous te racontons, en toute vérité, à l'intention d'un peuple qui croit, l'histoire de Moïse et de Pharaon. Pharaon était hautain sur la terre [d'Égypte]. Il avait réparti les habitants en sections (*shiya'an*). Il cherchait à affaiblir un groupe d'entre eux : il égorgeait leurs fils et laissait vivre leurs filles. C'était un fauteur de désordres. Mais nous voulions favoriser ceux qui avaient été humiliés sur la terre (*alladhîna stud'ifû fî l-ard*) ; nous voulions en faire des chefs (*a'imma*), des héritiers (*wârithûna*), nous voulions les établir sur la terre et montrer ainsi à Pharaon, à Haman et à leurs armées, *de leur part* (*minhum*), ce qu'ils redoutaient. »

Certains termes utilisés ici ont un sens technique pour les shî'ites, lesquels n'ont pas hésité à les exploiter pour les besoins de leur cause. Le mot *a'imma* (« chefs » ou « imâms ») est entendu comme des références à l'institution de l'imâmat et aux diverses doctrines qui s'y rattachent ; le mot *wârithûna* (« héritiers ») est compris comme désignant les Imâms, ceux que le shî'isme considère comme les seuls successeurs légitimes du prophète Muhammad. De la même façon, l'expression *alladhîna stud'ifû fî l-ard* (« ceux qui avaient été humiliés sur la terre ») est traditionnellement considérée comme faisant allusion aux shî'ites, minorité persécutée presque tout au long de l'histoire. 'Alî b. Ibrâhîm al-Qummî (mort au cours de la première moitié du xe siècle), l'un des commentateurs shî'ites les plus célèbres, propose l'interprétation suivante :

> Dieu a informé Son Prophète [Muhammad] des injustices et des persécutions que les compagnons de Moïse ont subies de la part de Pharaon, afin que ce [récit] le console de ce que lui et sa famille allaient subir de la part de son propre peuple. Après cette consolation, [Dieu] lui annonça que Sa Grâce les atteindrait [i.e. lui et sa famille) en faisant d'eux ses califes sur terre et les imâms de Son peuple. [À la fin des temps], Il les fera revenir à la vie, aussi bien eux que leurs ennemis afin que ces derniers subissent leur châtiment.... [L'expression coranique] « De leur part » (*minhum*) désigne la famille de Muhammad [...]. Dieu a mentionné Moïse et les fils d'Israël ainsi que leurs ennemis – Pharaon, Haman et leurs troupes – pour qu'ils servent d'exemple [aux shî'ites]. Dieu a dit : Pharaon tuait les fils d'Israël et leur faisait du mal, mais ensuite Dieu donna à Moïse la victoire sur Pharaon et les compagnons de celui-ci en anéantissant ces

derniers. De la même façon, la famille du Messager de Dieu endurera l'injustice et l'iniquité, mais par la suite Dieu les fera revenir en ce monde, eux et leurs ennemis, afin que les premiers puissent mettre à mort les seconds[38].

De tels parallélismes entre la destinée des Israélites de la Bible souffrant sous le joug de Pharaon et celles des shî'ites dominés par leurs ennemis sont récurrents dans les écrits shî'ites. Dans le commentaire coranique d'Abû 'Alî al-Fadl b. al-Hasan al-Tabrisî (mort en 1153), ce concept est exprimé en termes plus généraux : « "Nous voulions favoriser ceux qui avaient été humiliés sur la terre" [...] : Les justes qui sont parmi nous, nous la maisonnée [du Prophète] et nos fidèles, nous occupons le rang de Moïse et ses fidèles, tandis que nos ennemis et leurs partisans occupent le rang de Pharaon et ses partisans[39]. »

Une autre analogie entre la destinée du peuple d'Israël en Égypte et celle des shî'ites est établie à travers une tradition rapportée dans le commentaire coranique d'al-'Ayyâshî concernant le verset 11 : 72 : « Elle [Sarah] a dit : "Malheur à moi !... Enfanterai-je alors que je suis une vieille ?" » Ces paroles de Sarah, qui sont traditionnellement interprétées comme une mise en doute de la toute-puissance divine, ont été considérées par la tradition musulmane comme la cause de la condamnation de ses descendants, c'est-à-dire les Israélites, à l'esclavage sous le joug des Égyptiens pendant quatre cents ans. Mais après la repentance des Israélites, la tradition nous dit que Dieu a enlevé cent soixante-dix ans de la durée de leur esclavage. La morale de ce récit, selon une tradition remontant à l'Imâm al-Sâdiq, est que si les shî'ites suivaient l'exemple de leurs prédécesseurs israélites en se repentant, Dieu serait clément à leur égard et hâterait leur délivrance ; dans le cas contraire, leur souffrance se prolongera jusqu'à son terme[40].

L'épisode biblique de Gédéon soumettant ses guerriers à l'épreuve de l'eau à la source de Harod (Juges 7 : 4-7), dont on trouve un écho dans le Coran (2 : 247-250[41]), a fourni à nos auteurs une autre histoire édifiante. La conclusion de cette histoire coranique – « Combien de fois une petite troupe d'hommes a vaincu une troupe nombreuse, avec la permission de Dieu ! » – a manifestement contribué à faire percevoir ce récit comme une illustration supplémentaire de la victoire d'une minorité faible et juste sur une majorité puissante et inique[42].

Il est frappant de constater que des traditions shî'ites de ce genre se réfèrent principalement à l'époque de la servitude égyptienne et à celle des pérégrinations dans le désert. De fait, la plupart des figures bibliques choisies comme paradigmes remontent à cette période. Il en va de même pour les ennemis des Israélites que les shî'ites identifient à leurs propres adversaires. Parmi ces traditions se trouve la fameuse « tradition du rang » (*hadîth al-manzila*) selon laquelle Muhammad aurait dit au moment de désigner 'Alî comme son successeur : « ton rang par rapport au mien est semblable à celui d'Aaron par rapport à Moïse[43] ». Dans la tradition shî'ite, on trouve des appellations péjoratives pour désigner les trois premiers califes, considérés comme ayant usurpé la place de 'Alî, parmi lesquelles : Abû Bakr est *'ijl hâdhihi l-umma*, « le Veau [d'or] de cette communauté », 'Umar est *Fir'awn hâdhihi l-umma*, « le Pharaon de cette communauté », et 'Uthman est *Sâmirî hâdhihi l-umma*, « le Samaritain de cette communauté »[44]. Enfin, comme l'a montré Etan Kohlberg, le titre de *râfida* ou *rawâfid*, littéralement « ceux qui rejettent », l'une des appellations les plus usuelles par lesquelles sont désignés les shî'ites, aussi bien par eux-mêmes que par leurs adversaires[45], est notamment interprétée comme une reprise du titre donné aux soixante-dix fils d'Israël qui, après avoir accordé leur soutien à Pharaon, le rejetèrent (*rafadû*) lorsqu'ils découvrirent qu'il avait renié la vraie religion. Ils ajoutèrent alors foi à la religion de Moïse. Depuis lors, Dieu aurait réservé pour les shî'ites ce titre qui désignait à l'origine un groupe d'Israélites élus[46].

À mon sens, si cette période de l'histoire biblique a été particulièrement choisie comme modèle pour les shî'ites, c'est qu'elle comporte deux éléments susceptibles d'inspirer un sentiment d'identification : tout d'abord, l'histoire d'une persécution subie par une minorité ; ensuite, le fait que cette histoire se termine par la délivrance accordée par Dieu à cette minorité. Les shî'ites se donnaient ainsi une perspective optimiste au milieu des persécutions subies sous le joug de leurs ennemis, c'est-à-dire les califes des dynasties omeyyade et abbasside, pour ne citer qu'elles.

Conclusion

Le lien entre le shî'isme et l'Israël biblique tel qu'il se manifeste dans les traditions étudiées ici n'apporte qu'une explication partielle de l'attitude des shî'ites envers les juifs et leur religion. Tout comme le sunnisme, le shî'isme distingue nettement les fils d'Israël de la Bible des juifs postbibliques. Cette distinction, qui tire son origine du Coran même, est déjà nette dans la terminologie : alors que les premiers sont appelés *banû isrâ'îl* (Fils d'Israël), terme qui a généralement une signification positive, les seconds sont nommés *al-yahûd*, « les juifs », vocable souvent utilisé de manière péjorative. Communément, les musulmans en général et les shî‘ites en particulier entretiennent une attitude complexe et hétéroclite à l'égard des juifs : l'attitude qui prévaut dans le shî‘isme consiste à les considérer comme rituellement impurs, du point de vue juridique. Cette attitude a notamment pour conséquence le fait que les fidèles shî‘ites doivent se tenir physiquement à l'écart des juifs, s'abstenir de consommer des aliments cuisinés par eux, d'utiliser des ustensiles qu'ils ont touchés, de contracter des mariages avec les juives, etc. On peut penser également, en suivant la présentation que fait M. A. Amir-Moezzi de la vision du monde duelle du shî‘isme, que l'attitude du shî‘isme vis-à-vis des juifs et du judaïsme relève de la même division de la réalité en deux niveaux, exotérique (*zâhir*) et ésotérique (*bâtin*[47]) : dans cette optique, le droit et les règles juridiques négatives concernant les juifs correspondent à l'aspect exotérique alors que les données doctrinales positives correspondent à l'aspect ésotérique.

CONCLUSION

La religion musulmane est née d'un contrat persistant avec les traditions religieuses qui l'avaient précédée, au premier rang desquelles la religion juive. Nous avons essayé, dans ce livre, de rendre compte de la place qu'occupent les juifs et le judaïsme dans le Coran, sans négliger ni le contexte historique de la présence juive dans la péninsule Arabique au moment de la naissance de l'islam, ni les prolongements de ces thèmes coraniques dans la littérature islamique postérieure.

Le Coran porte sur les juifs, sur la Bible hébraïque et sur la littérature juive postbiblique un regard complexe. D'un côté, le Coran revendique un attachement sans faille à la Torah, aux prophètes et à leurs paroles en tant que révélations divines : ces sources doivent être révérées, et elles viennent en outre attester l'authenticité de la révélation coranique. D'un autre côté, le Coran met en doute l'authenticité des Écritures des juifs de son temps et accuse ces derniers de les avoir falsifiées, en particulier pour en supprimer ou en altérer les passages censés annoncer l'avènement de Muhammad et de l'islam, leur triomphe et leur supériorité sur toutes les religions antérieures, y compris le judaïsme.

Cette ambivalence du Coran se retrouve dans le domaine de la loi religieuse ou *sharî'a* : d'une part le Coran puise largement aux sources de la *halakha* juive, concernant des conceptions générales comme des points de détail, d'autre part la tradition islamique manifeste, tout au long de son histoire, une volonté de se distinguer nettement des pratiques juives, comme l'attestent de nombreux hadîths : « Ne ressemblez pas aux juifs et aux chrétiens », « Manifestez votre divergence avec les juifs », etc. Il s'agit de bien marquer le caractère indépendant de la religion islamique, sans qu'elle ait besoin de s'en référer aux religions qui l'ont précédée.

Cette attitude équivoque n'est nulle part plus patente que dans les *isrâ'îliyyât*, ces traditions orales dont le nom indique justement qu'elles trouvent leur source dans le patrimoine religieux juif et qui font l'objet, aujourd'hui comme hier, de polémiques à l'intérieur de l'islam. Nombreux sont les traditionnistes musulmans à avoir recouru à ces sources et à leur avoir accordé du crédit, conformément au célèbre hadîth : « Transmettez des enseignements issus des fils d'Israël et sachez que cela n'est pas répréhensible » (*haddithû 'an banî isrâ'îla wa-lâ haraja*[48]). D'autres y ont vu des influences étrangères dont la tradition musulmane doit absolument être purgée. Ils considèrent qu'elles ont été introduites en islam par des célèbres convertis juifs des premiers temps, parmi lesquels les Yéménites Ka'b al-Ahbâr et Wahb ibn Munabbih, et qu'il vaut mieux ne pas s'y fier.

Dans la mesure où le Coran est un texte vivant et dynamique sur lequel les musulmans règlent leur vie, il n'y a rien d'étonnant à ce que ses propos sur les juifs et le judaïsme influencent la manière dont les musulmans voient ces derniers, en tout temps et en tout lieu. Les musulmans, qui font l'expérience du Coran comme Parole divine, sont confrontés à travers lui – et à sa tradition exégétique longue de mille quatre cents ans – à l'omniprésence des juifs et de leurs ancêtres israélites. Ils sont transportés avec eux de verset en verset, connaissent parfaitement ceux qui évoquent l'élection du peuple d'Israël, le don de la Torah et l'entrée en Terre sainte, aussi bien que ceux qui relatent la colère divine dont ils ont été l'objet, eux les tueurs de prophètes, les idolâtres, les traîtres à l'alliance conclue avec Dieu et, partant, prompts à trahir toute alliance future avec les hommes. Ces paroles du Coran sont présentes aux lèvres de bien des croyants, qui énoncent : « Ô vous qui croyez ! Ne prenez pas les juifs et les chrétiens comme affiliés ; ils sont affiliés les uns avec les autres » (5 : 51).

Les rapports conflictuels qu'entretint Muhammad avec les juifs de Médine à partir de son hégire dans cette ville en 622, qui irriguent tant le Coran que les sources paracoraniques comme la *Sîra* et le Hadîth contribuent à alimenter l'image négative des juifs : ils auraient trahi Muhammad, auraient conspiré pour le faire assassiner, auraient raillé son message et auraient tenté de faire échouer sa mission.

Il faut bien être conscient que ces notions ne sont pas marginales, ni l'apanage d'un groupe d'initiés. Quiconque lit le Coran, quiconque même prête l'oreille aux sermons prononcés dans des mosquées, se familiarise avec ces thèmes et à l'interprétation qui en est donnée. Si cette « question juive » occupe une place si prééminente dans le discours musulman contemporain, c'est aussi parce que les juifs, à la différence d'autres groupes mentionnés dans le Coran, comme les sabéens (qu'on identifie parfois aux mandéens, une religion gnostique de Mésopotamie), sont un peuple qui existe toujours et qui est présent dans le vécu.

Les juifs, qui tout au long de l'histoire musulmane ont subsisté comme minorité « protégée » et soumise à la domination de l'islam, ont fait irruption dans l'arène géopolitique internationale avec les débuts du sionisme au XIXe siècle, lors de leur retour en Terre sainte, puis de la création de l'État d'Israël indépendant au milieu du XXe siècle, sur un territoire qui était jusqu'à récemment partie intégrante de l'Empire ottoman et du Califat. D'un point de vue musulman, cette situation est insupportable, tant sur le plan religieux que politique. Les juifs sont censés mener une vie d'humiliation et de pauvreté à l'ombre de l'islam ; que ce ne soit plus le cas constitue un scandale, nourrissant un discours incessant à ce sujet.

Rien de tout cela n'est non plus, comme on l'a vu, tout à fait spécifique à l'islam ; après tout, l'Église catholique, jusqu'à Vatican II, tenait aussi pour doctrine officielle que Dieu avait rejeté les juifs et que si ces derniers devaient continuer d'exister, c'est uniquement en tant que minorité opprimée, afin de bien manifester la différence entre l'Église élue de Dieu et la Synagogue réprouvée. Le Nouveau Testament ne se prête pas moins à une lecture « antijuive » que le Coran. À l'inverse, si le référent juif occupe une place majeure dans le discours coranique, ce n'est pas, comme on l'a vu, en tant que pur discours antagoniste, et la question des juifs est loin d'être au cœur des préoccupations du discours musulman classique. On a vu en outre que la tendance de l'exégèse traditionnelle était plutôt de spécifier les circonstances de validité de tel ou tel verset, tandis que la tendance moderne est à l'absolutisation du sens et à sa transformation en arme idéologique. Ce sont les vicissitudes de l'histoire qui ont poussé ce thème à l'avant-scène du discours actuel, et il serait faux d'extrapoler à partir de ce qu'on entend aujourd'hui quant à un islam qu'on dirait « irrévocablement » antijuif.

En naviguant sur Internet, on constate un flot constant de sources scripturaires, de cours et de sermons qui cherchent à rendre actuelles les paroles par lesquelles le Coran critique les juifs et les délégitimise. Ce sont toujours les mêmes versets, les mêmes hadîths qui sont mobilisés dans ce discours incendiaire. D'autres voix, plus posées, tentent cependant de se faire entendre au sein du monde musulman ; mais il faut bien constater qu'aujourd'hui elles sont loin d'être dominantes et rencontrent peu d'écho.

Notes

I. Le cadre historique

1. G. Newby, *A History of the Jews of Arabia : From Ancient Times to their Eclipse under Islam*, University of South Carolina Press, 1988, p. 7.

2. L. Ginzberg, *Les Légendes des Juifs,* traduit de l'anglais par G. Sed-Rajna, Paris, Le Cerf, 2006, vol. 6, p. 305.

3. Le texte est cité par C. J. Gadd, dans son article « The Harran Inscription of Nabonidus », *Anatolian Studies*, vol. 8, 1958, p. 80.

4. Voir Ch. Robin, « Arabia and Ethiopia », dans *The Oxford Handbook of Late Antiquity*, S. Fitzgerald Johnson éd., Oxford, 2012, p. 247–332.

5. Voir Procopius, *History of the Wars,* livres I et II, Londres, Havard University Press, 1914, p. 189-190.

6. Voir H. Z. Hirschberg, *Israël ba-'Arav : Qorôt Ha-Yéhûdîm be-Himyar ve-Hijâz* (« Israël en Arabie »), Tel-Aviv, 1946, p. 53-58 ; Y. Y. Toby, *Yahadût Teman be-tsel ha-Islâm me-reshito vé-'ad yamenu* (« Les Juifs du Yémen à l'ombre de l'islam, des origines à nos jours »), Jérusalem, 2018, p. 22, 26 et 200.

7. Voir Toby, *ibid.*, p. 19 et 185.

8. Voir P. Jule et K. Galor, « Zafar : Watershed of Late Pre-Islamic Culture », in *Le Judaïsme de l'Arabie antique* (Actes du Colloque de Jérusalem, février 2006), Christian Robin éd. p. 403-405.

9. Voir M. Lecker, *Muhammad ve-ha-Yehudim* (« Muhammad et les Juifs »), Jérusalem, 2014, p. 21-26.

10. Voir S. D. Goitein, *Jews and Arabs : Their Contacts through the Ages,* Schoken Books, New York, 1955, p. 49.

11. Voir Goitein, « Benei Israël u-mahloqtam : mehqar ba-Qur'ân » (« Les fils d'Israël et leurs controverses : étude sur le Coran »), *Tarbiz,* vol. 3 (1931), p. 412. Il convient de noter que les « villes de *cohanim* » ne constituent pas un phénomène propre à la péninsule Arabique. On en connaît bien d'autres exemples à travers l'histoire juive. La Bible, déjà, évoque « Nob, la ville de *cohanim* » (I Samuel 22, 19). À l'époque moderne, Djerba en Tunisie et Debdou au Maroc sont deux villes où les *cohanim* étaient très fortement représentés.

12. Lecker, « Muhammad et les Juifs », *op. cit.,* p. 36.

13. *Ibid.*, p. 38.

14. Newby, *A History of the Jews of Arabia, op. cit.*, p. 50.

15. *Ibid.*

16. S. D. Goitein, « Mi hayu rabbotav ha-muvhaqim shel Muhammad ? » (« Quels furent les maîtres à penser de Muhammad ? »), *Tarbiz* (*A quarterly for Jewish Studies*), vol. 23 (1962), p. 146-159 (en hébreu).

17. Voir Ch. Rabin, « Islam and the Qumran Sect », *Qumran Studies,* Londres, 1957, p. 112-130.

18. Le livre de Zellentin a paru chez Mohr Siebeck à Tübingen en 2013.

19. La thèse de doctorat de J. Witztum a été soutenue à l'université de Princeton en 2011.

20. M. Sharon, « The Decisive Battles in the Arab Conquest of Syria », *Studia Orientalia*, vol. 101, 2017, p. 297-357 (particulièrement p. 301).

21. Hirschberg, *Israël ba-'Arav, op. cit.*, p. 242-264 ; voir en particulier le débat sur l'authenticité, p. 262-264.

22. Voir Y. Perlman, « Ha-hitnaqqeshût ba-méshorérét ha-yéhudiyya 'Asmâ' bint Marwân » (« The Assassination of the Jewish Poetess 'Asmâ' bint Marwân »), *Pe'amim (Studies in Oriental Jewry)*, vol. 132, 2012, p. 149-169.

23. Goitein, « Les fils d'Israël et leurs controverses », p. 143.

24. Pour compliquer encore ces questions, notons que l'historiographie arabe traditionnelle tient que ces deux royaumes ont été fondés par des Arabes du Yémen ayant fui l'effondrement de leur ancien royaume. Pour tous ces aspects, voir A. L. de Prémare, *Les Fondations de l'islam. Entre écriture et histoire*, Paris, Le Seuil, 2002, p. 35-81.

25. Cf. R. Mantran, *L'Expansion musulmane*, Paris, PUF, 1991, p. 86.

26. Voir Mahmoud Hussein, *al-Sîra : Le Prophète de l'islam raconté par ses compagnons*, Paris, Grasset, 2007, tome 2, p. 177-367. Voir aussi M. Lecker, « Muhammad et les Juifs », *op. cit.*, p. 121-177.

27. Un examen détaillé de ce slogan, ainsi qu'un inventaire exhaustif des formules du même acabit, figurent dans le livre *Shi'ârât al-intifâda* (« Les slogans de l'intifâda »), dont j'ai eu connaissance par une version électronique, diffusée sur le site internet du Centre palestinien d'information (*al-markaz al-filastini li-l-i'lâm*, www.palinfo.com). Voir par exemple le site http://muslimcd.blogspot.com/2012/11/khiper.html et aussi : https://www.youtube.com/watch?v=IL-Zw-WVwTA8.

II. La représentation du judaïsme et des juifs dans le Coran

1. Voir H. Ben-Shammai, « *Suhuf* in the Qur'an – A Loan Translation for "Apocalypses" » dans *Exchange and Transmission across Cultural Boundaries : Philosophy, Mysticism and Science in the Mediterranean World – Proceedings of an International Workshop Held in Memory of Professor Shlomo Pines,* éd. H. Ben-Shammai, S. Shaked et S. Stroumsa, Jérusalem, 2013, p. 1-15.

2. Voir Abû Ja'far Muhammad b. Jarîr al-Tabarî, *Jâmi' al-bayân 'an ta'wîl ây al-qur'ān*, Mustafâ al-Bâbî al-Halabî éd., Le Caire, 1968, vol. 1, p. 75-78. Il est à noter que la même interprétation est répétée par plusieurs commentateurs de toutes les époques.

3. Voir aussi J. Chabbi, *Le Coran décrypté : Figures bibliques en Arabie*, Paris, Fayard, 2008, p. 347-349.

4. Cf. par exemple Tabarî, *Jâmi' al-bayân*, vol. 1, partie 1, p. 265.

5. Voir F. Dreyfus, « Reste d'Israël », *Supplément au Dictionnaire de la Bible* (H. Cazelle et A. Feuillet éd.), Paris, Letouzey & Ané, 1981, fascicule 55, p. 414-437.

6. Cf., par exemple, G. Dahan, *La Polémique chrétienne contre le judaïsme au Moyen Âge*, Albin Michel, « Présences du judaïsme », Paris, 1991, p. 126-129.

7. Voir H. Ben-Shammai, « L'idée de l'élection dans l'islam ancien » (Ra'ayon ha-behira ba-islam ha-qadum), dans *L'Idée de l'élection chez le peuple d'Israël et les autres peuples* (*Ra'ayon ha-behira be-Israel u-va-'ammim*), S. Almog et M. Heyd éd., Jérusalem, 1991, p. 159-160 (en hébreu).

8. Voir Tabarî, *Jâmi' al-bayân*, vol. 3, partie 4, p. 265.

9. Cf. M. M. Bar-Asher, *Scripture and Exegesis in Early Imâmî Shiism*, Leyde et Jérusalem, 1999, p. 102.

10. Cf. aussi A. I. Katsh, *Judaism in Islam : Biblical and Talmudic Backgrounds of the Koran and its Commentaries*, New York, NY University Press, 1954, p. 65-66 ; G. S. Reynolds, *The Qur'an and the Bible* : *Text and Commentary*, New Haven, Yale University Press, 2018, p. 51.

11. Voir aussi J. Chabbi, *Le Coran décrypté, op. cit.*, p. 325-365.

12. Cf. le commentaire d'al-Tabarî sur le verset 5 : 21, *Jâmi' al-bayân*, vol. 4, partie 6, p. 171-173.

13. Cf. par exemple R. Blachère dans sa traduction de ces versets : « Ce verset fait allusion soit aux intrigues des Juifs Qaynuqâ' soit à la trahison des Juifs Qurayza, lors de la bataille de Ohod » in *Le Coran*, p. 209, note au verset 58.

14. *Ibid.*, p. 342, note 87. Voir aussi la note importante de D. Masson à sa traduction du Coran : « Le prophète Osée (VIII, 5-6) fait allusion au "veau de Samarie". Le culte du Veau d'or s'est maintenu dans le royaume du Nord, au temps des Rois (cf. I Rois, XII, 28 ; II Rois, X, 29 ; XVII, 16) » in *Le Coran : Introduction, traduction et notes*, Paris, Gallimard, 1967, p. 883, note 85. Voir aussi l'entrée « Veau d'or » (par Daniel de Smet), dans le *Dictionnaire du Coran*, M. A. Amir-Moezzi éd., Paris, Robert Laffont, 2007, p. 897-899.

15. Voir R. Comerro, « Esdras est-il le fils de Dieu ? », *Arabica*, vol. 52, 2005, p. 165-181 ; M. Ayoub, « 'Uzayr in the Qur'ân and Muslin Tradition », W.M. Brinner et S. D. Ricks éd., *Studies in Islamic and Judaic Traditions*, Atlanta, 1986, vol. 1, p. 3-18.

16. Cf. Ch. Mopsik, « La datation du *Chi'our Qomah* d'après un texte néotestamentaire », in *Revue des sciences religieuses*, 68e année, n° 2, 1994, p. 131-144, repris dans Ch. Mopsik, *Chemins de la cabale*, Paris, Éclat, 2004, p. 309-324.

17. Abû Ishâq Ahmad b. Muhammad al-Naysâbûri al-Tha'labî, *Qisas al-anbiyâ' al-musamma 'arâis al-majâlis*, Beyrouth, 1985, p. 346.

18. Le texte d'Ibn Hazm est cité par H. Lazarus-Yafeh, « Ezra-'Uzayr : The Metamorphosis of a Polemical Motif », dans *id.*, *Intertwined Worlds : Medieval Islam and Bible Criticism*, Princeton, 1992, p. 68.

19. *Ibid.*, p. 68-70.

20. Cf. Shelomo ben Adret, *Ma'amar 'al Ishma'el* (« Dissertation sur l'islam »), Betzalel Naor éd., Orot, Spring Vally, NY, 2008.

21. Voir A. Kofsky, « Zechariah of Caphar-Zechariah in the Crux of Theology and Hermeneutics », *Proche-Orient Chrétien*, vol. 6 (2011); p. 34-44 et voir aussi B. Halpern Amaru, « The Killing of the Prophets : Unravelling a Midrash », Hebrew Union College Annual, vol. 54 (1983), p. 153-180.

22. Voir J. Horovitz, *Koranische Untersuchungen,* Berlin et Leipzig, 1926, p. 40.

23. Voir l'entrée « Crucifixion » (par Daniel de Smet), dans le *Dictionnaire du Coran*, M. A. Amir-Moezzi éd., p. 197-199.

24. Ce thème est traité ci-dessous, p. 177-180.

25. Pour une discussion générale de ces thèmes, cf. P. Lory, *La Dignité de l'homme face aux anges, aux animaux et aux djinns*, Paris, 2018, p. 31-36.

26. Pour une discussion de ces termes de la métempsychose dans le contexte de l'islam en général, voir H. Ben-Shammai, « Transmigration des âmes dans la pensée juive en Orient au xe siècle » (*« Gilgul neshamot ba-mahashava ha-yehudit ba-mizrah ba-me'a ha-'asirit »*), dans *Sefunot (Études et sources sur l'histoire des communautés juives en Orient*, 20 (1991), p. 118-124 (en hébreu).

27. L'article a paru dans S. Almog éd., *Antisemitism Through the Ages*, Oxford, 1988, p. 161-170.

28. *Sahîh Muslim* 41 : 6985 (54 : 7376). Voir aussi Mohamed Lakhdar-Bahlouli, « Le *gharqad*... l'arbre que les sionistes aiment bien... », *Centrale Info algérienne,* 26 novembre 2016 (https://lakhdarbahlouli.wordpress.com/). Voir aussi A.-M. Olivier et P. F. Steinberg, *The Road to Martyr's Square ; A Journey into the World of the Suicide Bomber*, Oxford, 2005, p. 19-24 (« The Gharqad Tree »).

29. http://www.crif.org/sites/default/fichiers/images/documents/ Charte%20du%20Hamas.pdf.

30. Le KKL est une institution sioniste créée en 1901 afin d'acheter des terres en Palestine et d'aménager le territoire en plantant des forêts, construisant des ponts et des barrages, développant l'agriculture, etc.

31. http://www.assadtamimi.net/Israelstate1.htm.

III. Les récits bibliques et leurs prolongements postbibliques dans le Coran

1. D'après une autre interprétation, répandue dans l'exégèse du Coran, le mot est dérivé de la racine *s-k-n* signifiant « quiétude », « tranquillité », « grand paix ». Voir l'entrée « sakîna » (par E. G. Geoffroy), dans le *Dictionnaire du Coran*, *op. cit.*, p. 784-785.

2. Geiger le faisait déjà remarquer. Voir A. Geiger, *Was hat Mohammed aus dem Judenthume aufgenommen ?*, Bonn, 1833, p. 101-102 (*Judaism and Islam*, traduit en anglais par F. M. Young, Madras, 1898, p. 80-81) ; Blachère, *Le Coran*, p. 137 ; H. Speyer, *Die biblischen Erzählungen im Qoran*, Gräfenhairichen, 1931, p. 84-88 ; Voir aussi Reynolds, *The Qur'an and the Bible*, *op. cit.*, p. 199.

3. Le texte standard de cette mishna que l'on trouve aujourd'hui dans les éditions du Talmud, notamment, donne la version « une seule personne *juive* » et l'on a souvent fait le procès du « racisme » du Talmud. Il faut cependant se rappeler que le texte du Talmud, et donc de la mishna qui s'y trouve incluse, a depuis le Moyen Âge fait l'objet de censure et de « corrections » de la part de l'Église catholique. En tout état de cause, les plus anciens manuscrits de la Mishna parlent bien d' « une seule personne » sans préciser « juive ».

4. Voir D. Sidersky, *Les Origines des légendes musulmanes*, p. 18, et Speyer, *Die biblischen Erzählungen*, *op. cit.*, p. 84-88.

5. Voir l'entrée « Abraham » (par P. Lory), dans le *Dictionnaire du Coran*, *op. cit.*, p. 13.

6. Voir l'entrée « hanîf » (par G. Gobillot), *ibid.*, p. 381-384.

7. Voir A. Jeffery, *Materials for the History of the Text of the Qur'ān*, Leyde, 1937, p. 32.

8. Voir Geiger, *Was hat Mohammed aus den Judenthume aufgenommen ?*, p. 42 (*Judaism and Islam*, p. 111-112) ; voir aussi Sidersky, *Les Origines des légendes musulmanes*, p. 59-61 et Speyer, *Die biblischen Erzählungen im Qoran*, p. 202-203 ; Reynolds, *The Qur'an and the Bible*, p. 368-369.

9. Voir al-Tabarî, *Jâmi' al-bayân*, vol. 7, partie 12, p. 187 et 189.

10. La traduction française de ce passage du Midrash est celle de D. Sidersky, *Les Origines des légendes musulmanes*, p. 62-63, avec des changements légers.

11. L'article est publié dans : *New Perspectives on the Qur'ān*, éd. G. S. Reynolds, Londres, 2011, p. 425-448.

12. Sur le développement de cette doctrine en islam, voir Bar-Asher, *Scripture and Exegesis in Early Imami Shiism*, Leyde et Jérusalem, 1999, p. 159-179.

13. Talmud de Babylone, traité *Shabbat* 56a. Voir aussi A. Shinan, « L'image de David dans la littérature talmudique » (« Demuto shel David be-sifrut haza ») dans Y. Jacovitch, *David, de berger à messie* (*David – me-ro'eh le-mashiah*), Jérusalem, 1995, p. 181-199 (en hébreu).

14. Voir l'entrée « David », dans le *Dictionnaire du Coran*, p. 202. Et voir aussi Z. Maghen, « Intertwined Triangles : Remarks on the Relationship between Two Prophetic Scandals », *Jerusalem Studies in Arabic and Islam*, vol. 33 (2007), p. 17-92.

15. A. H. Johns, « David and Batsheba : A Study in the Exegesis Quranic Story-Telling », *Mélanges de l'Institut dominicain d'études orientales*, vol. 19 (1989), p. 225-266 ; voir particulièrement p. 226-227.

16. Abû Ishâq Ahmad b. Muhammad al-Naysâbûri al-Tha'labî, *Qisas al-anbiyâ' al-musamma 'arâis al-majâlis*, p. 265.

17. Voir Geiger, *Was hat Mohammed aus den Judenthume aufgenommen ?*, p. 178-180 (*Judaism and Islam*, p. 143-144) ; Katsh, *Judaism in Islam*, p. 161-171.

18. Voir aussi Sidersky, *Les Origines des légendes musulmanes*, p. 109-111.

19. Blachère, *Le Coran*, *op. cit.*, p. 67, note au verset 2 : 248.

20. Voir Katsh, *Judaism in Islam*, p. 71-73.

21. Sur les *isrâ'îliyyât* voir entre autres les études suivantes : B. Heller, « Récits et personnages bibliques dans la légende mahométane », *Revue des études juives*, vol. 85 (1928), p. 113-136. ; M.J. Kister, « *hadditĥû 'an banî isrâ'îla wa-lâ haraja* », *Israel Oriental Studies*, vol. 2 (1972), p. 215-239 ; G. Vajda, « Isrâ'îliyyât », *Encyclopédie de l'islam*, vol. 5, p. 221-222.

22. Pour l'exégèse sunnite, voir par ex. al-Tabarî, *Jâmi' al-bayân*, dans son commentaire de la sourate 12 ; pour

l'exégèse shi'ite voir par ex. 'Alî b. Ibrâhîm al-Qummî, *Tafsîr al-Qummî*, éd. al-Tayyib al-Mûsawî al-Jazâ'irî, Najaf, 1386-1387 H, vol. 1, p. 339-358 ; Muhammad b. Mas'ûd al-Ayyâshî, *Tafsîr al-'Ayyâshî*, éd. Hâshim al-Rasûlî al-Mahallâtî, Qom 1380H, vol. 2, p. 166-201. Cf. *Genèse Rabba*, chap. 84-85.

23. Voir par exemple *Tafsîr al-Qummî*, vol. 1, p. 85 (dans son commentaire du « verset du Trône » [2 : 255]) et cf. Ezekiel, chap. 1.

IV. Loi coranique et loi juive

1. Publié dans *Atti della Accademia Nazionlae dei Lincei*, Rome, 1975.

2. Publié dans *Hommage à Georges Vajda*, G. Nahon et Ch. Touati éd., Louvain, 1980, p. 125-134.

3. On doit à Gideon Libson une monographie importante dans ce domaine, *Jewish and Islamic Law : A Comparative Study of Custom During the Geonic Period* (Cambridge, MA, 2003). Mais comme l'indique le titre de l'ouvrage, il se concentre surtout sur le développement de l'islam à l'époque où son centre n'est plus en Arabie mais en Irak, où les communautés juives se trouvaient déjà depuis plus d'un millénaire. Il consacre cependant quelques pages (p. 1-7) à la période formative.

4. Pour une discussion pertinente de ces hadîths, voir l'étude magistrale de M. J. Kister, « Do Not Assimilate Yourselves… : *Lā Tashabbahū* », *Jerusalem Studies in Arabic and Islam*, vol. 12 (1989), p. 321-371.

5. U. Rubin, « Les directions de la prière (*qibla*) dans l'espace sacré » (« Kivvuné ha-tefilla [ha-qibla] be-merhan ha-qedushsha »), in *idem*, *Entre Jérusalem et La Mecque : Sainteté*

et salut dans le Coran (et la tradition musulmane) (= *Beyn Yerushalayim le-Mecca : Qedushsha u-Gueula ba-Qur'an u-ve-massoret ha-islam*), Jérusalem, 2019, p. 226-242.

6. Ces traditions se rencontrent beaucoup dans les hadîths. Voir par exemple Bukhârî, *Sahîh*, *Kitâb al-sawm* (« Livre sur le jeûne »), chap. 69.

7. Voir S. D. Goitein, « Ramadan : The Muslim Month of Fasting », dans *Studies in Islamic History and Institutions*, Leyde, 1966, p. 90-110.

8. Voir Katsh, *Judaism and Islam*, p. 132. Et voir aussi la note de D. Masson à sa traduction du Coran, p. 794.

9. Par exemple chez Justin Martyr, *Le Dialogue avec Tryphon*, édition critique, traduction et commentaire par Philippe Bobichon, Fribourg, 2003, chap. 18, § 2.

10. Voir Ch. Torrey, *The Jewish Foundation of Islam*, New York, Jewish Institute of Religion Press, 1933, p. 151-152.

11. Pour une étude approfondie des lois alimentaires en islam, voir M. Cook, « Early Islamic Dietary Law », *Jerusalem Studies in Arabic and Islam*, vol. 7 (1986), p. 216-277.

12. Pour une discussion détaillée de ce verset, voir ci-dessous, p. 193-194.

13. Ce verset est discuté au chapitre précédent.

14. Bîrûnî, *Al-Âthâr al-bâqiya*, C. E. Sachau éd., Leipzig, 1923, p. 62.

V. Les sources coraniques de la dhimma

1. Ismâ'îl b. 'Umar Ibn Kathîr, *Tafsîr*, Beyrouth, 1998, vol. N, p. 1174.

2. Pour un exposé détaillé d'autres versets coraniques considérés comme justifiant la *dhimma* accordée aux non-

musulmans, voir Ibn Qayyim al-Jawziyya, *Ahkâm ahl al-dhimma,* Beyrouth, 1961, vol. 1, p. 238-242. Ce texte est discuté plus loin.

3. Voir M. R. Cohen, *Under Crescent and Cross : The Jews in the Middle Ages*, Princeton 1994, p. 68-72. Pour une discussion détaillée de l'exégèse de ce verset, voir M. J. Kister, « 'An Yadin (Qur'an, IX/29). An Attempt at Interpretation, », *Arabica*, vol. 11 (1964), p. 272-278 ; U. Rubin, « Quran and *tafsîr* : The Case of *'an yadin* », *Der Islam,* vol. 70 (1993), p. 133-144.

4. Sur la conception musulmane de la supériorité de l'islam sur les autres religions, voir Yohanan Friedmann, *Tolerance and Coercion in Islam: Interfaith Relations in the Muslim Tradition*, Cambridge University Press, 2003, p. 37-39.

5. C. Cahen, « Dhimma », *Encyclopédie de l'islam*, vol. 2, p. 235.

6. La traduction française du pacte de 'Umar citée ici est extraite de son livre *Le Statut légal des non-musulmans en pays d'Islam*, Beyrouth, 1958, p. 61-63. Le texte a été réimprimé et discuté attentivement par Marc Cohen dans le volume magistral *Histoire des relations entre juifs et musulmans des origines à nos jours*, A. Meddeb et B. Stora éd., Paris, Albin Michel, 2013, p. 72-73 (le document) ; p. 58-71 et tout particulièrement p. 67-69 (une analyse du document).

7. Pour une discussion détaillée et approfondie du « pacte de 'Umar » basée, *inter alia*, sur l'œuvre d'Ibn Qayyim al-Jawziyya, voir M. R. Cohen, *Under Crescent and Cross*, p. 54-74.

8. B. Lewis, *Juifs en terre d'Islam*, traduit de l'anglais par J. Caranaud, Paris, Calmann-Lévy, 1986, p. 17.

9. M. Abitbol, *Le Passé d'une discorde : Juifs et Arabes du VIIe siècle à nos jours*, Paris, Perrin, 1999.

10. Bat Ye'or, *Le Dhimmi : Profil de l'opprimé en Orient et en Afrique du Nord depuis la conquête arabe*, Paris, Anthropos, 1980.

11. Voir, par exemple, D. Tsadik, *Between Foreigners and Shi'is : Nineteenth-Century Iran and its Jewish Minority*, Stanford University Press, 2007 ; M. M. Bar-Asher, « Le statut des juifs chez les malikites du Maroc, » dans *Relations judéo-musulmanes au Maroc : Perceptions et réalités,* M. Abitbol éd., Paris, 1997, p. 57-71.

12. P. Fenton, *Le Pogrome de Fès ou le tritel 17-19 avril 1912,* Étude et documents, Jérusalem, 2012.

VI. La place du judaisme et des juifs dans le shî'isme duodécimain

1. Voir, par exemple, I. Goldziher, « Islamisme et Parsisme, » dans *Gesammmelte Schriften*, Hildesheim, 1970, vol. 4, p. 232-260 ; W. Ivanow, *Studies in Early Persian Ismailism*, Leyde, 1948, p. 29-30.

2. Pour la notion de *Verus Israël*, voir *supra*, p. 71 et note 6.

3. Tabarî, *Jâmi' al-bayân,* vol. 10, p. 105-109. Il est à noter cependant que parmi les traditions citées par Tabarî, certaines distinguent entre juifs et chrétiens d'une part et les autres infidèles ou polythéistes (nommés *mushrikûn*) d'autre part. Les premiers bénéficient d'une discrimination moins marquée par rapport aux autres infidèles. (Voir par exemple *ibid.*, p. 108-109.)

4. Muhammad Bâqir al-Majlisî, *Bihâr al-anwâr*, Beyrouth, 1983, vol. 77, p. 42 *sqq*.

5. Ayatu'llâh Muhammad al-Husaynî Shirâzî, *Mawsû'a fiqhiyya istidlâliyya*, Beyrouth, 1987-1989, vol. 4, p. 182, *sqq*.

6. Voir *Bihâr al-anwâr*, vol. 77, p. 44, ligne 18.

7. *Ibid.*

8. *Ibid.*, ligne 6.

9. Pour les détails voir les références citées dans les notes suivantes.

10. Voir Shirâzî, *Mawsû'a fiqhiyya istidlâliyya*, vol. 4, p. 184.

11. *Bihâr al-anwâr*, vol. 77, p. 46, lignes 11-14 ; *Mawsû'a fiqhiyya istidlâliyya*, *ibid.*

12. Voir Shirâzî, *Mawsû'a fiqhiyya istidlâliyya*, p. 194-196.

13. *Ibid.*, p. 194.

14. *Ibid.*, p.194-195.

15. *Ibid.*, p. 194, lignes 3-7.

16. *Bihâr al-anwâr*, vol. 74, p. 47. Notre auteur cite ici une source ancienne, le *Kitâb al-mahâsin* d'Ahmad b. Muhammad al-Barqî (mort en 274/887 ou 280/893).

17. Le sujet a été finement étudié par N. Tsafrir dans son mémoire de maîtrise (sous la direction de Y. Friedmann), « L'attitude de la loi islamique vis-à-vis des autres religions : Le problème de l'abattage rituel et du mariage » (« *Yahas ha-halakha ha-muslémit kelappé datot ahérot : 'inyéné shéhîta ve-nisû'îm* »), Université hébraïque de Jérusalem, 1988, p. 12-15 et 37-45 (en hébreu).

18. Voir Abû Ja'far al-Tûsî, *Al-Tibyân fî tafsîr al-qur'ân*, Najaf, 1957-1981, vol. 3, p. 444.

19. Voir, par exemple, *Bihâr al-anwâr*, vol. 77, p. 43, ligne 5 ; Shîrâzî, *Mawsû'a fiqhiyya istidlâliyya*, vol. 4, p. 189, ligne 18 ; p. 19, ligne 13.

20. Ce mariage n'est licite que dans le droit shî'ite duodécimain. Sur le mariage *mut'a* dans le shî'isme, voir

Y. Richard, *Le Shi'isme en Iran : Imam et Révolution*, Paris, Jean Maisonneuve, 1980, p. 32 et surtout A. Gribetz, *Strange Bedfellows : mut'at al-nisâ' and mut'at al-hajj*, Berlin, 1984.

21. S. Souroudi, « The Concept of Jewish Impurity and its Reflexion in Persian and Judeo-Persian Traditions », *Irano Judaica,* vol. 3 (1993), p. 1-29.

22. Ces questions ont été abordées plus récemment dans D. Tsadik, *Between Foreigners and Shi'is, op. cit.*, p. 20-21 et p. 240-241 (les notes).

23. *Bihâr al-anwâr*, vol. 67, p. 44 ; Shîrâzî, *Mawsû'a fiqhiyya istidlâliyya*, vol. 4, p. 182-208.

24. Voir la formulation d'al-Tûsî : « L'urgence d'une situation permet [la consommation de] la chair de l'animal [non rituellement abattu]. Elle permet même [la consommation de bêtes abattues] par une personne hostile à l'islam » (Abû Ja'far al-Tûsî, *al-Istibsâr fî mâ ukhtulifa min al-akhbâr*, vol. 4, p. 88). Concernant les positions permissives vis-à-vis des *ahl-al kitâb*, voir p. 81-82 du même volume.

25. Voir Goldziher « Islamisme et Parsisme », p. 232-260.

26. Soroudi, « The Concept of Jewish Impurity », p. 8-13.

27. Voir A. J. Wensinck, « Nadjis », *Encyclopédie de l'islam*, vol. 7, p. 871-872.

28. Voir M. Cook, « Early Islamic Dietary Law, » *Jerusalem Studies in Arabic and Islam*, vol. 7 (1986), p. 217-277.

29. Y. Elman, « Contrasting Intellectual Trajectories : Iran and Israel in Mesopotamia », dans U. Gabbay et S. Secunda éd., *Encounters by the Rivers of Babylon : Scholarly Conversations Between Jews, Iranians and Babylonians in Antiquity*, Tübingen, 2014, p. 7-105 ; P.O. Skjaero et Y. Elman, « Concepts of Pollution in Late Sasanian Iran: Does

Pollution Need Stairs, and Does It Fill Space? » ARAM, vol. 26 (2014), p. 21-45.

30. S. Secunda éd., *The Iranian Talmud : Reading the Bavli in its Sassanian Context*, Philadelphia, Penn Press, 2013.

31. Il s'agit de la principale prise de position des shî'ites mais il existe des traditions qui la nuancent, par exemple la tradition sur le mélange des argiles (*ikhtilât al-tînatayn*). Voir M. A. Amir-Moezzi, *La Religion discrète : Croyances et pratiques spirituelles dans l'islam shi'ite*, Paris, Vrin, 2006, p. 218.

32. Sur ces fondements de la foi et des doctrines shî'ites, voir par ex. M. A. Amir-Moezzi, *Le Guide divin dans le shî'isme originel. Aux sources de l'ésotérisme en islam*, Paris, Verdier, 1992, p. 73-111 ; Bar-Asher, *Scripture and Exegesis in Early Imami Shiism*, p. 130-140.

33. M. Boyce, *A History of Zoroastrianism*, vol. 1 (« The Early Period »), Londres, 1975, p. 295-296.

34. Pour les lois de pureté des sectes de la mer Morte, voir par ex. L. H. Schiffman, *Sectarian Law in the Dead Sea Scrolls : Courts, Testimony and the Penal Code*, Californie, 1983, p. 161-162, 167-168, 172-173. Nous ne faisons ici qu'une allusion aux ressemblances entre les croyances messianiques des sectes de la mer Morte et celles du shî'isme. Le sujet mérite une étude à part.

35. Voir Muhammad b. Mas'ûd al-'Ayyâshî, *Tafsîr al-'Ayyâshî*, Hâshim al-Rasûlî al-Mahallâtî, éd. Qom, 1380H, vol. 1, p. 44, traditions 43 et 44.

36. Al-'Ayyâshî, *Tafsîr al-'Ayyâshî*, vol. 1, p. 44.

37. Al-Majlisî, *Bihâr al-anwâr*, vol. 24, p. 397-398.

38. 'Alî b. Ibrâhîm al-Qummî, *Tafsîr al-Qummî*, al-Tayyib al-Mûsawî al-Jazâ'irî éd., Najaf, 1386-1387 H, vol. 2, p. 134.

39. Abû ʿAlî al-Fadl b. al-Hasan al-Tabrisî, *Majmaʿ al-bayân fî tafsîr al-Qur'ân*, Beyrouth, n.d., vol. 5, partie 20, p. 264.

40. *Tafsîr al-ʿAyyâshî*, vol 2, p. 154, tradition 49.

41. Il faut noter cependant que dans le récit coranique, Gédéon est remplacé par Saül nommé Tâlût ; voir Speyer, *Die biblischen Erzählungen, op. cit.*, p. 368.

42. Muhammad b. Yaʿqûb Al-Kulaynî, *Al-Kâfî*, ʿA. A. Ghaffârî éd., Téhéran 1955-1957, vol. 8, p. 292-293, tradition 498. Un récit biblique similaire raconte comment la tribu d'Ephraïm fut postée sur les gués du Jourdain pour mettre les Galaadites à l'épreuve (Juges 12 : 5-6). Pour une étude pertinente de ce récit et de ses parallèles éventuels dans le Coran, voir U. Rubin, *Between Bible and Qur'ân : The Children of Israel and the Islamic Self-Image*, Princeton, The Darwin Press, 1999, p. 83-99.

43. Sur ce fameux hadîth shiʿite, voir par ex. Y. Friedman, *Prophecy Continuous* : *Aspects of Ahmadī Religious Thoughts and its Medieval Background*, Berkeley-Los Angeles-Londres, 1989, p. 58-59 ; Bar-Asher, *Scripture and Exegesis, op. cit.*, p. 156-157.

44. Sur ces appellations péjoratives dans l'exégèse duodécimaine, voir Bar-Asher, *Scripture and Exegesis, op. cit.,* p. 113-120.

45. Dans son article « The Term Râfida in Early Imâmî Shîʿî Usage » in *Journal of the American Oriental Society*, vol. 99 (1979), p. 1-9 (réimprimé dans E. Kohlberg, *Belief and Law in Imâmî Shîʿism*, chap. IV).

46. *Ibid.*, p. 3.

47. M. A. Amir-Moezzi et Ch. Jambet, *Qu'est-ce que le shîʿisme ?*, Paris, Fayard, p. 31-35 ; ainsi que « L'Imam dans le ciel : Ascension et initiation, » dans M. A. Amir-Moezzi, *La Religion discrète, op. cit.*, p. 135-150, surtout p. 148, note 64.

48. *Sahîh al-Bukhârî* 3461 (livre 60, hadîth 128) et voir aussi l'étude pertinente de M. J. Kister, déjà citée, « *Haddithû 'an banî isrâ'îla wa-lâ haraja* : A Study of an Early Tradition », p. 215-239.

Bibliographie

Abitbol, M., *Le Passé d'une discorde : Juifs et Arabes du VIIe siècle à nos jours*, Paris, Perrin, « Tempus », 2003.

Almog, S. éd., *Antisemitism Through the Ages*, Oxford, Pergamon Press, 1988.

Amir-Moezzi, M. A., *Le Guide divin dans le shî'isme originel. Aux sources de l'ésotérisme en Islam*, Lagrasse, Verdier, 1992 (nouvelle édition : 2007).

–, *La Religion discrète. Croyances et pratiques spirituelles dans l'islam shî'ite*, Paris, Vrin, 2006.

–, « L'Imam dans le ciel : Ascension et initiation (Aspects de l'imamologie duodécimaine III) », dans *id.* (éd.), *Le Voyage initiatique en terre d'islam. Ascensions célestes et itinéraires spirituels*, Louvain-Paris, 1996 (*La Religion discrète*, p. 135-150).

–, « Note à propos de la *walâya* imamite (Aspects de l'imamologie duodécimaine X) », *Journal of the American Oriental Society*, vol. 122 (2002), p. 722-741 (*La Religion discrète*, p. 177-207).

– (sous la direction de), *Dictionnaire du Coran*, Paris, Robert Laffont, 2007.

– et Ch. Jambet, *Qu'est-ce que le shî'isme ?*, Paris, Fayard, 2004.

M. Ayoub, « 'Uzayr in the Qur'ân and Muslim Tradition », W. M. Brinner et S. D. Ricks éd., *Studies in Islamic and Judaic Traditions*, Atlanta, 1986, vol. 1, p. 3-18.

Al-'Ayyâshî, Muhammad b. Mas'ûd, *Tafsîr al-'Ayyâshî*, Hâshim al-Rasûlî al-Mahallâtî éd., Qom, 1380 H.

Bakhos, C. et Shayegan, M. Rahim (dir.), *The Talmud in its Iranian Context*, Tübingen, Mohr Siebeck, 2010.

Bar-Asher, M. M., *Scripture and Exegesis in Early Imami Shiism*, Leyde et Jérusalem, 1999.

–, « Le statut des juifs chez les malikites du Maroc », dans *Relations judéo-musulmanes au Maroc : Perceptions et réalités,* éd. M. Abitbol, Paris, Stavit, 1997, p. 57-71.

Bat-Ye'or, M., *Le Dhimmi : Profil de l'opprimé en Orient et en Afrique du Nord depuis la conquête arabe*, Paris, Les Provinciales, 1980.

Ben-Shammai, H., « L'idée de l'élection dans l'islam ancien » [= Ra'ayon ha-behira ba-islam ha-qadûm], dans *L'Idée de l'élection chez le peuple d'Israël et les autres peuples* [= *Ra'ayon ha-behira be-Israel u-va-'ammîm*], S. Almog et M. Heyd éd., Jérusalem, 1991, p. 147-177 (en hébreu).

–, « Jew-Hatred in the Islamic Tradition and the Koranic Exegesis », dans *Antisemitism through the Ages*, S. Almog éd., Oxford, Pergamon Press, 1988, p. 161-170.

–, « *Suhuf* in the Qur'an – A Loan Translation for "Apocalypses" », dans *Exchange and Transmission across Cultural Boundaries : Philosophy, Mysticism and Science in the Mediterranean World – Proceedings of an International Workshop Held in Memory of Professor Shlomo Pines,* H. Ben-Shammai, S. Shaked et S. Stroumsa éd., Jérusalem, 2013, p. 1-15.

–, « Transmigration des âmes dans la pensée juive en Orient au xe siècle » [= *Gilgul neshamot ba-mahashava ha-yehudit ba-mizrah ba-me'a ha-'asirit*], dans *Sefunot, Études et sources sur l'histoire des communautés juives en Orient*, 20 (1991), p. 118-124 (en hébreu).

Bîrûnî, Abû Rayhân, *Al-Âthâr al-bâqiya*, C. E. Sachau éd., Leipzig, 1923.

Blachère, R., *Le Coran*, Paris, Maisonneuve et Larose, 1980.

Boyce, M., *A History of Zoroastrianism*, Leyde, Brill, 1975.

Brunschvig, R. « Herméneutique normative dans le judaïsme et dans l'islam », dans *Atti della Accademia Nazionale dei Lincei*, Rome, 1975.

–, « Vœu ou serment : Droit comparé du judaïsme et de l'islam », dans *Hommage à Georges Vajda,* éd. G. Nahon et Ch. Touati, Louvain, 1980, p. 125-134.

Bukhari, Muhammad b. Ismâ'îl, *Sahîh*, Leyde, 1864.

Cahen, C., « Dhimma », *Encyclopédie de l'islam*, vol. 2, p. 227-231.

Chabbi, J., *Le Coran décrypté. figures bibliques en Arabie*, Paris, 2008.

Cohen, M. A., *Under Crescent and Cross : The Jews in the Middle Ages*, Princeton, 1994.

Comerro, R., « Esdras est-il le fils de Dieu ? », *Arabica*, vol. 52 (2005), p. 165-181.

Cook, M., « Early Islamic Dietary Law », *Jerusalem Studies in Arabic and Islam*, vol. 7 (1986), p. 217-277.

Dahan, G., *La Polémique chrétienne contre le judaïsme au Moyen Âge*, Albin Michel, « Présences du judaïsme », Paris, 1991.

Dozy, R., *Suppléments aux dictionnaires arabes*, Leyde, 1881.

Dreyfus, F., « Reste d'Israël », dans *Supplément au Dictionnaire de la Bible*, H. Cazelle et A. Feuillet éd., Paris, 1981, p. 414-437.

Elman, Y., « Contrasting Intellectual Trajectories : Iran and Israel in Mesopotamia », dans U. Gabbay et S. Secunda éd., *Encounters by the Rivers of Babylon : Scholarly Conversations Between Jews, Iranians and Babylonians in Antiquity*, Tübingen, Mohr Siebeck, 2014, p. 7-105.

Fattal, A., *Le Statut légal des non-musulmans en pays d'Islam*, Beyrouth, 1958.

Fenton, P., *Le Pogrome de Fès ou le tritel 17-19 avril 1912,* Étude et documents, Jérusalem, 2012.

Friedman, Y., *Prophecy Continuous* : *Aspects of Ahmadî Religious Thoughts and its Medieval Background*, Berkeley et Londres, University of California Press, 1989.

Furât b. Ibrâhîm al-Kûfî, *Tafsîr Furât*, Muhammad al-Kâzim éd., Téhéran, 1990.

Gadd, C. J., « The Harran Inscription of Nabonidus », *Anatolian Studies*, vol. 8 (1958), p. 35-92.

Geiger, A., *Was hat Mohammed aus dem Judenthume aufgenommen ?*, Bonn, 1833 (= *Judaism and Islam*, tr. F. M. Young, Madras, 1898).

Geoffroy E. G., « Sakîna », in *Dictionnaire du Coran*, *op. cit.*, p. 784-785.

Ginzberg, L., *Les Légendes des juifs*, vol. 6, traduit de l'anglais par G. Sed-Rajna, Paris, 2006.

Gobillot, G., « Hanîf », dans le *Dictionnaire du Coran*, p. 381-384.

Goitein, S. D., « *Isrâ'îliyyât* », *Tarbiz* (*A Quarterly for Jewish Studies*), vol. 6 (1931), p. 89-101 et p. 510-522 (en hébreu).

–, *Jews and Arabs : Their Contacts Through the Ages*, New York, 1955.

–, « Les fils d'Israël et leurs controverses : étude sur le Coran » [= *Bene Israël u-mahloqtâm : mehqar ba-Qur'an*], *Tarbiz* (*A Quarterly for Jewish Studies*), vol. 3 (1931), p. 410-422 (en hébreu).

« Quels furent les maîtres à penser de Muhammad ? », [= *Mi hagu rabhotav ha-muvhaqim shel Muhammad?*] *Tarbiz* (*A Quaterly for Jewish Studies*), 1962, vol. 23, p. 146-149 (en hébreu).

–, « Ramadan : The Muslim Month of Fasting », in *id.*, *Studies in Islamic History and Institutions*, Leyde, 1966, p. 90-110.

Goldziher, I., « Islamisme et Parsisme », in *id.*, *Gesammmelte Schriften*, J. De Somogyi éd., Hildesheim, 1970 (réédition), vol. 4, p. 232-260.

Gribetz, A., *Strange Bedfellows : Mut'at al-nisâ' and mut'at al-hajj*, Berlin, 1984.

Griffith, S., *The Bible in Arabic : The Scriptures of the « People of the Book » in the Language of Islam*, Princeton, 2013.

Halpern Amaru, B., « The Killing of the Prophets : Unravelling a Midrash », *Hebrew Union College Annual*, vol. 54 (1983), p. 153-180.

Heller, B., « Récits et personnages bibliques dans la légende mahométane », *Revue des Études juives*, vol. 85, 1928, p. 113-136.

Hirschberg, H. Z., *Israël en Arabie (= Israël ba-'Arav : Qorôt Ha-Yéhûdîm be-Himyar ve-Hijâz)*, Tel-Aviv, 1946 (en hébreu).

Horovitz, J., *Koranische Untursuchungen,* Berlin et Leipzig, 1926.

Ibn Kathîr, Ismâ'îl b. 'Umar, *Tafsîr*, Beyrouth, 1998.

Ibn Qayyim al-Jawziyya, *Ahkâm ahl al-dhimma,* Beyrouth, 1961.

Ivanow, W., *Studies in Early Persian Ismailism*, Leyde, 1948.

Jeffery, A., *The Foreign Vocabulary of the Qur'ān*, Baroda, 1938.

–, *Materials for the History of the Text of the Qur'ān*, Leyde, 1937.

Johns, A. H., « David and Batsheba : A Study in the Exegesis of a Quranic Story », *Mélanges de l'Institut dominicain d'études orientales*, vol. 19 (1989), p. 225-266.

Jule, P. et Galor, K., « Zafar : Watershed of Late Pre-Islamic Culture », dans *Le Judaïsme de l'Arabie antique* (Actes du Colloque de Jérusalem [février 2006]), Ch. Robin éd., Turnhout, 2015, p. 387-421.

Justin Martyr, *Le Dialogue avec Tryphon*, édition critique, traduction et commentaire par Philippe Bobichon, Fribourg, Academic Press Fribourg, 2003.

Katsh, A. I., *Judaism in Islam : Biblical and Talmudic Backgrounds of the Koran and its Commentaries*, New York, 1954.

Kister, M. J., « 'An Yadin (Qur'ân, IX/29) : An Attempt at Interpretation, », *Arabica*, vol. 11 (1964), p. 272-278

–, « *Hadditһû 'an banî isrâ'îla wa-lâ haraja* : A Study of an Early Tradition », *Israel Oriental Studies*, vol. 2 (1972), p. 215-239.

–, « Do Not Assimilate Yourselves… : *Lā Tashabbahū* », *Jerusalem Studies in Arabic and Islam*, vol. 12 (1989), p. 321-371

Kofsky, A., « Zechariah of Caphar-Zechariah in the Crux of theology and Hermeneutics », *Proche-Orient Chrétien*, vol. 61 (2011), p. 34-44.

Kohlberg, E., *Belief and Law in Imâmî Shî'ism*, Variorum, Aldershot, 1991.

–, « The Term Râfida in Early Imâmî Shî'î Usage », *Journal of the American Oriental Society*, vol. 99 (1979), p. 1-9 (= *Belief and Law in Imâmî Shî'ism*, chap. IV).

Al-Kulaynî, Muhammad b. Ya'qûb, *al-Kâfî*, 'A. A. Ghaffârî éd., Téhéran, 1955-1957.

Lazarus-Yafeh, H., « Ezra-'Uzayr : Metamorphosis of a Polemical Motif », in *id.*, *Intertwined Worlds : Medieval Islam and Bible Criticism*, p. 50-74.

–, *Intertwined Worlds : Medieval Islam and Bible Criticism*, Princeton, 1992.

Lecker, M., « Muhammad et les juifs » [= *Muhammad ve-ha-Yehudim*], Jérusalem, 2014 (en hébreu).

Lewis B., *Juifs en terre d'Islam*, traduit de l'anglais par J. Caranaud, Paris, Calmann-Lévy, 1986.

Libson, G., *Jewish and Islamic Law : A Comparative Study of Custom During the Geonic Period*, Cambridge (Massachusetts), 2003.

Lory, P. « Abraham », dans le *Dictionnaire du Coran*, p. 9-14.

–, « David », *ibid.*, p. 201-203.

–, *La Dignité de l'homme face aux anges, aux animaux et aux djinns*, Paris, Albin Michel, 2018.

Hussein, Mahmoud, *Al-Sîra : Le Prophète de l'islam raconté par ses compagnons*, Paris, Grasset, 2007.

Al-Majlisî, Muhammad Bâqir, *Bihâr al-anwâr*, Beyrouth, 1983.

Maghen, Z., « Intertwined Triangles : Remarks on the Relationship between Two Prophetic Scandals », *Jerusalem Studies in Arabic and Islam,* vol. 33 (2007), p. 17-92.

Mantran, R., *L'Expansion musulmane*, Paris, PUF, 1991.

Masson, D., *Le Coran* : *Introduction, traduction et notes*, Paris, Gallimard, « Bibliothèque de la Pléiade », 1963.

Mazuz, H., *The Religious and Spiritual Life of the Jews of Medina*, Leyde, 2014.

Meddeb, A. et Stora, B. éd., *Histoire des relations entre juifs et musulmans des origines à nos jours*, Paris, Albin Michel, 2013.

Mopsik, Ch., « La datation du *Chi'our Qomah* d'après un texte néotestamentaire », *Revue des sciences religieuses*, 68ᵉ année, n° 2 (1994), p. 131-144, repris dans Ch. Mopsik, *Chemins de la cabale*, Éditions de l'Éclat, Paris, 2004, p. 309-324.

Muslim, ibn al-Hajjâj, *Sahîh*, éd. F. 'Abd al-Bâqî, Beyrouth, 1983.

Newby, G., *A History of the Jews of Arabia : From Ancient Times to their Eclipse under Islam*, Columbia, University of South Carolina Press, 1988.

Olivier, A.-M. and Steinberg, P. F., The Road to Martyr's Square : A Journey into the World of the Suicide Bomber, Oxford, 2005.

Perlman, Y., « The Assassination of the Jewish Poetess 'Asmâ' bint Marwân » (*Ha-hitnaqqeshut ba-meshoreret ha-yehudiyya 'Asmâ' bint Marwân*), *Pe'amim (Studies in Oriental Jewry)*, vol. 132 (2012), p. 149-169.

De Prémare, A.-L., *Les Fondations de l'islam. Entre écriture et histoire*, Paris, Le Seuil, 2002.

Procopius, *History of the Wars*, vol. I et II, Londres, 1914.

Al-Qummî, 'Alî b. Ibrâhîm, *Tafsîr al-Qummî*, éd. al-Tayyib al-Mûsawî al-Jazâ'irî, Najaf, 1386-1387 H.

Rabin, Ch., « Islam and the Qumran Sect », dans *Qumran Studies*, Londres, 1957, p. 112-130.

Reynolds, G. S., *The Qur'an and the Bible : Text and Commentary*, New Haven, Yale University Press, 2018.

Richard, Y., *Le Shi'sme en Iran : Imam et Révolution*, Paris, Jean Maisonneuve, 1980.

Robin, Ch., « Arabia and Ethiopia », dans *The Oxford Handbook of Late Antiquity*, S. Fitzgerald Johnson éd., Oxford, 2012, p. 247-332.

– (éd.), *Le Judaïsme de l'Arabie antique*, Turnhout, Brepols, 2015.

Rubin, U., « Quran and *tafsîr :* The Case of *'an yadin,* » *Der Islam,* vol. 70 (1993), p. 133-144.

–, *Between Bible and Qur'ân : The Children of Israel and the Islamic Self-Image*, Princeton, N. J. Darwin Press, 1999.

–, « Les directions de prière (*qibla*) dans l'espace sacré » (« *Kivvuné hatefilla [ha-qibla] be-merhav ha-qedushsha* »), in *idem*, *Entre Jérusalem et La Mecque : Sainteté et salut dans le Coran et la tradition musulmane* [= *Beyn Yerushalayim le-Mecca : Qedushsha u-Gueula ba-qur'an u-vemassoret ha-islam*], Jérusalem, 2019, p. 226-242 (en hébreu).

–, « Become you apes, repelled ! » (Quran 7 : 166) : The transformation of the Israelites into apes and its biblical and midrashic background », *Bulletin of the School of Oriental and African Studies*, vol. 78 (2015), p. 25-40.

Schiffman, L. H., *Sectarian Law in the Dead Sea Scrolls : Courts, Testimony and the Penal Code*, Californie, Scholars Press, 1983.

Secunda, S. éd., *The Iranian Talmud : Reading the Bavli in its Sassanian Context*, Philadelphie, Penn Press, 2013.

Sharon, M., « The Decisive Battles in the Arab Conquest of Syria », *Studia Orientalia*, vol. 101 (2017), p. 297-357.

Shelomo Ben Adret, *Ma'amar 'al Ishma'el* (« Dissertation sur l'islam »), B. Naor ed., Orot, Spring Valley, NY, 2008.

Shinan, A., « L'image de David dans la littérature talmudique » (Demuto shel David be-sifrut haza"l) dans Y. Jacovitch, *David – d'un pasteur au Messie* (*David – me-ro'eh le-mashiah*), Jérusalem, 1995, p. 181-199 (en hébreu).

Shirâzî, Ayatu'llâh Muhammad al-Husaynî, *Mawsû'a fiqhiyya istidlâliyya*, Beyrouth, 1987-1989.

Sidersky, D., *Les Origines des légendes musulmanes dans le Coran et dans les vies des prophètes*, Paris, Paul Genthner, 1933.

Skjaero, P. O., et Elman, Y., « Concepts of Pollution in Late Sasanian Iran : Does Pollution Need Stairs, and Does It Fill Space ? », *ARAM*, vol. 26 (2014), p. 21-45.

De Smet, D., « Crucifixion », dans M. A. Amir-Moezzi, éd., *Dictionnaire du Coran*, p. 197-199.

–, « Veau d'or », *ibid.*, p. 897-899.

Soroudi, S., « The Concept of Jewish Impurity and its Reflection in Persian and Judeo-Persian Traditions », *Irano Judaica*, vol. 3 (1993), p. 1-29.

Speyer, H., *Die biblischen Erzählungen im Qoran*, Gräfenhairichen, 1931.

Al-Tabarî, Abû Ja'far Muhammad b. Jarîr, *Jâmi' al-bayân 'an ta'wîl ây al-qur'ān*, Mustafâ al-Bâbî al-Halabî éd., Le Caire, 1968.

Al-Tabrisî, Abû 'Alî al-Fadl b. al-Hasan, *Majma' al-bayân fî tafsîr al-qur'ān*, Beyrouth, n.d.

Al-Tha'labî, Abû Ishâq Ahmad b. Muhammad al-Naysâbûri, *Qisas al-anbiyâ' al-musamma 'arâi's al-majâlis*, Beyrouth, 1985.

Toby, Y. Y., *Les Juifs du Yémen à l'ombre de l'Islam, des origines à nos jours* [= *Yahadut Teman be-tsel ha-Islam me-reshito ve-'ad yamenu*], Jérusalem, 2018.

Torrey, Ch., *The Jewish Foundation of Islam*, New York, Jewish Institute of Religion Press, 1933.

Tsadik, D., *Between Foreigners and Shi'is : Nineteenth-Century Iran and its Jewish Minority*, Stanford, University Press, 2007.

Tsafrir, N., « L'attitude de la loi islamique vis-à-vis des autres religions : Le problème de l'abattage rituel et du mariage » [= *Yahas ha-halakha ha-muslémit kelappé datot ahérot : 'inyéné shéhîta ve-nisû'îm*], mémoire de maîtrise, sous la direction de Y. Friedmann, université hébraïque de Jérusalem, 1988 (en hébreu).

Al-Tûsî, Abû Ja'far, *al-Istibsâr fî mâ ukhtulifa min al-akhbâr*, Najaf, 1956-1957.

–, *Al-Tibyân fî tafsîr al-Qur'ân,* Najaf, 1957-1981.

Vajda, G., « Isrâ'îliyyât », *Encyclopédie de l'Islam*, vol. 5, p. 221-222.

Wensinck, A. W., *Muhammad and the Jews of Medina*, Berlin, 1975 (version originale en néerlandais : *Mohammed en de Joden te Medina*, Leyde, 1908).

–, « Nadjis, » *Encyclopédie de l'islam*, vol. 7, p. 871-872.

Wieder, N., *The Judean Scrolls and Karaism*, Leyde, 1962.

Witztum, J. « Joseph among the Ishmaelites : Q 12 in light of Syriac sources », dans *New Perspectives on the Qur'ān*, G. S. Reynolds éd., Londres, 2011, p. 425-448.

–, *The Syriac Milieu of the Quran : The Recasting of the Biblical Narratives*, thèse de doctorat, université de Princeton, 2011.

Zellentin, H. M., *The Qur'ân's Legal Culture. The Didascalia Apostolorum*, Tübingen, Mohr Siebeck, 2013.

Table

ESPACES *libres*

TITRES PARUS

Psychologie

Marie Thirion, *Pourquoi j'ai faim ? De la peur de manquer à la folie des régimes*

Serge Tisseron, *Empathie et manipulations. Les pièges de la compassion*

Didier Lauru, *Père-fille, une histoire de regard*

Joëlle Desjardins-Simon et Sylvie Debras, *Les verrous inconscients de la fécondité*

Gérard Bonnet, *La pornographie. Une agression sexuelle sur mineurs*

Eudes Séméria, *Le harcèlement fusionnel. Les ressorts cachés de la dépendance affective*

Idées

Ali Benmakhlouf, *Pourquoi lire les philosophes arabes. L'héritage oublié*

Roger-Pol Droit, *Et si Platon revenait... Un regard philosophique sur le monde d'aujourd'hui*

Emmanuel Faye, *Arendt et Heidegger. La destruction dans la pensée*

Pierre Hadot, *N'oublie pas de vivre. Goethe et la tradition des exercices spirituels*

Françoise Vergès, *Le ventre des femmes. Capitalisme, racialisation, féminisme*

Sciences

Jean-Michel Oughourlian, *Notre troisième cerveau. La nouvelle révolution psychologique*

Gauthier Chapelle et Michèle Decoust, *Le vivant comme modèle. Pour un biomimétisme radical*

Patrick Blandin, *Biodiversité. L'avenir du vivant*

Karl von Frisch, *Vie et mœurs des abeilles*

Etienne Klein, *Conversation avec le Sphinx. Les paradoxes en physique*

Spiritualités vivantes

Michel Fromaget, *Les Quatre Vivants de l'Apocalypse*

Jacques Berque, *Le Coran. Essai de traduction*

Jean-Yves Leloup, *L'Apocalypse de Jean*

Thich Nhat Hanh, *La respiration essentielle,* suivi de *Notre rendez-vous avec la vie*

Shrî Aurobindo, *Le guide du Yoga*

Annick de Souzenelle, *Le féminin de l'être. Pour en finir avec la côte d'Adam*

Gisèle Siguier-Sauné, *La Bhagavad-Gîtâ ou le grand Chant de l'Unité*

Farîd-ud-Dîn ʿAttar, *Le langage des oiseaux*

Jean-Yves Leloup, *L'Évangile de Jean*

Jean-Yves Leloup, *L'Évangile de Philippe*

Meir M. Bar-Asher, *Les Juifs dans le Coran*

Ibn ʿArabî, *Les illuminations de La Mecque*

Annick de Souzenelle, *L'Égypte intérieure ou les dix plaies de l'âme*

Christiane Rancé, *La passion de Thérèse d'Avila*

Histoire

Catherine Coquery-Vidrovitch, *Les routes de l'esclavage. Histoire des traites africaines*

Composition : Nord Compo
Impression : Black Print en février 2021
Éditions Albin Michel
22, rue Huyghens, 75014 Paris
www.albin-michel.fr

ISBN : 978-2-226-45984-8
ISSN : 1147-3762
N° d'édition : 24175/03
Dépôt légal : mars 2021
Imprimé en Espagne